AUTOPSY

AUTOPSY

The Memoirs of Milton Helpern, the World's Greatest Medical Detective

by Milton Helpern, M.D.,
with Bernard Knight, M.D.

St. Martin's Press   New York

Library of Congress Cataloging in Publication Data

Helpern, Milton, 1902-1977
Autopsy.

Includes index.
1. Helpern, Milton, 1902-1977   2. Medical examiners
(Law)—New York (City)—Biography.   I. Knight, Bernard,
joint author.   II. Title.   [DNLM: 1. Autopsy—Personal narratives.   2. Forensic medicine—Personal
narratives.   W825 H483a]
RA1025.HA3   614′.19′0924   [B]   77-76639
ISBN 0-312-06211-7

MILTON HELPERN
(1902 - 1977)

What kind of man is he we
    honor here,
A doctor who has served his
    science well?
Why, yes, of course, but most
    of us could tell
Of science or profession served.
    A peer
Without a peer in his own field
    and sphere?
Why, yes, that too, but more than
    this, his spell
Is cast by greatness of the mind.
    We dwell
On inner strengths of character
    so dear
To all who know him, radiance
    that springs
From hidden depths of manliness
    and truth.
These are the constant hallmarks
    of the soul
That draw us to the man, these
    are the things
Of which we offer now as
    humble proof
The heartfelt testimony of
    this scroll.

Contents

Foreword

by Bernard Knight, M.D.

Although Milton Helpern, retired Chief Medical Examiner of the City of New York, was probably the world's best known forensic pathologist, this professional supremacy was not his only major attribute. Above all else, he was a gentleman—and a gentle man.

This very quality gave rise to some difficulty when I was helping Dr. Helpern to put together his memoirs, for his natural reticence made it more than a little difficult to draw out some of the more personal matters that are the stock-in-trade of biography. If one steered Milton onto an interesting homicide, he would talk for hours. Get him on the subject of improving the legal medicine system in the country and he would talk for days! But when I would gently edge him toward personal matters, his characteristically mischievous grin would appear as he would shake his head and say, "Ah, who wants to know about that stuff!" Autobiography in these circumstances is harder to unfold than the third-person approach of a biography. This is the reason for these few introductory words, to say just a few of the thngs that would never have fallen from the lips of "Milt" himself.

Sadly, we shall never hear that mellow voice again, for regretfully these preliminary pages have had to be re-written in the past tense. Between the completion of the manuscript and the date of publication, this gentle giant of a personality died, on April 22, 1977, a few days after his seventy-fifth birthday. He passed away in San Diego, far from his beloved New York City. Characteristically, he had travelled across the continent, age and ill-health notwithstanding, in order to attend the annual convention of one of the forensic organizations that he had been largely instrumental in founding. His own city, his country and worldwide legal medicine are the poorer for his passing.

At his funeral service in New York, ex-Mayor Robert Wagner headed the list of eminent men who praised his memory, but even the original draft of this foreword sounded dangerously like a eulogy—a parade of all the nice things that so many distinguished people have had to say about Milton Helpern during his lifetime. It could so easily have become a catalogue of all the honors bestowed upon him and a precis of the literally millions of words written about him during almost half a century at the top of his profession. But it is Milton the man that I will remember, rather than Professor Helpern, the doyen of crime doctors.

As Dr. Howard Reid Craig, Director of the New York Academy of Medicine, has said, "Milton Helpern is smart, he is tough, he is incredibly dedicated—and he is a very sweet man." Perhaps quite naturally, all the descriptions by newpapermen absorbed in dramas of the death scene or the court room, uniformly fail to do justice to the true character of this man. Already the trap of eulogy again yawns wide before me, but how can one avoid saying that Milton was extraordinarily kind, he was unfailingly considerate, he was unbendingly honest and his devotion to good manners amounted almost to a fetish.

One manifestation of this trait was particularly noticeable— in conversation or when reminiscing about a case: Milton Helpern had an extraordinary delicacy of expression. This man, who had probably seen more bloodied corpses and more violated bodies than anyone else in history, deliberately sidestepped the obvious but more brutally descriptive words to pick less abrasive and traumatic ones. This was not motivated by any mealy-mouthed puritanism, but to me seemed like a wish to avoid adding to the brutality of the business by the relishing of explicit descriptions, quite a common habit amongst some crime pathologists, as it is with many police and newspapermen. Some use this half-jesting crudeness as a safety valve against the pressures of their horrific occupation, but Milt seemed to have no need of it.

His gentleness, however, must never be mistaken for softness. This amiable lion would roar if he saw injustice, incompetence or corruption. Milton Helpern had his own strict principles and abhorred anyone falling short of those standards. As the *Washington Post* said some years ago: "His mild manner and benevolent gaze through his half glasses belie his impatience with imperfection—even sloppy janitor work makes him a little grumpy."

But for much of the time, Milt was his deceptively sleepy self, rather slow moving and slow talking—though this was given the lie by those bright eyes and the razor-sharp mind behind them. Many a time, newswriters and others have described him in terms of "a typical grandfather figure" or likened him to a Midwestern farmer sitting on the stoop in a rocking chair. The word "avuncular" crops up in the feature columns with almost monotonous regularity, and there is some justification for it, for Milt was everyone's idea of their favorite uncle.

This aspect has been seen many times when Milton was giving testimony in court. Whereas many an expert witness has been blustering, rattled, or just plain crushed under the onslaught of some aggressive attorney, Milt always had the whole thing under control, and not uncommonly turned the whole drama backwards. He would smile amiably at some ranting lawyer and stop him in full spate. "Now wait a minute, Counselor, let me help you to phrase that question more precisely." Beautiful, but only Helpern could get away with it! The New York *Sunday News*, reporting him in a Brooklyn courtroom, said, "absorbed, the jurors never took their eyes off him—he talked to them like a learned friend."

Dr. Helpern was first and foremost a medical man, not a lawyer, but he commanded the greatest respect amongst members of the legal profession. This is borne out by Judge Bernard Botein, President of New York's Bar Association. In the editorial of an issue of the New York State *Journal of Medicine* devoted entirely to Helpern he said:

I know no man of medicine who has captured the respect

and affection of men of law so completely and deservedly as Dr. Milton Helpern, Chief Medical Examiner of the City of New York. In the area of forensic medicine, lawyers and judges view doctors with as much skepticism as doctors view them. The faith, at times reverence, which lawyers have for their family doctors and which doctors in turn often have for their family lawyers, does not find professional parallel in the courtroom. The "battle of the experts" is a frustrating and can even be an unsavory courtroom spectacle.

In medical terms unintelligible to judge and jury, one expert diagnoses the plaintiff's injuries as black, and the other expert testifies they are white! One states the plaintiff suffered a linear fracture of the skull: the other that it only was the suture line he was born with. A charlatan may be a much more impressive witness than the competent, honorable physician. And the jury is driven to groping for the truth.

Doctor Helpern, on the other hand, takes the extra trouble to translate enigmatic medical terms into lay language understandable by jurors. His impregnable integrity, scholarship and articulateness have become legendary. His loyalty is to truth, to the validity of his findings and not to any person involved in a law suit or other situations. As he himself has so aptly put it, "We are strictly a discovery agency. We are not interested in whodunit. All we want to know is *what* did it."

Doctor Helpern seldom testifies for the defense in a criminal case. Certainly not because of lack of sympathy for defendants—this kindly, modest man has devoted a lifetime to his arduous specialty because of an abiding love for mankind. But few prosecutors will dare seek an indictment when Doctor Helpern has ruled out a cause of death upon which they would have to rely.

Milton Helpern had an uncanny knack of slowly and lovingly unfolding any story, any case however old—so let him tell his story himself....

Chapter 1

Beginnings

Professionally, I have been around a long time, so perhaps there are people who might want to pick up a book to see what Milton Helpern actually did with himself all these years, how he got started, and how he evolved as a physician and forensic scientist.

I said "professionally," as I assume that no one wants a complete run-down on my childhood or memories of my school days. Personally, I become a little impatient with the kind of biography that purports to give detailed conversations the subject had when he was six years old, with a blow by blow description of what he had for lunch one day in 1911.

Let's face it: I have been a forensic pathologist and medical examiner for a long time, and that's where the interest lies.

Well, my life story has been played out almost entirely in the city of New York, where I was born and where I have lived for three-quarters of a century. I have been a city official for most of that time, and I have been proud to be a public servant all these years, even though at times New York can be a difficult mistress.

To get the ordinary details over and done with: I was born in 1902, in a tenement house up on 114th Street, next to Central Park, in East Harlem. My birthday was April 17, and that particular day seems to have been packed with news of disasters—the *New York Times* had headlines like "Russian Situation Grave"; "Coercion in Ireland"; "Revolutionary Movement Widespread." Maybe it was an augury that much of my life would be spent in nosing around trouble associated with sudden death.

My father, Moses Helpern, worked ten hours a day, six days a week, as a cutter in a clothing factory in Lower Manhattan, and my mother, Bertha, had four children besides myself; I had three brothers and a sister, Edna, who was the oldest. She had a great fondness for the theater and was a fan of Maude Adams and Sarah Bernhardt. Theater was cheap, and I used to tag along. I can recall seeing Adams in Barrie's *Peter Pan* and Bernhardt in *L'Aiglon*. Herman, my youngest brother, is a physician and an internist, who practices not far away from where I now live, on Manhattan's Upper East Side.

I suppose it is customary in a book of this kind to write about the effect that one's childhood home and parents had on shaping one's later character and career, but I can sum up by saying that it was a good home. No one either discouraged us or pressured us into anything because it was socially the thing to do. My home was a typical working-class New York household of the early part of the century, and I got on with the interesting job of growing up, in the best way I knew. I started learning at Public School 25 and finished at Public School 23 on 165th Street, after which I spent three years at Townsend Harris Hall or high school, the prep school of City College, which I entered in 1918, just before the end of World War I. A growing interest in all things connected with science sent me there, where I majored in biology and received a Bachelor of Science degree in 1922.

Up to this point, I had had no particular leaning toward any future professional specialty, but I was admitted to the Cornell University Medical College, which had been founded in 1878. I spent the next four years studying medicine, exposed to the influence of a magnificent group of inspiring full and part-time, pre-clinical and clinical medical teachers. In the evenings I taught biology to help pay my way through college, along with other medical students and classmates who studied at Cornell, including Harold Wolff, Bill Menninger, Julius Chasnoff, and Arthur Antenucci. I received my M.D., graduating as one of sixty-three students, on June 11, 1926, and became an intern in the Cornell (or Second) Medical Division of Bellevue Hospital. From then on it was pathology all the way, and I completed a residency in this specialty at Bellevue Hospital after finishing my clinical internship.

In those days, training in pathology was considered essential for subsequent training in medicine, surgery or any of the surgical or clinical medical specialties. My residency in pathology was under the direction of Dr. Douglas Symmers, a younger brother of Dr. William Symmers, who was professor of pathology at Belfast, in Northern Ireland, and the father of William St. Clair Symmers, now professor of pathology at Charing Cross Hospital in London.

Now the way I got into legal medicine was almost casual. People often ask professional men, especially doctors, how they decided to pick their particular discipline—well, often they don't pick it at all—it more or less picks them. Chance and being in a certain place at a certain time are far more common processes than some undeviating devotion or obsessive determination. A man may be equally well-suited to be, say, a neurosurgeon or general pathologist, or a gastroenterologist or skin specialist. But chance may well dictate which one he becomes, and from then on, the normal interaction between ambition and opportunity carry him along.

And so it was with me—I was devoted to clinical medicine and general pathology, once I had started my internship and residency at Bellevue, but certainly at that time I had no burning desire, or undertook any vocational crusade, to become a forensic pathologist.

In fact, at the start I never gave it a thought, but as the twenties ended, I found myself in daily contact with medical examiners' autopsies, for in those days—and for many years later—they were performed in the large, many-tabled autopsy rooms on the second floor of the pathology building designed by Dr. Charles Norris when he was director of the pathological laboratory of Bellevue. The same large mortuary, or morgue, served the Department of Pathology and the Office of the Medical Examiner, just as the old city morgue at the foot of East Twenty-sixth Street had served the coroners prior to 1918. Interns in pathology or "pathological interns," as we were called, and the resident pathologist often assisted the medical examiner with autopsies on cases from Bellevue Hospital and on other routine cases.

I quite enjoyed pathology but had no intention then of taking it up as a full-time speciality. In fact, I was hoping to get a full-time job as head of a new surgical pathology laboratory at Bellevue; but the Great Depression killed the financing of that project, and the expected job did not materialize, to my disappointment and that of Dr. Symmers, who had offered me the job.

While helping with the medical examiner's cases, I got to know Dr. Charles Norris, the first chief medical examiner of New York City, and his devoted, loyal staff, but I never dreamed then that I would one day be sitting behind his desk. Dr. Norris was a very able and kind man, a graduate of Yale, who received his M.D. at the Columbia University College of Physicians and Surgeons and interned at Roosevelt Hospital in New York. He had studied abroad in Scotland and Vienna, and specialized in pathology and bacteriology.

At that time, Dr. Norris became interested in medico-legal institutes on the Continent. He had been recommended for the directorship of pathology at Bellevue Hospital by none other than Dr. William H. Welch, professor of pathology at the Bellevue Hospital Medical School and later at Johns Hopkins. Dr. Norris seemed to take a liking to me, but he thought I was going into surgical pathology.

My good friend Dr. Jerome Silverman had suggested that I take the Civil Service examination for assistant medical examiner. (Dr. Norris had obtained some new openings for this position.) I was not too keen and put off making a decision, until the other job I wanted evaporated.

I submitted my application to take the examination in the last hour of the last day after which applications would be too late. If Jerome Silverman had not insisted on my doing this, I would not have become a medical examiner, and my career might have been in clinical medicine, for which I had great liking and good opportunities. I passed the examination and joined Norris's staff on April 15, 1931—two days before my twenty-ninth birthday.

Those were very difficult days economically, in the worst period of the Depression, and, along with everyone else in city employment, we soon had to take a cut in our annual salary, from $4,100 to $3,800. The following year there was another cut, to $3,600. We worked seven days a week, which was the pace Dr. Norris had set for himself. Charles Norris was also an expert forensic pathologist, familiar with the high standards of the European institutes of legal medicine, and he must have secretly vowed to develop an institute even before he became director of laboratories at Bellevue in 1904. It was not until 1918 that he became the first chief medical examiner of the City of New York. In 1954 I was to become the third.

The origin of the office of medical examiner derives from the function of coroner. To trace the origin of the death investigation systems in the United States, we must go back many hundreds of years in time and cross the Atlantic Ocean. In England—and later in Wales and Ireland (but never in Scotland)—there were officials called "coroners" from very early times. The first mention of this public office was before the Norman Conquest, in the reign of Alfred the Great, but the appointment was revived in 1194, during the reign of King Richard I. He is usually held out in story books to be a great man, friend of Robin Hood, Richard the "Lion-hearted," and all that—but in fact, he never bothered to learn to speak English and only spent four months of his reign in England. Well, King Richard was very fond of crusading, and this cost him and his country a great deal of money. Even worse, he got himself kidnapped by Leopold of Austria, and England had to rustle up one hundred thousand marks as a ransom—a gigantic sum in those days. In order to save the royal treasury from insolvency, his chief minister of justice, Hubert Walter, thought up a scheme to raise whatever money he could from the impoverished peasantry: he revived the old Saxon office of "coroner," a name derived from *coronae custodium regis*, meaning "keeper of the royal pleas."

In each shire or county, a man of substance—usually a knight—was appointed to see that any money due to the king actually reached the treasury and was not diverted into the pockets of the local "shire-reeve" (sheriff) who, until then, had been the king's representative in the counties. The sheriffs were a corrupt, rapacious lot, and the coroner was most unpopular with them at first, as he was a check on their greed.

The coroners collected money for the king by a variety of methods, but they were all basically financial officers—

primitive internal revenue men, if you like. The investigation of unnatural deaths was merely one of the means by which they helped to raise the royal bank balance.

The coroner had to make sure that the property of "felons"— those who were hanged (the bulk of criminal offenses carried the death penalty)—was confiscated for the crown. Also, any object causing death might be sold for the king; for instance, if a man was killed with a sword, or run down by a horse, or gored by a bull, the fatal object could be confiscated for the benefit of the crown. Finds of "treasure trove" were subject to a coroner's inquiry—the "inquest"—as were stranded royal fish, the whale and the sturgeon. Fires in the City of London were a threat to royal property and also required investigation by the coroner.

In those days, Norman and Saxon were still at odds with each other, and the Saxons were not averse to stabbing a Norman in the back on a dark night. So anyone found dead in suspicious circumstances was held to be a Norman, unless the local villagers could prove otherwise. If they could not substantiate this "presentment of Englishry," the coroner imposed a heavy fine on them, again for the benefit of the royal purse. This fine was called the "murdrum," and from it we get the word "murder". So crushing was this penalty, that the local population used to conceal dead bodies or drag them over the boundary into the next district in order to avoid it. The coroner would summon a jury to his inquest to inquire into any suspicious death. In those days, the jury was a panel, not of impartial decision makers, but of real witnesses, neighbors who had known the dead man and his circumstances.

Oddly enough, though Britain abandoned this type of jury centuries ago, it still persists in the United States in the grand jury system, where theoretically, neighbors of a suspect come together to decide if there is a prima facie case to go forward for trial.

Thus, the medieval coroner was really a fiscal officer, whose investigation of sudden deaths was only a sideline. But as the English "justice of the peace" and judicial system developed, the other functions of the coroner fell away, and he was left with the primary duty of investigating those deaths in the community that were not obviously due to some well-recognized disease process.

The status of the English coroner declined in the fifteenth

through eighteenth centuries, until in the nineteenth century his functions were recognized as a necessary part of the great urban resurgence of the Industrial Revolution. From then until recent years, the English coroner system has progressed, and it now provides an efficient death investigation service.

Unfortunately, the very time when the thirteen American colonies were founded was the period when the coroner's system in England was deteriorating. Thus, when the American colonists adopted almost all the English institutions, a rather poor breed of coroners was transplanted here, and initially, the colonial coroners were unqualified for their positions. But at that time, how many doctors were really *qualified* physicians in any case? There certainly weren't any pathologists in those days!

The early American coroners, like their English counterparts, tried to use as much common sense as possible, in place of professional advice. Juries were impounded to advise the coroner as to what they thought about a case; the coroner would guide them. The jurors were made up of any persons in the community who could be tapped by the coroner to serve on the jury and view the body. This viewing was the precursor of a pathologist's autopsy, and in England the coroner is still supposed to view the body himself before an inquest, to confirm or eliminate the question of marks of violence.

Back in the time of the colonies, the same principle applied, and if there was evidence of injury or violence, the jury would produce a verdict. But in all other cases, not understanding medicine, they made hazardous guesses—it must be remembered that the coroner was not a doctor.

At that time in the United States, the only qualification required of the candidate for coroner, in order to run for office, was proof that he was not an ex-convict! Anyone who could appear on the ballot was eligible to run for coroner, usually the lowest position on the list. Actually, there was not too much for coroners to do, except to use a layman's judgment, which was not too different in those days from a medical decision. There was no one around at that time who knew anything about the medical aspects of a case, except when there was recognizable violence. So again, many of the more subtle cases were grossly misinterpreted.

This situation continued, and with the growth of the country after the Revolutionary War, the same coroner system was used.

Coroners were elected in the original thirteen colonies, and then, as new states and territories developed, were established as elected county officers, comparable to sheriffs, with whom they often traded places.

By 1877, the coroner system had become so unsatisfactory in the commonwealth of Massachusetts that it was abolished. In its place, a medical examiner system was established for the first time, under which the governor would appoint "discreet physicians" in the various counties and districts, who were in no way responsible to each other or, indeed, to anybody except the governor. They had a seven-year appointment and then had to seek reappointment. Those physicians who were appointed in the Boston area received salaries, but the others received fees per case. They were called "medical examiners", but, in all but name, they were much more like the coroners, whom they had replaced. They were physicians, but they had no special attributes fitting them for the job of investigating deaths; they were certainly not pathologists.

Of course, a good "discreet physician" could find out a great deal. In those days, no autopsy at all was better than one attempted by these physicians ignorant of what they were trying to demonstrate. When there wasn't an autopsy, at least you *knew* you didn't know, but when one was supposedly done, then everyone was in trouble. The only appointed medical examiners who were also pathologists and knew what they were looking at were associated with the Harvard and Tufts Medical Schools in the Boston area. In 1932, Harvard established a consulting autopsy service for the entire state, but its use was optional on the part of the counties. The availability of this important service was a great improvement over the previous insulated situation.

The medical examiner system in Massachusetts was a very loose one, despite significant efforts to improve it. When it started, autopsies could not—and even today cannot—be done by the medical examiner without approval from the district attorney, who controlled the show with regard to the need for autopsies; the medical examiner had no autonomy in this regard. Not too long ago, there was a much publicized example of this, the Kopechne case in Chappaquiddick, where the local medical examiner was so overwhelmed by the authority of the representatives and advisors of an individual that he signed the case out without autopsy. Presumably, he did not realize the difficult situation he was creating by giving opportunity for unnecessary, reckless, and unfair speculation about the incident.

On the night of July 18, 1969, Mary Jo Kopechne died at Chappaquiddick Creek, on Martha's Vineyard Island in Massachusetts, after a car driven by Senator Edward M. Kennedy plunged off a bridge into the water. If ever a case needed clarifying, it was that one. The twenty-eight-year-old former secretary to Robert Kennedy was found submerged in the car. Death was attributed to drowning, but blood was found in the mouth and nose (she had a fractured nose, probably sustained when the car rolled over).

To sort out all the rumors and insinuations, the medical examiner should have insisted on an immediate autopsy—he had all the authority to do so, had he wished. The Kennedy entourage persuaded him to issue a certificate for "drowning"— and I'm satisfied that this was the correct cause of death, but there's more to an autopsy than the mere determination of the principal cause of death.

So Mary Jo's body was taken to Pennsylvania and buried in Larksville, where her Polish family, devout Catholics, and not very keen on autopsies, lived. Later, when all the rumors started flying around, the Kennedy faction turned around and *wanted* an autopsy, to clear things up. But the family refused. In August 1969, Kennedy's lawyers went to Common Pleas Court in Wilkes-Barre, Pennsylvania and were granted a hearing, but the petition was dismissed. The judge said that he had no authority to direct that the body be exhumed unless someone would come forward and swear that he was convinced that a crime was committed—and the only crime to which Edward Kennedy pleaded guilty was the minor one of leaving the scene of an accident.

The judge said there was nothing but delayed curiosity at this late stage, and that he had no right to order the examination. What I thought was kind of silly was that a lot of people were called in to testify either for or against the autopsy, depending on which side had retained them for their opinion. The one side got all emotional about why there should be an autopsy. Sure, there should have been an autopsy, but they were missing the point! If there had been an autopsy, it would have laid all those baseless rumors to rest, right at the start.

Many people said, "Maybe Mary Jo was pregnant." Well there

was no basis for such a conjecture, which no autopsy would have permitted. Even assuming a pregnancy, it would have been part of the autopsy record and therefore not subject to public inspection, whereas then, everybody was speculating without grounds about that and about why the whole thing happened. So instead of doing Kennedy a service, his friends did him the greatest *disservice*. They should have gone straight to the medical examiner and said, "Look, we want to have an autopsy." How could an autopsy have hurt? It would have shown that she drowned (for I'm pretty sure that's what happened to the girl)—and whatever else they found would not have been anyone's business.

So it was not that the certified cause of death was not correct, but that it should have been verified at the time by an autopsy, a simple and proper procedure that would have put an end to the vile scandal-mongering that occurred in its absence. The Massachusetts system has become obsolete, and legislation is being sought to bring it up to date as a statewide system.

Coming nearer home as far as I am concerned, the state of New York had coroners dating back to colonial times. In the early years of this century, back in the nineties, in fact, a lot of dissatisfaction arose with the coroners in New York, especially in the five counties that made up the city. They were inevitably lay people—political hacks. They belonged to the political clubs but had no professional qualifications for the job. They didn't even try to understand their responsibilities, but they were empowered to sign cases out and certify deaths, often *despite* the evidence, rather than *because* of it.

Theoretically, the coroners held inquests, but these were carried through by juries packed with members selected by the coroners, members being given the chance to pick up a few dollars as a coroner's juror. There was a great demand for these jobs; originally, there may not have been corruption, but it developed. As diagnoses and conclusions as to the cause of death were so blatantly wrong, there arose suspicion of bribery or of helping a friend, but sheer ineptitude was often responsible.

It became very evident that the coroner system was not good, even for the early 1900's. A short-ballot association in New York City was trying to reduce the long list of names on these ballots, and the disquiet about the coroner being an elected official with no qualifications of any sort grew. The scandals in criminal investigations began to be discussed around the town. For instance, a man would be shot in the back, and the verdict of the coroner's jury would be inconclusive as to the manner of death— the district attorney might not even be notified. The district attorney soon became concerned about the detection and prosecution of crime and came to realize that the coroners' inquests were doing a lot of harm by holding unnecessary investigations, which should have been carried out under the auspices of the district attorney.

Public dissatisfaction and anger increased, until various individuals and groups of New York citizens began to take action. One of these, Richard S. Childs, is still alive and active after more than seventy years of helping to establish good municipal and county government. Now a gallant old man of ninety-four, Childs was later associated with the founding of the National Association of Medical Examiners. He and others like him became interested in reforming the coroner system.

One particular incident is said to have brought the ferment to a boil. In 1914, an elderly distinguished citizen died suddenly at the Century Club of Manhattan. He happened to be a personal friend of the mayor, John Purroy Mitchell. Well, everyone was aghast at having a member die in their club—in fact, there is nothing more upsetting to a group of people than to have someone die in its midst, no matter how old he might be. It's a delicate situation that has to be handled correctly. In this instance, the coroner was notified and came by, and though it was apparently a natural death, he refused to issue a death certificate unless a certain undertaker he recommended was called to handle the funeral. Everyone at the club was incensed by the coroner's behavior. The next day, they went to the mayor and complained.

Mitchell was a reform mayor only twenty-nine years old at the time; he had appointed a group of commissioners who were also very young and energetic. He was incensed by the incident and summoned his commissioner of accounts (today he is called commissioner of investigation), Leonard Wallstein, and asked for a full investigation of the incident and of the coroner system in New York City. Wallstein immediately began a most thorough inquiry. At that time, there were separate coroners' offices in each of the five counties corresponding to the boroughs. The coroners were all elected, and each received a stipend. But more important than the stipend, there were in some instances more irregular methods of obtaining payment. This did not mean that all the coroners were dishonest, but several of them were. When questioned by Wallstein, they simply collapsed and admitted the irregularities.

By the time the investigation was over, everyone agreed that the only course was to get rid of the coroners and install a new system. Wallstein prepared a report, which is still available and which makes very interesting reading as a study in civics. It exposed many scandals and much dissatisfaction on the part of the public and designated the coroner system as antiquated and ill-fitting the needs of the city.

Up to this time, the district attorneys had to have their own physicians and pathologists look into cases, because apart from the poor investigations carried out by the coroners, they did not keep sufficiently detailed records. All the coroner kept was a card with a name and possibly a cause of death on it. Sometimes, the coroners would show off a bit by affecting a French language designation. For instance, a sunstroke case would be written up on the card as *coup de soleil*. Other meaningless jargon would be added to create a spurious air of knowledge.

The coroners were not qualified to do anything, let alone an autopsy, but sometimes they had physicians perform the operations. The only autopsies done before the abolition of the coroners were performed by pathologists on the staff of the large teaching hospitals and medical schools, the detailed reports being contained in the hospital records. Only the cause of death appeared on the coroner's card, often written in a fine Spencerian hand; these brief records can still be seen in the Municipal Archives of New York City and go back incompletely as far as the Slocum disaster on the East River, in which many people on a neighborhood excursion boat outing were drowned.

Professor Leo Hershkowitz of Queens College was able to retrieve some of the old coroners' records from the last century and early part of this one. Many had been destroyed as waste paper, and some were pilfered by trespasser derelicts. They make interesting reading and show the inadequacy of the examinations of those cases. The Wallstein Report of 1914 revealed that many coroners had been bartenders, plumbers, and bricklayers, prone to record their "favorite" causes of death.

When this report by the commissioner of accounts was

published, its strong recommendations that the offices of coroner be abolished were approved and sent to the state legislature in Albany. Section 284 of the New York State Laws of 1915 actually abolished the coroners' offices in the five counties constituting New York City. The succeeding section established a medical examiner's office for New York City. That Medical Examiner Law is the best that has been devised and is the prototype of the new laws since that time. It is no more than three or four pages long but has in it all that is necessary for a fully comprehensive death investigative system. It is so clearly defined that one could go out into the wilderness and set up a medical examiner's office. In fact, sometimes this has had to be done!

For the first time, it was required by law that the chief medical examiner and his assistants and deputies had to be not only doctors of medicine, but also *skilled pathologists and microscopists.* Thus, as far back as 1915, it was recognized that the microscope was an important tool and that only qualified pathologists were able to do this basic work. The Medical Examiner Law is important in that it established the independence of the Office of Chief Medical Examiner as a separate agency of government. The chief was directly responsible to the mayor of New York City who appointed him, but the mayor could not summarily dismiss him without preferring and sustaining charges against him. At one time, the chief medical examiner was the only city agency head who enjoyed Civil Service tenure. In 1915, this was felt to be the best way to get and retain suitably qualified persons, and it has continued until the present day, but I am disturbed at some recent proposals that would place the Office of the Medical Examiner, because it is small, in the larger Department of Health where it does not belong.

The state law of 1915 went into effect on the first day of January, 1918, on which day the offices of coroner were simultaneously abolished. The chief medical examiner, though himself appointed by the mayor, has the power to appoint and remove his deputies and assistants, who, as mentioned earlier, had to have the same scientific qualifications as their chief. Such appointments and removals have to conform to Civil Service rules; there can be no arbitrary appointments or dismissals. The Office is required to be open for business every day of the year and to have at least a clerk in attendance both day and night.

The chief medical examiner's powers and duties are clearly defined and relate to persons dying from criminal violence; casualty; suicide; suddenly when in apparent health; when unattended by a physician; in prison; in any suspicious or unusual manner; and when an application was made for cremation. These categories of death for many years had been reported to the coroners, but the reporting was haphazard. All citizens in New York have a duty to report such deaths to the chief medical examiner or to a police officer. Some of the displaced coroners challenged the Wallstein Report, but not effectively. It should be pointed out that the New York State Assembly had among its members Robert F. Wagner Sr., later senator from New York State, and Alfred E. Smith, who was to become governor. These were men of action.

Dr. Charles Norris was appointed the first chief medical examiner at the end of 1917 by Mayor John F. Hylan. Dr. Norris was a distinguished physician and pathologist, who had been director of laboratories at Bellevue Hospital from 1904 to 1918. Dr. Alexander Gettler, principal chemist at Bellevue, became the part-time toxicologist of the Office but received his salary from Bellevue Hospital. Later he was appointed director of the toxicological laboratories in the Office. The first headquarters for the new agency was in the Bellevue Hospital pathology building located at 400 East Twenty-ninth Street, with the administrative office at first in the Municipal Building and later at 125 Worth Street.

When our new building at 520 First Avenue was opened in 1961, all divisions were combined under one roof. The mortuary and autopsy facilities in the old Bellevue pathology building, which had played such an important, historic role in our development, had become quite unsuitable for our needs. The work and case load had been increasing tremendously for many years before we had the opportunity to move into better quarters. At Bellevue, there were four autopsy tables in the large upstairs room, which was needed more and more by the pathology department. Upon Dr. Norris' death in 1935, Dr. Thomas A. Gonzales became acting chief and later was appointed second chief medical examiner by Mayor Fiorello LaGuardia.

The close and very welcome association between our Office, a city establishment, and the academic faculty of New York

University School of Medicine began early, since the medical staff and pathologists were closely associated with the work of the medical examiner. Until recently, the medical staffs were made up of representatives from the three medical schools—Columbia, Cornell, and New York University—which staffed the four divisions of Bellevue Hospital. In 1932, the association between city and university was further strengthened, when the Department of Forensic Medicine, the first of its kind in any American medical school, was established at the New York University Medical School. Dr. Charles Norris was appointed its first professor and chairman. Upon his death in 1935, Dr. Harrison S. Martland, an outstanding pathologist and forensic pathologist, director of laboratories of the Newark City Hospital, and since 1927 chief medical examiner of Essex County, became its chairman. On his death, Dr. Thomas A. Gonzales, the second chief medical examiner, assumed Dr. Martland's post as professor and chairman. The initiative was carried on in 1954, when I became chief, on Dr. Gonzales's retirement, as the New York University School of Medicine appointed me professor and chairman of the Department of Forensic Medicine.

Chapter 2

Poison Without a Trace—
The Coppolino Trials

When people ask me the obvious question: "Which was your most memorable case?", I have no difficulty answering at all. Although forty-two years in the New York Chief Medical Examiner's Office (and a few more active years since I left) have cast up literally hundreds of memorable cases, the one that leads the field is the Coppolino case. Not only was the medico-legal aspect unique—it broke new ground in forensic toxicology—but the ballyhoo surrounding the trials was of an intensity that beat anything ever witnessed.

Now the first thing that I should explain about my involvement with the Coppolino case is that I wasn't just called in at a late stage to give expert testimony on behalf of the district attorney, either in New Jersey or Florida (the two states concerned in this bizarre affair). I was mixed up in the business long before any trials started; in fact, before the question of exhumations or autopsies had been considered.

I first heard of the case through a telephone call I received in November 1965. It was from Dr. Malcolm Gilman, the medical examiner of Monmouth County, New Jersey. He was almost a contemporary of mine at Cornell, for he graduated in 1927, just a year after I did, and I remembered him well.

Dr. Gilman said that the district attorney in Monmouth County had asked him to call me to ask if I would discuss two somewhat unusual death reports with them. One concerned a retired army officer who had died in New Jersey in 1963, and the other a woman who had died in Florida, but who had formerly lived in New Jersey and was now buried there.

They wanted some advice as to what they should do about the strange story they had been told about these deaths and wondered if I would be prepared to help them, as I was a pretty well-known person in this kind of problem, and New York City was just across the river from them. This was not the first time I had been asked to advise the authorities in New Jersey.

I can never say 'no' to an intriguing problem in the medico-legal sphere, so I said, "Certainly, come over to our Office and we'll have a talk about it." That casual invitation catapulted me into the most extraordinary case ever to come my way.

They came across to our Office on First Avenue. Dr. Gilman brought along the county prosecutor and the sheriff from New Jersey. Also present were the D.A. and Sheriff Boyer from Sarasota County, near Tampa, Florida.

They all met with me and some of my associates from the medical school across the way, around the long conference table in the Chief Medical Examiner's Office, and showed me the remarkable document which started the whole affair.

I am emphasizing the way in which I came into this case because some people have been under a misapprehension about the relationship of our Office to this particular case—they tend to think that I was consulted just because a district attorney had decided to prosecute and wanted me to add weight to the evidence. This was not so: the prosecutions were brought *because* of what we found at the autopsies, after many months of exacting laboratory work.

Well, to get back to our roundtable conference. The extraordinary document that had brought us together had been prepared by a Mrs. Majorie Farber, who used to be a New Jersey resident but now lived in Sarasota County, near Tampa, Florida. She had become very uneasy about the death of someone she knew there, and so agitated had she become, that she talked to the doctor who had certified the death and then went to her religious minister and told him the story. He was aghast and said that she must tell the authorities—he suggested the Federal Bureau of Investigation. So Mrs. Farber went to the local branch of the F.B.I., but they informed her that they had no jurisdiction in the matter and directed her to the local authorities. Many people have the idea that the F.B.I. exists to investigate particularly serious crimes, but in fact, they are powerless to intervene in anything but federal offenses or cases in which criminal acts transgress state boundaries.

Marjorie Farber was directed to the local custodian of the law in Sarasota County, Sheriff Ross Boyer. Now you have to see Sheriff Boyer to really appreciate him. He is a very large man indeed. He wears a ten-gallon hat, is very straightforward in his manner, and is not inclined to listen to nonsense stories.

This lady had gone to him earlier that month and said, "Sheriff Boyer, you remember that young woman doctor, Carmela Coppolino, who died last August at her home at Longboat Key, Sarasota?"

The sheriff had some recollection of the case, which had been certified as a heart attack, and said, yes, he did.

"Well, she didn't have a heart attack," announced Mrs. Farber, "She was murdered."

Now Sheriff Boyer was used to dealing with all sorts of people, some less sane than others, so he didn't just throw his hands up in the air.

"Come on now," he said. "That's not a nice thing to say. Both those good people were doctors, the wife and her husband."

But Marjorie Farber was unmoved. "She was murdered," she repeated. "Murdered by her husband, Carl Coppolino. And what's more, two and a half years ago, he murdered my husband. I know he did, because I was present when he did it."

All Sheriff Boyer could do was to say, "Well, I'll be God damned!"

He contacted the authorities in New Jersey, and soon afterward they arranged to see me, to decide the best course of action.

They then went on to tell me the facts as they knew them, but in putting the story together here, it makes more coherent reading if I piece the whole together from what was known subsequently. The details of the Coppolino saga, then, were these.

Carl Coppolino, a lean, dark, good-looking fellow in his early thirties, had qualified as a doctor of medicine at the Downstate Medical School in New York—formerly Long Island Medical School—in the year 1958. He had become engaged, before graduating, to another student, Carmela Musetto, who was the daughter of a successful internist in New Jersey. Carmela was the apple of her father's eye, especially as she turned out to be an exceptionally gifted medical student. Carl was quite bright, too, but a colleague in their medical faculty once told me that the girl was possibly the best student they had ever had.

Anyway, Dr. Musetto took quite a liking to his daughter's fiancé, but he prevailed on him to postpone their marriage until they had graduated. In return for this, he promised to finance Carl's progress through medical school. Shortly after their graduation, Carl and Carmela were married and settled in New Jersey. The husband did a residency in anesthesiology and then became a staff anesthesiologist at Riverview Hospital in Red Bank, New Jersey.

His wife, Carmela, took a post with a large pharmaceutical company, Hoffman-La Roche Inc., working as a research physician. They had two young children, and for a time, all seemed to be working out normally. Carl continued to work as an anesthesiologist and became interested in hypnosis as a means of anesthesia—he even wrote several books on the subject.

It was around 1961 when some trouble developed at the hospital where Carl worked. A nurse-anesthetist there suddenly received four anonymous, typewritten letters, threatening her that if she didn't stop working in the hospital, she would be mutilated and have all sorts of dire things happen to her.

She immediately went to the F.B.I. with these letters, as this was a matter within the jurisdiction of the federal agency.

They very soon traced the letters to the typewriter in the office next door to the operating room, and it soon became very obvious that the author of the letters was Dr. Carl Coppolino.

He admitted making the threats but said that he had never carried them out. The root of the trouble appeared to be that he was very jealous of his position as anesthesiologist in the hospital and wanted to eliminate any possible competition.

The hospital administration thought it would be better to just let him go, as they wanted no trouble; though they later admitted that future events might have been prevented if appropriate action had been taken. Anyway, Carl was allowed to resign without any scandal. Just before this happened, he anticipated that he was heading for trouble, so he took out a $20,000 annual disability insurance policy with the group insurance plan of the New Jersey Medical Society.

He then declared that he had coronary heart disease—this was in January 1963—and declared himself disabled as a cardiac patient. Reluctantly, the insurance company paid out on his $20,000 policy, but they watched him like a hawk to make sure that he didn't practice on the quiet.

Carmela was still working at Hoffman-La Roche, bringing in about $15,000 a year; so with his disability benefit, they managed to get along.

The drama continued with the appearance of new neighbors on Wallace Road in Middletown, where they lived. These were the Farbers—the husband was a retired army colonel, William Farber, who was fifty-four years old, and the wife was the lady who was so to surprise Sheriff Boyer, Mrs. Marjorie Farber, a lady of about fifty, but still quite attractive.

The Coppolinos and the Farbers had first met on the street in Middletown, then at a Christmas party, and from then on their social contact rapidly widened—though it would seem that the mainstay of the friendship was between Carl and Marjorie. Marjorie Farber suffered from a chest condition and was always coughing, a disorder she blamed on her compulsive smoking. She said one day that she wished she could find a way of giving up the habit, and it was Carmela who suggested that she consult Carl about her problem, as he was a proficient hypnotist. The next day she rang Carl, who was not at home. She left a message, and within fifteen minutes he was at her home, giving her the first of his mesmeric treatments.

From then on, their intimacy grew rapidly, and they later admitted that they became lovers from about February 1963. In March, Carl decided that he needed a holiday in Florida for the sake of his heart. When Carmela said she couldn't take time off from her job to go along with him, Marjorie Farber took him south "to look after him," apparently with the knowledge and consent of Colonel Farber and Carmela.

What the colonel thought of this arrangement we never really got to discover. He had been a line officer in the service and had been very active in the war in the South Pacific. After leaving the army, he took a degree at the University of Maryland and then moved to New Jersey. He had a job with an insurance company in Manhattan and commuted to the city every day.

As Carmela also went every day to her work at the Hoffman-La Roche plant in Nutley, New Jersey, Carl and Marjorie had plenty of opportunity to indulge in propinquity, or whatever you like to call it. She later testified that he continued to practice hypnosis on her, and it was this that caused her to remain infatuated with him. According to Mrs. Farber, she was a little worried about his heart complaint, especially the effect of all his amorous activity, which occurred at least once a day, and more often when they were in Florida or Puerto Rico.

Well, the convalescence trips began to multiply because of Carl's poor heart, which prevented him from working, though it didn't seem to stop him from indulging his passions. He went to Florida, Bermuda, and Puerto Rico during the first half of 1963, each time taking Mrs. Farber with him. The insurance company eventually began to get a little disgruntled, and apparently so did Colonel Bill Farber.

It seems that there never had been much liking between the two men, as might easily have been expected. Carl disliked Farber, and according to Marjorie's later testimony, he once said, "That man has got to go."

Now I'll just relate what was reported to have happened in Middletown on July 30, 1963.

During the evening, the two Farber children came across to the Coppolino house, in search of their mother. They said that they couldn't wake up their father, and there was a notice on his door which said: "Don't disturb Daddy. He's sleeping." This story was confirmed later by the maid at the Farber house.

Now Carl, who was afraid to be seen practicing any sort of medicine because of his disability pension, sends over his wife, a currently licensed physician, to see what is wrong at the Farber's. She telephones back shortly afterwards to say that she had found Bill Farber dead.

"He must have had a heart attack," says Carl, though in fact the colonel had led a very active life, with no signs or symptoms whatsoever of any cardiac trouble.

Carl then told Carmela to issue a death certificate, even though she was not Farber's regular physician and had never attended him for any ailment. Legally, she had no right to sign out the death. It should have been reported to the medical examiner as a sudden, unexpected death of someone not under a physician's care.

But Carmela did as her husband told her and wrote a death certificate for "occlusive coronary artery disease."

"You know *I* can't sign it," said Carl to her, "I'm on total disability." He told her to use coronary disease as the cause, as he knew these deaths are most common, especially in men of fifty-four. They rarely get questioned, and the certificate was accepted without query by the health department.

A funeral director came and removed the body, and eventually it was buried with military honors in Arlington National Cemetery.

So now we have the colonel, decked out in his best dress uniform, his medals pinned on his chest, mouldering in a wet grave in Virginia.

Almost two years later, in the middle of 1965, the Coppolinos moved to Florida. Carmela's father, Dr. Musetto, loaned them the money to build a new house at Longboat Key, Sarasota County, not far from Tampa, in northwest Florida.

It seems that the affair between Carl and Marjorie Farber had continued for most of the intervening time, but it cooled off at the time of the move. She said she had not been intimate with him since leaving New Jersey—a few weeks after the Coppolinos relocated, Marjorie also shifted to Sarasota and actually bought a plot of land for a house right next door to Carl and Carmela!

There was a month between the move of the two families. Carl, being a fast worker, had in this time already discovered another lady, Mrs. Mary Gibson, an attractive brunette in her late thirties. She had met Carl at a bridge club, and very soon they were going around together.

It seems that Carl asked Carmela for a divorce, but being a devout Italian Catholic, she would not consent and became very upset. According to Marjorie Farber, it was on the very next day that Carmela was found dead.

To go back a little, Carmela was a physician licensed to practice in New Jersey, but not in Florida. She wanted to take the state medical board examinations, so that she could take a job there. Another local woman doctor, Juliette Karow, was helping Carmela prepare for the Florida examinations. Carl was still on his disability and was not working. Carmela had had to leave Hoffman-La Roche on leaving Middletown, so they would have virtually no additional income until she could get another medical post.

At six o'clock on the morning of August 28, 1965, Carl Coppolino rang Dr. Karow and asked her to come over right away, as he had found his wife dead in bed.

The local doctor hurried to the new house on Bowsprit Lane, in Longboat Key. She got there twenty minutes after the phone call, and Carl met her at the door. "She's dead," he said, leading her to the bedroom.

Dr. Karow found Carmela dead in bed, lying on her right side. The bed looked undisturbed, but the body seemed to be in a most uncomfortable position, according to Juliette Karow. She had some initial misgivings, as the upper surface of Carmela's face was discolored, rather than the lower part where blood would be expected to settle after death, due to gravity. The doctor was also puzzled that the hand on the lower side of the corpse was not swollen, in comparison with the other one, though I don't really see the relevance of that.

Once again, Carl claimed that his wife had complained of chest pains the previous night, but had refused to call a doctor.

He also said that he and Carmela had gone to bed at about ten the previous night (in their separate twin beds) and had each drunk one bloody mary at that time. He had slept all night, and when he woke just before six o'clock, she was dead in her bed, just as Dr. Karow saw her. "She must have had a heart attack," he said.

Well, Dr. Karow was rather concerned. She knew nothing of the medical history of these new arrivals in Florida, and as far as she knew, Dr. Carmela Coppolino was a healthy thirty-two-year-old woman. But her husband was also a physician; there was nothing at all suspicious about the family situation. They seemed a normal young couple with two small children, recently established in this new housing development. Who was she to argue with the physician-husband's diagnosis? The only odd thing was that fatal coronary disease is very uncommon in women of Carmela Coppolino's age—much less common than in men of comparable years.

Dr. Karow felt that it was probably all O.K.; physicians generally, by inclination and training, have a low suspicion index and are conditioned into believing most of what their patients tell them. But she did the right thing in the circumstances and called the sheriff's department to report the death. They told her that they would send an investigator and also an escort to remove the body for an autopsy.

Dr. Karow then called the county medical examiner, Dr. Millard White, but he said the sheriff's office had not referred the case to him, so he suggested that they get a funeral director to remove the body to a funeral home.

There was an administrative mix-up right off the bat. Dr. Karow rang the sheriff's office and was told that Bowsprit Lane was not in the county area of jurisdiction, so she phoned the Longboat Key police department, and they came over. In fact, Chief Corsi himself came, but he arrived just as the undertakers were trundling out the body. He asked to see Carl Coppolino but was told he was too distressed. Now the police officer knew that the deceased was a doctor; that the husband was a doctor; that there was another doctor on the premises; and that she had already phoned the medical examiner, who had authorized the removal of the body. So Corsi understandably was satisfied that all the doctors must be on the level and therefore did not apply the strict letter of the law, which required that Dr. Millard White perform an autopsy. He should have done so, because a few years earlier a law was passed in Sarasota County making an autopsy mandatory in all cases where the deceased had not been attended by a physician. This legislation followed an embarrassing case, where a physician had certified the death of a fat lady as being due to coronary disease, but her "heart complaint" was later traced to a stab wound in the chest from an ice pick!

Now in that county, an unsatisfactory state of affairs existed whereby the medical examiner could not himself order an autopsy but had to await a police or D.A.'s request. As Chief Corsi did not do this, Carmela Coppolino's body went unexamined by anyone.

All this points up the moral that when you fragment responsibility, something is sure to go wrong. In the New York system, all the responsibility is held by one person, the chief medical examiner, and if there is a foul-up, then everyone knows immediately where the blame lies.

By now, Dr. Karow felt she had fulfilled all her legal obligations in the matter, as she had notified all three, the sheriff, the police and the medical examiner—and no doubt she was justified in feeling that she could do no more.

Carmela had been found dead early in the morning. The Coppolino children were taken in by a neighbor, but later in the day, they went to stay with Mary Gibson, who was soon to become the second Mrs. Coppolino. Carl did not get in touch with Carmela's parents in New Jersey until that evening, though they had been informed of the death by another daughter, Angela Imhof, about six o'clock that evening.

The father, Dr. Musetto, had two rather obscure telephone conversations with Carl, who was in a highly emotional state and incoherent. But the elder doctor managed to ask him what the cause of death was and was told "a heart attack, a massive myocardial infarction."

Then he asked Carl if the medical examiner had seen the body and performed an autopsy. Carl said, "Yes, Doctor White has done an autopsy—he just called to tell me that it was a massive coronary occlusion."

Now this was significant—however emotionally upset Coppolino might have been, no mere confusion or slip of the tongue could have led him to lie about the autopsy. Dr. White had never telephoned him about the results of any autopsy, because there had never been one—by Dr. White or anyone else.

Carmela's father was himself an experienced physician, with a lot of background in cardiology. He found it hard to accept that a previously healthy girl like his daughter had suddenly died of a coronary attack, which is virtually unknown in women of her age. But he had little grounds to dispute it, as he had just been told that the official medical examiner had done an autopsy and discovered a heart condition. So arrangements were made for the embalmed body to be shipped back to New Jersey for burial.

Five weeks later, Carl Coppolino was married again—not to Marjorie Farber, his former mistress, but to the rich divorcée, Mary Gibson.

In the subsequent trial, Coppolino's defense counsel, F. Lee Bailey, used the phrase "Hell hath no fury like a woman scorned" as one of the main planks of his defense. He was referring, of course, to the state of mind of Mrs. Farber when she found that her ex-lover, for whom she had moved from New Jersey to Florida, had suddenly married a comparative stranger, right under her nose! Bailey contended that Marjorie's accusations were all fabricated in order to railroad her boyfriend into a murder charge. But the Farber denunciation was worth being taken seriously by the authorities, especially as it meant that Mrs. Farber was putting herself in dire peril of suspected involvement in a murderous conspiracy to kill her own husband.

The story she narrated to Sheriff Boyer (and later testified to at Coppolino's trial) was sufficient to rock him out of his usual imperturbability and make him exclaim, "Well, I'll be God damned!"

She told him that back in New Jersey, just over two years earlier, Carl had decided that her husband, Colonel Bill, had to go.

You remember that I said earlier that Carl felt that William Farber had become antagonistic and insulting toward him over the developing affair with his wife. At Coppolino's trial for Farber's murder, Mrs. Farber testified that Coppolino gave her an undetectable drug which was supposed to kill instantly. It was called succinylcholine and is used to cause muscle relaxation during surgery, so that the abdomen and other areas can be operated upon without difficulty. Too much of the drug will cause widespread paralysis of all muscles, and this can cause death by failure of the chest muscles to maintain breathing movements.

Marjorie testified that Carl gave her a syringe and needle and some white powder. He told her to dissolve the powder in water and inject it into her husband when he was asleep. She said that she was still under a hypnotic spell that had begun when he had used hypnosis to cure her of smoking.

She was in a great state of conflict within herself, her natural abhorrence of this act clashing with the mesmeric state that Coppolino had induced in her. Marjorie was supposed to administer the injection on a Sunday night, but when she had gone as far as taking the hypodermic and powder out of the envelope, she couldn't continue.

On the next night, she paced the house trying to decide what to do, then filled the syringe and went to the bedroom where her husband was asleep. Colonel Farber was lying on his side, and she jabbed the needle into the top of his leg and started to push the plunger down. Then she froze and couldn't bring herself to carry on. At that point, Bill Farber woke up and complained of having a charley-horse in his leg. He staggered to the bathroom and was immediately ill with diarrhea, gasping and in general very distressed.

His wife phoned Carl to come, and he hurried over in the middle of the night. He gave Farber another type of injection to quiet him, and asked Marjorie to get a plastic bag. She says she didn't know what he wanted it for, but she fetched one that had come from the dry cleaners. He put it over Farber's head and started to suffocate him, but the poor victim began vomiting.

According to Marjorie's testimony she was now yelling at Carl to "stop doing that," so Coppolino left Farber alone. It seems that he went home then, after telling Marjorie not to wash the pillow case upon which Farber had just vomited.

Carl came back to the house about one o'clock the following afternoon and gave Bill Farber another injection of a sedative, which made him sleepy, but soon Marjorie testified that she heard a violent argument going on. Farber was apparently telling Coppolino to clear out.

Carl stalked out of the bedroom to the room where Marjorie was and in great anger said, "The bastard's got to go. He's threatened me and my family. Nobody is going to talk to me like that!"

He began taking out his syringe again, but Mrs. Farber begged him to go and leave them both alone. Carl went back into the bedroom and she followed, by which time she thought that he had given Bill another injection.

Coppolino said, "He's a hard one to kill; he's taking a long time to die."

Then, she testified, he took a pillow and placed it on Farber's face, leaning on it with both his hands so that the weight of his body was pressing on the pillow. After a time, he told Marjorie to wipe some blood off Farber's hand, perhaps where the injection had been given. Then he removed the pillow and lifted an eyelid, to make sure Farber was dead.

Carl turned the body onto its side, saying, "I want him to look like he died in his sleep."

He told Marjorie to write the note about "Daddy is sleeping— do not disturb," and pin it to the door.

This was the incredible story that Marjorie Farber brought to Sheriff Boyer, two and a half years after the event. She said that she did not believe that Carmela had died a natural death, and she had already spoken to Dr. Karow and others before coming to Boyer.

Well, that was the story—but what to do about it?

After this conference in our Office in New York, it was agreed that a disinterrment of Carmela's body would be the best way to start. She was the more recently dead, only three and a half months had elapsed when I eventually performed the autopsy in the middle of December 1965.

It was suggested that the examination be done in New Jersey, but as the death took place outside the state anyway—in Florida—and we had much better facilities in New York, it was decided that the autopsy would be performed in the Manhattan Office of the Chief Medical Examiner, where there is so much activity that the case would not excite any curiosity.

As the story concerning Carmela's death revolved around the possible use of succinylcholine, a drug used in anesthesia, I got in touch with a colleague to get the best possible expert advice. This is one of the advantages of a medical examiner's office being in a close geographical and professional relationship with various university and hospital departments. You just can't work in isolation, and on many occasions I have been very glad of the available advice of anesthesiologists, dentists, radiologists, neurologists, anatomists, and a host of other specialists that I can call upon when some special need arises. This time, I was glad of the help of my good friend, Dr. Valentino D.B. Mazzia, who was professor and chairman of the Department of Anesthesiology at New York University School of Medicine, with whom my office had been working on a project concerned with operating room fatalities. I asked him to sit in on the conference as a consultant and to give his opinion on the possibility of proving the presence or absence of the drug in the body.

Dr. Mazzia told us that succinylcholine was rapidly broken down in the body into succinic acid and choline, both of which are normal constituents of the tissues. As far as he knew, this rapid breakdown had so far prevented any chemical detection of the drug in the body, and he was not too optimistic about recovering proof, especially in an embalmed body that had been buried for over three months.

However, we had to investigate the case and to look for the alleged coronary disease already revealed by Carl's imaginary .

autopsy, as well as for any other disease or injury.

As far as the drug aspect was concerned, this was an all-time first, an autopsy search for a medicinal chemical compound never before detected in a body, alive or dead. Furthermore, it might be the main evidence in a trial for murder, which at that time still carried the death penalty. Thus, a heavy responsibility lay on our shoulders.

I began the examination on December 17 in the special well-ventilated, air conditioned autopsy room in the big new department on First Avenue. We did it in the accessible special room where all the routine cases with any decomposition were done, so that no suspicion or comment would be aroused, as it might have had we hidden ourselves away in a closed room. No one was particularly curious or came in to ask what was going on that was so special.

I began by cleaning off the macerated skin to look for a needle puncture, though I was a bit pessimistic about finding one after the body had been in the ground for three and a half months. However, it was in a fairly good state of preservation, and as I took the surface film off the skin, I hoped to get a glimpse of some suspicious mark. Had I been doing this autopsy without knowing the history of the case, I might well have missed the perforation which shows how important it is to have all possible information at hand before you begin.

Well, we turned the body onto its front as it was rolled on the table, washed the skin, and examined the buttocks. There was the puncture as plain as the nose on your face: a tiny pink spot, marking the skin of the outer upper quadrant of the left buttock.

I pointed it out to my assistants, who asked skeptically, "How do you know it's a needle puncture mark?"

"Because it looks like one," I said. "Let me take a photograph and then we'll see what it is."

I made an incision through the skin, right down through the fat of the buttock—and there, extending down from the surface, was a red streak right into the tissues under the skin—as obvious as the day it was made. It penetrated the skin and passed right through the fatty layer of the buttock, leaving a little trail of hemorrhage that terminated in the gluteal fasci like the exhaust of a high-flying airplane. After perforating the fascia (the fibrous layer beneath the fat), it passed into the gluteal muscle where it was obscured, but no doubt it entered the muscles of the buttock. The embalming of the tissue had preserved it sufficiently so that the typical appearance one sees from an intramuscular injection on a fresh corpse was easily evident even three and a half months after death.

Now nothing at all in Carmela's medical history suggested that she had had a deep intramuscular injection shortly before death. (It had to be shortly before death, for the track would have healed up and been absorbed within a few days.) She was supposed to have been in perfect health, which was why people were so surprised to hear of her sudden, unexpected demise.

So what had been the purpose of this injection? For the streak could be nothing other than the track of a needle.

The track was about one and a half inches long, and I saved all the tissues we needed for the most extensive analysis. I took the skin from around the puncture mark and all the fat and muscle from the region. I also preserved corresponding material from the opposite, unpunctured buttock, to act as a control for any analytical techniques that might be carried out.

The rest of the autopsy revealed absolutely nothing in the way of abnormalities. Carmela's heart—which allegedly had killed her—could not have been healthier. This was never even raised at the subsequent trial as an issue—the defense knew that with a heart as healthy as that, they had not the slightest hope of clouding the issue by trying to assert that she had died of natural causes. There was nothing anywhere else in the body that suggested any disease or injury that might have contributed to death. Carmela was a perfectly fit young woman—except that she was dead!

I refrigerated at low temperature all the tissues saved for analysis and turned them over to my chief toxicologist, Dr. Charles ("Joe") Umberger.

Now Joe is a man who will not be pushed. Believe me, he can be like a Missouri mule; he cannot be hurried or intimidated into doing something or finding something, unless it is done at his pace and to his satisfaction. It was later insinuated that I told him, "Your job is to find succinylcholine, Joe," but if you knew Dr. Umberger, you'd know how laughable that suggestion is.

Joe Umberger worked on the tissues for a long time. There was a heavy load of other routine laboratory work to get through, and you must remember that this was an absolute first.

He had to develop methods to detect the breakdown products of succinylcholine, apply them to the tissues, and satisfy himself beyond any doubt that they were present and that they were not merely normal constituents in the quantity found. These tests took a number of months to complete. As Joe later explained, it was impossible by the methods of toxicologic analysis to find the original substance in the body, as succinylcholine is broken down within minutes to succinic acid and choline. Although these two compounds are normally present in dead tissue, they are there in such small quantities that ordinary techniques fail to detect them.

Joe Umberger devised a method that would show up abnormally large amounts of the two substances but would not react with the minute quantities normally present. Using this technique, he eventually proved to his satisfaction that there was an abnormally high concentration of succinic acid in the organs of the body. He could not show that there was an excess in the left buttock itself, as he could not apply the technique to fatty tissue.

Now we had another break, again thanks to the proximity of a large medical school like New York University. Dr. Valentino— or "Tino" as we called him—Mazzia continued to be a great help to me; he even volunteered to test the effect of succinylcholine on an unanesthetised person—himself! He already knew a lot about the drug, but Tino is one of those enterprising people who— when he wants to know something about a substance— experiments first hand. He injected himself with a paralyzing dose of succinylcholine, keeping a mechanical respirator alongside in case of emergency. Subsequently, he was able to describe exactly what happened—it rendered him completely helpless, but he retained consciousness. Eventually his breathing stopped, so if the respirator had not been available while the drug wore off, he might well have died from asphyxia. This very important piece of evidence was introduced at the trial.

But even more important was Dr. Mazzia's help in putting us in touch with yet another expert on the faculty of medicine at N.Y.U. Tino was a good friend of Dr. Bert LaDu, professor and chairman of the Department of Pharmacology. Now Bert LaDu was an expert on succinylcholine and undoubtedly knew more about its pharmacology than anyone else in the country. He had been working on the recovery of the drug from the body tissues and especially on perfecting methods of recovering it from fatty tissues—a research project tailor-made for our urgent need in the Coppolino case.

A shy man, Dr. LaDu asked Mazzia to inquire whether I would allow him to work on the buttock material, which had so far been useless to our own toxicologists.

I was only too glad to let him have it, both the sample with the needle mark and the opposite buttock, which was intact except for some small bruises. They had been under lock and key in a deepfreeze since the autopsy and were in good condition, even after storage for a year or so.

So Bert LaDu went off with the tissues and worked away in his own laboratory at the medical school. I carefully made a point of not going near him or asking him about his progress, as I didn't want any insinuations or suggestions made that I was hounding him into providing an answer that would suit the prosecution's purposes.

About a month before the trial, I ran into Dr. Mazzia, who asked me if I had heard from Dr. LaDu. I said no, I hadn't heard a thing. "Well, Bert's found the stuff around the needle tract in the left buttock," he disclosed.

This was the clincher. Apparently, succinyldicholine breaks down into a monocholine derivative that is stable in fat, and Dr. LaDu had found a positive reaction for this around the needle track and a less intense reaction in the surrounding fat of the buttock, fading out as the distance from the needle puncture increased. In the right buttock, there was no reaction at all. The embalming process had actually helped preserve the monocholine by its acid effect on the tissues.

This, together with Joe Umberger's discovery of abnormal amounts of succinic acid in the other organs, was cast-iron proof that a large dose of succinylcholine had been injected into Carmela's left buttock shortly before her death. Many experiments were run on patients who had died in the operating room after having received succinylcholine in therapeutic doses, with negative results, and the analytical technique was so accurate that there could be no doubt that a large amount of the drug had been given.

Now I was the *pathologist* in the case—I knew little or nothing of the complicated chemistry involved in the analyses—but when I received the test results, I used them, in conjunction with the story of the circumstances and with the completely negative findings at the autopsy, to arrive at the cause of death. Much was made at the trial of the fact that I had not run the tests myself—well, of course not!

But it was not the chemists who inferred the cause of death—they supplied me with information about certain analyses they had performed at my request, and I used this information in conjunction with the rest of my knowledge to arrive at a conclusion. A perfectly commonsense procedure, but not to lawyers eager to tear you to bits in order to destroy your credibility as a witness.

Well, long before the results of the toxicologic study on Carmela had become available, the law enforcement authorities wanted to know what had happened to William Farber. The autopsy on Carmela had already shown that she certainly hadn't died of a coronary, and she had a needle mark in her buttock, so Marjorie Farber's accusations seemed to have a considerable foundation of truth, sufficient to warrant having a good look at the body of the colonel in Arlington Cemetery. This was done a few months after the autopsy on Carmela, in July 1966.

William Farber had been in the ground at Arlington for three years and his cadaver was not in good shape. The skin was all rotted away, so it was impossible to find any injection marks, though we did our best to search for signs of them. Thanks to the embalming, some parts of the body were quite well-preserved, including the internal organs, but much of the body had been converted to *adipocere*, a white waxy substance that is formed by the action of damp on the body fat.

The authorities were very careful when the grave was opened and the body removed from the coffin. It was suggested later that the injuries we found on Bill Farber's throat might have been caused by the lid of the coffin caving in or a careless gravedigger hitting it with his shovel. Nothing of the kind occurred, and I personally supervised the removal of the coffin lining and the uniform. In this situation I never let the mortuary attendant undress the body, because of the possibility of damage and because the clothing can sometimes provide more pertinent information than the autopsy itself.

I undressed the body and found no evidence of any accidents that might have contributed to Bill Farber's damaged throat. During the autopsy, I found a double fracture of the cricoid cartilage, which is the ring of gristle that forms the upper part of the windpipe immediately below the larynx, in the front of the neck. It is commonly fractured during strangulation or violence to the throat.

Later, at the trial, Lee Bailey kept insinuating that the injuries were the result of violence during burial or exhumation. They could not have occurred in this way since although the sides of the coffin had given way, the lid was in place. The fabric of the uniform was intact except for the rotting of the cotton threads. The tissues of the extremities were rotted away, but the fabric was unmistakable. The cotton shirt was also rotted, but the nylon tie was undisturbed, and the shirt-buttons and celluloid collar stays were all there. Therefore, the insinuation that a spade had broken the larynx was pure surmise and speculation, unsupported by the slightest evidence. The coffin had not collapsed on the Colonel, and nothing had pressed on his neck after he died.

I did not expect to find any residual signs of the alleged death by smothering, as the body had been buried for over three years and was beyond any hope of providing recognizable signs of smothering. These signs are subtle enough in a fresh body—even completely absent in certain circumstances. There was no positive way of confirming Marjorie Farber's accusations against Carl Coppolino, apart from the very significant discovery of the double fracture of the cricoid cartilage. I found these fractures toward the end of my autopsy—the last thing I did was to take out the throat organs—but before removing them from the body, I felt them with my fingers. This is always a wise precaution, to avoid the later accusation that the very act of physically removing the throat structures was the cause of the damage.

But in William Farber's autopsy, I felt a queer sensation when I gently touched the front of the larynx—it felt like a cracked ping-pong ball, with no resilience in the region of the cricoid cartilage ring above the top of the windpipe.

I removed the larynx and dissected the soft tissues, carefully avoiding opening the larynx either before or after its removal from the body, so that no one could accuse me of breaking it myself. But the defense merely transferred the blame from me to the funeral director or to the supposedly collapsed coffin, which hadn't collapsed on the body at all.

Later, during the trial two pathologists for the defense hurriedly looked at the cricoid and declared that this exquisitely characteristic injury was a post-mortem artifact! How they could tell that better than I could tell it had happened during life never came to light. There was talk of the absence of blood at the fracture site, implying that the damage had been done after the heart stopped, but in my experience—which you must admit is not inconsiderable—the amount of blood found in these little fractures after strangulation is very small indeed, even when you have the tissues in the fresh state. So what hope was there of finding it after three years under the sod?

Nevertheless, the double fracture was good enough for me to offer it as a sign of violence applied to the front of the neck—which was what Mrs. Farber had described as the heels of Coppolino's hands pressing on the pillow. She thought her husband was being smothered, but the autopsy clearly indicated that he was strangled manually.

Now Colonel Farber had been certified—by Carl's wife, no less—as having died of coronary artery disease, so the state of his coronary arteries became a crucial issue at the trial.

I looked at them with great care and kept numerous samples for microscopic examination. Yes, there was coronary artery disease—it would be a rare fifty-four-year-old American male who didn't have some. But the *degree* was what counted, and in my estimation (and I have been looking at coronary arteries since about 1927, including a number of research projects on the subject) the degree of narrowing was not a competing cause of death in view of the signs of violence to the neck, classic signs of manual strangulation.

I looked at Farber's heart before I examined his larynx, and I experienced the frustration familiar to all pathologists, that I was going to terminate this autopsy without determining any satisfactory cause of death. The coronary arteries showed patches of atherosclerosis, but none was seriously blocking the bore of the blood vessels. There was certainly no complete shut-off of the coronary supply, nor even any serious deprivation of the flow of blood due to narrowing. The heart muscle was normal and did not reveal a single scar.

But of course the defense pathologists came to exactly the opposite conclusion. They considered the state of the coronary arteries such that heart disease had to have caused death. Well, it's up to the jury to decide among the expert medical witnesses, once they qualify themselves as such to the court.

This was the state of affairs then, around the middle of 1966. An autopsy had been performed on Carmela Coppolino back in the winter and one on William Farber in July.

In the first case, my report, dated six months after the exhumation of Carl's wife, gave the cause of death as succinylcholine poisoning. The actual report read: *Liver and brain tissue showed positive chemical findings for both choline and succinic acid. Control cases examined by the same analytical procedure did not show either compound to be present. The positive chemical findings by the method employed indicated significant quantities of these substances, which, when present in normal or medicinal amounts, are not detectable. Systematic analyses of liver, brain and kidney for toxic substances other than those found in the embalming fluid or as a result of decomposition, were negative.*

Of course, at this time the results of the special researches of Dr. Bert LaDu on the buttock fat were not known or even suspected, and they came to light only shortly before the actual trial in Florida. The conclusions from the exhumation of Bill Farber, just completed, were that he had died from pressure on the neck producing a double fracture of the cricoid cartilage of the larynx, and no hope existed of identifying any possible drugs in the decomposed body. Neither did I consider his alleged coronary disease a factor in the death.

Almost simultaneously, in August 1966, two separate grand juries, one in New Jersey and one in Florida, indicted Dr. Carl Coppolino on separate charges of first degree murder. There was a legal hassle about who was to get him first, but New Jersey ultimately won the day.

However, before his trial for the murder of Bill Farber, Coppolino appeared at a preliminary hearing in Sarasota, Florida, in connection with the charge of killing his wife. His counsel, headed by the renowned and flamboyant Boston attorney F. Lee Bailey, asked for this hearing, hoping to have the case dismissed on the evidence without being sent on for a full jury trial. On the first day of September 1966, the hearing began—coincidentally exactly one year to the day from when Carmela had been buried in Boonton, New Jersey.

A few days later, I encountered the fabled F. Lee Bailey for the first time. Although we both reside in the northeast, chance had decreed that our paths never cross in court, and in fact, I could not recall having seen him before.

I'll say at once that Bailey is an excellent lawyer. To say that he leaves no stone unturned in his fight for his client, is the understatement of the century. But his methods, I'm afraid, are jarring to the senses.

I gave my testimony about the autopsy on Carmela and the chemical findings. Then Bailey got up to cross-examine me. He eyed me rather warily and for a time proceeded with caution. Then he started to employ tactics that didn't accord with the way I was accustomed to being treated in a court of law. Perhaps an objective description may be quoted from John MacDonald's excellent account of the case in his book *No Deadly Drug*:

"How much choline?" asked Bailey. "I want to know if you have any estimation."

"I'm sorry. There was no quantitation carried out. They had all they could do to come up with the qualitative. It was a great deal of work to analyze for this substance."

"You mean the men were *instructed* to come up with the findings?" Bailey's tone was one of incredulity and indignation.

Milton Helpern was shocked, affronted, and furious. "Counsellor, that's not fair! You know I didn't say that. I resent that."

Bailey persisted in asking me what constituted a lethal dose of succinylcholine. Well, it's impossible to say. Many factors determine the amount: the speed of administration, personal susceptibility; the different rates at which individuals break it down. I knew only that if detectable amounts could be found of the two substances, choline and succinic acid, then a quantity far greater than a legitimate dose must have been given in a very short time. But Bailey kept trying to lever a fixed quantity out of me.

I said to him, "I know the drug is lethal in excess, and that is sufficient. I am not interested in the amount of it; I am interested in the effect of it. I don't have to carry the figures around in my head to say it is lethal."

At this, he snapped back at me. "This is not a carrying-around-in-your head case. You are testifying in a *capital* case!"

I nearly exploded. In MacDonald's book he says, "Bailey's

response made Helpern so angry that he came dangerously close to incoherence."

What annoyed me was Bailey's assumption that because the case was capital, the standard of evidence should be different from that in any lesser case. Why should I take the oath and change my testimony just because it was a homicide case and not a small insurance claim? Is the truth any truer in murder than in shoplifting? It makes no difference whatsoever to me if the accused person is an alleged sadistic child slayer or a poor henpecked guy who once in his life lashed out at his nagging wife. It's all the same to me. I'm there to present the medical facts as well as I can, and I deeply resented Bailey's attempt to tell me how to testify—an activity that I was engaged in some four years before he was even born.

This kind of verbal wrangling occurred now and then throughout the Coppolino affair. All the same, I had to admire Bailey's expertise, although he could be utterly ruthless as far as witnesses were concerned.

Well, the preliminary hearing didn't achieve Bailey's object, and the case was sent for trial. Already New Jersey had set the legal machine in operation to get Coppolino up there to be tried for Farber's death, and on October 5, he was escorted to Monmouth County Jail, New Jersey.

The reason for this extradition was that back in July the New Jersey grand jury had beat the one in Florida by the narrow margin of four days, so it had precedence in bringing him to trial.

In December 1966, after a long bail hearing and jury selection, the trial began, with Bailey still acting as Coppolino's counsel. He knew that if he beat the Farber charge—which was the weaker one for the prosecution—he would have a far better crack at acquittal in Florida than if the trials had been in the reverse order.

I had been ill in the hospital immediately before testifying at the Farber trial, but I was well enough by the time I arrived at the little courthouse in Freehold, New Jersey. The place was teeming with reporters, who must have doubled the population of the place for the duration of the trial.

During both the preliminary hearing in Florida and the first part of this trial, Bailey had been in frequent conflict with his opponents on the prosecution, and everyone was anticipating that I would be raked over the coals on cross-examination. Bailey started quietly enough by asking me if my involvement in 20,000 autopsies meant that I had only supervised them. I told him gently that if he wanted to add the number I had only supervised, then he must increase the total to 60,000. He immediately diverted to another subject, as he had the clever knack of rapidly dropping any line of questioning that was proving unprofitable.

It would be tedious even to summarize all the cross-examination that went on that afternoon and again the next day, but it was a constant battle of wits; we fought every inch of the way over every facet of all the autopsy evidence and my opinion on those facts. The next morning, some of my colleagues from the Office set up a screen and projector in the courtroom and I showed pictures of the coronary arteries at numerous points, to prove that there was no place where significant blockage could explain William Farber's death.

Bailey seized on the broken cricoid cartilage and emphasized that post-mortem damage, including that caused by a grave-digger's spade or a collapsed coffin, could have caused the fracture. Equally dogged, I gave my opinion that no such explanation was valid.

After all those hours of verbal slugging, my last words were, "If I didn't have the larynx in this case, I would have to say I didn't know what this man died of."

I was the last witness for the prosecution, and when I left the stand, the state rested its case against Carl Coppolino.

The defense called two pathologists—both now deceased—to counter my evidence. The first was Joe Spelman, the chief medical examiner of Philadelphia, and the second was Richard Ford, from the legal medicine department at Harvard.

Both said more or less the same thing, that Farber had died of severe coronary artery disease, and that the absence of hemorrhage at the site of the cricoid fractures proved that they occurred after death.

This was exactly the reverse of what I had maintained during my testimony.

Well, what was the jury to do? One doctor said one thing and two younger doctors said the diametric opposite.

Perhaps they just did some arithmetic and said, "Two say this, but only one said that, so the majority wins."

I don't know and I don't care. I was there to tell the truth, the whole truth, and nothing but the truth, as I saw it. Once I've delivered my testimony, my interest is academic. The jury can do what they like with all the information they have before them.

In the Farber case, they chose to decide that the burden of proof of Coppolino's guilt was not discharged. Their foreman eventually delivered a verdict of "not guilty." According to the newspapers that wormed the story out of the jurors later, there were five ballots, starting at eight to four for acquittal, until the four eventually came across to the majority side.

While the celebrations were going on later among the defense team, Dr. Coppolino, the man it was all about, was still in the local jail. The next day, he was flying south again, under escort, to be handed over from the custody of New Jersey to Sheriff Boyer in Florida.

He had beaten one charge and was now on the launching pad for the other. During the journey, he told a reporter that for him the low point of the Farber trial was my testimony. He told F. Lee Bailey that if they lost, it would be because of my testimony. Well, that neither pleased or distressed me, for as I've said, I go to court to say my piece, and what comes of it is none of my business. Perhaps naturally enough, people (especially those in peril or their lawyers) are ready enough to accuse me of bias and partiality or succumbing to pressure from the prosecutors. The worst example of this was not in the Coppolino case, but in the long, drawn out affair of Alice Crimmins.

From the medical point of view, the second Coppolino trial was more interesting—and certainly more hectic and vituperative—than the Farber trial.

It was April 1967 by the time it took place, in Naples, Florida, and by then the whole world seemed to be homing in on the courthouse there. But my involvement began some time before the trial, and again F. Lee Bailey played a major role in the activities. He had quite properly obtained a court order to see the exhibits I had saved from the autopsy on Carmela Coppolino.

He came up to New York to examine them, with his usual colorful entourage. This took place at our Office, and I made sure that the occasion was played strictly by the legal rules. In a case of this sort, I do not like anyone working under my supervision to indulge in any small talk or chitchat about the case with the defense attorney. If he wants to find out about the case, he must go through the proper legal channels, subpoena the witness, and have a hearing before trial in a court of record.

I do not like to have any attorneys talking to the doctors informally and then saying later, "Didn't you say this, that, or the other, Doctor?" Before you know where you are, there's a hassle, and nobody knows who said what to whom. It's not a good idea, when the case has reached this advanced stage, to encourage or indulge in loose talk, and as head of the agency, I was legally responsible for this autopsy and had to carry the can for anything that went wrong.

Now when Bailey came around to the Office with his team, Umberger was rather too willing to expand on all aspects of the case. Joe is a great chemist, but a rather unconventional guy. He would work his own hours and sometimes be up in his laboratory almost all night, working alone on a case. But in the daytime, when you wanted to get at him for some routine matter, he was often missing. Well, you can put up with that kind of thing quite a bit, as many brilliant men in the world of science have been somewhat eccentric in their life styles, but Joe tended to be a little too forthcoming and perhaps easily led into saying things that were *ex officio*.

I knew this, and I watched rather warily as Bailey got talking to Umberger. The lawyer had come with an expert of his own, and they began questioning Joe rather intensively as to what he had done, how he had done it, and what he hadn't done. Now the place for all this is the witness stand in a court of law, before a judge who will see that the rules of evidence and admissibility are strictly observed. The place for it certainly was *not* a chatty session in an office in New York. So I said to Mr. Bailey, "If you want to get Dr. Umberger into court, you are welcome to do so and to talk to him from now until next week, but not here, and not in this way."

I went on to insist that there be no further informal discussion unless we recorded the conversation and got a court stenographer to take a record of what was said. I didn't want wild versions of anything that Joe Umberger or anyone else might say being bandied about when we got to trial, so I pulled my rank as chief medical examiner in charge of the Office and forbade any further questioning of Umberger.

Bailey got mad at me and said, "Doctor Helpern, you are depriving my client of his civil rights by not allowing me to question Dr. Umberger, a material witness in the case."

Though I was pretty much concerned about the situation at the time, looking back on it now, the scene in the Office that day was rather ludicrous. It reminded me for all the world of one of the old Marx Brothers' films, it was such a crazy situation!

Well anyway, it was his right to object, and he sure took advantage of it. He brought a civil suit against me for the deprivation of Carl Coppolino's civil rights, and I was brought into federal court in New York.

When I was served with this suit, I went to the corporation counsel for the city of New York, my employer, and asked them if they would represent me or if I should get my own private lawyer. The city asked me, was this a private case, or was I doing it officially? I told them that my Office was doing it officially as a courtesy for another state; and that we were called on occasion for advice and expertise; and that our findings were not disclosed to the media. I wasn't getting a dime out of it—I was just offering our special facilities to another jurisdiction that needed expert help.

When they heard this, the city agreed to represent me in the suit, and we went to court. The federal judge was a woman; it was the first case she had ever handled. She was very nice and understood why I was making this stand, but she nevertheless decided that I had violated Coppolino's civil rights and instructed me not to further forbid Umberger from talking to Bailey, if the need should arise. (It never did.) I agreed and let the matter go—if it had been a New York case, I would have pressed the city to appeal, but as it was a Florida case, it was somewhat awkward to persist.

I was warned by the court that I would have to pay $250 if I broke the ruling. (Incidentally, I was also sued for $15,000 over this, and the money was kept in a bank, pending my behavior in the case.) Well, the whole episode evaporated after that, but this was the way F. Lee Bailey seemed to work.

This was by no means the end of the circus surrounding the second trial. When Professor Bert LaDu, the pharmacologist who detected succinylcholine in the needle track and buttock, went down to Naples to give evidence, he was approached at his hotel before the trial by Teri Plaut, a particularly attractive young woman who acted as Bailey's personal assistant. At the side of the swimming pool, she sweetly asked him, "Are you

Doctor LaDu? I'm Miss Plaut. Would you mind telling me what you found in the buttock of the deceased?''

Bert LaDu, though quite unused to court appearances, was no mug. "I'm going to testify tomorrow," he answered. "You'll hear all about it then."

The next day, when I was through testifying, Bert LaDu went on the stand and meticulously described all the tests he had done and how he had found the drug in the left buttock, most abundantly around the needle track.

Bailey was unprepared for this degree of certainty, I think. He must have figured that if Dr. LaDu had found anything really significant, he would have been put on the stand ahead of me, not after me. He began badgering him in cross-examination, asking "Didn't Miss Teri Plaut talk to you yesterday and ask you what you found?''

"Yes, she did," replied Bert LaDu, "But I didn't take that as a very formal meeting. I was in swimming, when this girl in very short shorts came up to me and began chatting about the case."

Bailey then asked him, "Did anybody tell you not to tell her anything?'' He was wondering whether I had violated the order of the federal court about not forbidding anyone to talk to the defense, but of course, I'd done no such thing. Thankfully, Dr. LaDu's answer to that was "no". His evidence was so effective because it was independent, direct confirmation of Umberger's indirect findings, which had not discovered the original compound and had been done by different methods in an entirely different laboratory in the medical school. It also localized the drug to the left buttock and even to the needle track, whereas Umberger's tests only showed that a large amount must have been introduced generally into the body. The two results complemented each other and left nothing to conjecture.

The medical evidence was no doubt the major factor in bringing the jury to a verdict of "guilty of murder in the second degree," which raised a howl of protest from Bailey, who said, "How can you have a poison case and get a verdict of murder in the second degree?'' It does seem a little odd, when poison murders are almost by definition premeditated, but in Florida law, the judge apparently charges the jury with the highest possible verdict, and they can bring in any other verdict below that ceiling if they think fit.

Well, Carl Coppolino went to a Florida prison on a life

sentence, but the most acrimonious proceedings were yet to come. Bitterly disappointed at the outcome, Bailey lashed out at the prosecutor's team and the witnesses on "the other side". He went on a T.V. late night talk show, and later gave newspaper interviews, saying that Umberger would publicly announce that his testimony was in error. Mr. Bailey called my New York Office "a scandal and the source of some peremptory and sloppy opinions." He alleged that three junior chemists in Umberger's laboratory were fired because they cooperated with the defense. This was untrue, as they had been suspended for quite different reasons, but they started talking of bringing an action against me in the federal court for loss of civil rights—that gambit seemed to be getting contagious—!

Since Coppolino had been convicted, the state attorney in the case, Frank Schaub, asked for a "full investigation of Bailey and his ridiculous and highly publicized claims about the trial." (Bailey was eventually suspended from practice in New Jersey for one year.)

Bailey said that he was coming to New York with a letter for Mayor John Lindsay demanding a full investigation of my Office and its activities. He alleged that the issue affected "every criminal case" that emanates from my Office and that "any verdict based on evidence coming from the New York Office of the Chief Medical Examiner should be scrutinized by defense lawyers."

A real war of words built up, which dragged on for weeks before fizzling out because there was just nothing to substantiate Bailey's disgruntled allegations. At the end, Bailey and I were threatening to sue each other, though nothing came of it.

Well, that's all water under the bridge now, I guess, but I was pretty mad at the time. All the same, he's a very good lawyer—especially if he's on your side. And I hear that he has mellowed considerably in recent years.

Chapter 3

I Call It The Office

I was on the staff of the Chief Medical Examiner's Office in New York City for almost forty-three years, but my final twenty as chief were preceded by twenty-three years as an assistant and then a deputy chief medical examiner.

All those earlier years, as well as my first seven as chief, were spent in what was commonly known as "the Bellevue morgue," though "morgue" is a word that I dislike intensely. I have always encouraged my colleagues and employees to avoid using such a crude and gruesome term. Unfortunately, many people, especially those who work in law enforcement and the news media, tend to use the word, usually without any intention to offend. Sometimes this type of speech is used almost as bravado, perhaps as a safety valve for the rather distasteful job that constantly reminds us of our mortality. This rather aggressive, distasteful style of speech, which includes the even more obnoxious description of the mortuary ambulance as the "meat wagon," is sometimes heard among policemen, mortuary attendants, and even some doctors. The same people in another environment may act in quite a considerate manner, so I'm sure it is at least partly an overreaction to the situation, perhaps to prove an indifference to the aura of death. This is understandable, but it shouldn't become so overt as to distress bereaved relatives and friends, so I always make the effort to use the term "mortuary" or preferably, the even less evocative word "office".

In the beginning, the Medical Examiner's Office in New York City was fragmented and scattered. Its Manhattan mortuary, autopsy rooms, and laboratories were housed in the Department of Pathology building of Bellevue Hospital, at Twenty-ninth Street and First Avenue. The large, skylighted autopsy room was on the second floor, and its many marble tables were shared by the hospital pathologists and by the medical examiners. I always felt that having many tables in the same room provided those who worked there with an opportunity to compare the normal with the abnormal and one abnormal condition with another.

There were also facilities for autopsies in the basement, used occasionally when the elevator to the main autopsy room on the second floor broke down. There were several hundred centrally refrigerated storage compartments for bodies. These included unclaimed ones brought in from other hospitals for storage and then burial by the city in its cemetery on Hart's Island. This was sometimes designated as the "potter's field," from which a body could always be claimed for private burial by the deceased's family or friends at a later time.

Among the assistant medical examiners, Morgan Vance was a scholar, a graduate of Harvard and the University of Pennsylvania, and an avid handball player. He contributed excellent papers on the subject of fat embolism and thrombotic embolism, fractures of the skull, and blunt force injuries. Thomas A. Gonzales made detailed studies on strangulation and asphyxia. Robert Fisher contributed papers on sickle cell disease. I was involved in sudden natural death, malaria, and other complications of intravenous heroin addiction.

When I joined the Office in 1931 I sometimes was able to get a histology technician to prepare sections for microscopic study, but for many years Dr. Vance and I would cut our own sections. Vance was a talented artist in watercolors and oil. I was the photographer and took all the pictures. (Dr. Norris purchased the camera and microscope.)

When I became assistant medical examiner, there was no laboratory space available. Dr. Douglas Symmers, the director of laboratories, was kind enough to turn over a large room on the second floor, originally designed as an X-Ray room but never used for that purpose. This very large room became our single laboratory, which Dr. Norris equipped with a desk and other furniture, including a coat rack and the microscope he had purchased out of his own funds.

The scene of a murder in the Hatfield house, on Lexington Avenue, provided a large carpet. This was taken as evidence, sent to the cleaners to remove the bloodstains, and then placed on the floor of our large room. One day, Dr. Symmers saw all this luxury in the room he had provided and called the whole thing "the country club," a name we could never live down.

However, the old arrangement, while extremely important to the development of the Office, did not provide enough space. There were not enough mortuary compartments for the increasing number of cases in the Medical Examiner's Office, and there were inadequate facilities for the public, who had to visit the Office to make identifications and for many other reasons. The existing arrangement made it evident that there would not be sufficient space for the scientific expansion of legal medicine in the city.

Years passed before the Medical Examiner's Office had truly adequate facilities. It was a great day for me when the new building for which I had fought for so long was finally finished and dedicated with appropriate ceremonies late in 1960. The new six-story headquarters of the Medical Examiner's Office, located north of our old laboratories at Bellevue, had cost $3.7 million to erect, and the interior furnishings and equipment added the better part of three-quarters of a million dollars. Due to unavoidable construction delays, we were not able to occupy the building on schedule for the dedication, but the occasion was none the less impressive, especially as we had present a great gathering of medico-legal personalities from forty-two countries of the world and other parts of the United States, as well as our own New York colleagues.

The new Office at 520 First Avenue was dedicated in great style, and we moved into our new quarters in the early part of 1961. The contrast to the old premises at Bellevue was extraordinary, but we soon got used to the space and modernity. The outside of the building has a facade of blue and white glazed brick with aluminum panelling. There are six floors above ground; the autopsy rooms and body storage place are in the easily accessible, well-lighted basement. There is a cellar floor containing air-conditioning and heating equipment and a large storage room for equipment and supplies. All the autopsy work from the other boroughs, with the exception of Brooklyn, is centralized here, and there is also a unit of the Missing Persons Bureau of the New York City Police Department located in the building to make for better coordination in identifying bodies.

The entire building, including the autopsy rooms, is air-conditioned, a feature that means a great deal for the public, who may suddenly be called there in connection with a death. Storage space for 128 bodies is provided by large refrigerated compartments lining the basement. The shrouded bodies are placed on individual trays easily reached through individual stainless steel doors. There is a large walk-in refrigerator with shelves for storage of children's and infants' bodies. Seven thousand autopsies are performed each year in the new building from a total of about 30,000 cases accepted each year for investigation, which make up one-third of New York City's 90,000 deaths.

Gone are the old days when distressed relatives had to suffer the additional unpleasantness of the sights and smells of the old Bellevue mortuary. Now, when a body has to be viewed for identification purposes, a special elevator lifts it from the basement level to a glass-enclosed chamber inside a waiting room on the main floor, divorcing the procedure as much as possible from the old traditional atmosphere of the charnel house.

On the high ground floor, to which entrance steps lead up from First Avenue, much of the space is taken up with offices for the medical examiners, administrative clerks and stenographers. There is a public lobby with marbled walls displaying a Latin motto. This lobby leads to an identification room, the Missing Persons Bureau of the police department, a business office handling the cases of the day, and a large communications room with five desks, each receiving and dispatching the notifications of cases from the five boroughs. Even when activity quiets down elsewhere in the building, this office always remains open.

Beyond it, there is another large room with a series of office cubicles where during the day typists transcribe autopsy findings, and clerks compile and collate records.

At the far end of this room there are offices for the statisticians who analyze and classify data from the records of the 30,000 investigations carried out by the Office. Every case which has been investigated by the Medical Examiner's Office since its inception is preserved here or in the City Archives, an important source of statistical data, revealing changing trends in the incidence of death from different causes.

Thus, in the case of the influenza pandemic of 1918, the high mortality figures are readily available for study. The statistics for the twenties and thirties reflect the large number of deaths from carbon monoxide poisoning (10 percent of the total deaths reported, both suicidal and accidental), a situation which has diminished in recent years. The statistics also reflect the large increase in homicidal deaths and reveal that the largest number now stem from the use of handguns.

After 1950, we encounter an increasing incidence of narcotics addiction deaths, especially from intravenous heroin addiction, and in more recent years a pattern has emerged of narcotic addiction deaths in which multiple drugs are involved. Deaths from the battered child syndrome have also increased greatly in recent years. Autopsy studies distinguish the sudden infant death syndrome or "crib death," for which no evident cause can be found, from death resulting from congenital malformations, infection, and tumors: these conditions cannot be differentiated except by the mandatory reporting of such deaths and inclusion of a careful autopsy.

The sudden, unexpected deaths from natural causes occurring in different age groups, most commonly from coronary artery disease in middle-aged white men, become evident in the statistical analysis of autopsied, medically unattended deaths.

Vehicular fatalities among drivers, car occupants, and pedestrians are also revealed in the statistics compiled from the case records of such deaths. The high correlation between alcoholic intoxication and traumatic death of all kinds— suicidal, homicidal, and accidental—is striking when such chemical studies are carried out in connection with the autopsies. The Medical Examiner's Office of New York City has carried out routine alcohol testing of fatalities since its beginning in 1918.

The other floors of the building are mainly devoted to laboratory space. The second floor contains large storage rooms for case records. The third and fourth floors contain laboratories mainly used for toxicology, and the fifth floor has a series of laboratories where the medical examiners can study their cases and prepare their reports. A laboratory for the study of sudden infant death—"crib death"—was equipped a number of years ago on the fifth floor and has been funded by Lou and Vicky Menschell and their friends, who have set up the Andrew Menschell Infant Survival Foundation. This project utilizes the case material in the Medical Examiner's Office, which is also conducting studies in collaboration with the Department of Forensic Medicine of the New York University School of Medicine.

On the top or sixth floor, are the rooms that attract the greatest curiosity among visiting doctors and guests, for here is the museum, containing exhibits which I have been collecting assiduously since 1931, when I began my career in legal medicine. Like the proverbial magpie, I've accumulated all manner of things, which can help to instruct new generations of doctors, pathologists, lawyers, and law enforcement agents, mainly in the field of sudden and violent death.

Weapons, from hatchets to the traditional blunt instruments, stand among demonstrations of identification techniques. Specimens from autopsies of the past forty-five years revealing a variety of modes of death always excite the interest of those who come to visit.

One of the exhibits most widely described in the medical press is the famous "stabbed skull case," in which a lad of fifteen was struck on the head with a knife by an attacker. The boy then chased his assailant for a whole block before collapsing, even though at autopsy the knife blade was shown to have penetrated the scalp, skull, coverings of the brain, and the brain itself, causing a subdural hemorrhage (a collection of the blood in the space between the brain and the lining inside the skull). The most interesting feature, however, was that the end of the blade had snapped off, leaving a large portion embedded in the bone of the skull. At autopsy I removed a segment of skull that contained the broken-off blade, and when the perpetrator came to trial, I could show that the broken blade exactly matched the stump of the pocket knife found in his possession.

Other exhibits in this "Black Museum," to copy a name from the Old Scotland Yard collection in London, include a big display about narcotic drug deaths in the city, dating back to the 1930's; a tailor's dummy dressed in the tattered clothes of a boy who was struck by lightning; and a host of formaldehyde-preserved specimens from autopsies.

The icepick seems to figure quite often in New York deaths—the museum houses one sample which came from a man found dead in bed from what was assumed by the physicians to be a stroke. Yet at autopsy we found a wound-track starting in the depths of his brain. Following this outwards, I traced the track up through the brain-covering membranes, through a small hole in the side of the skull, to a little hole in the scalp, concealed in the hair. The fellow had been hit in the head with the sharp point of an icepick, and if he had not been subjected to a good autopsy, the death would have been written off as a natural stroke. If I had just kept that brain in preservative for later examination by a neuropathologist, the body would have been buried or cremated, and we would never have been able to reconstruct the true cause of death. You always have to be alert for any eventuality—and the case showed the error of those pathologists who don't bother to examine the head if they find sufficient cause of death elsewhere. In the greater proportion of cadavers over middle age, you can usually find enough coronary disease to satisfy your requirements, unless you maintain the critical faculties that are vital in this job.

Another icepick affair sits a little farther along the museum shelf; this was a man who died in the hospital from an infection of the lining of his heart—and with good cause, because at autopsy we found the broken-off tip of an icepick embedded in his heart muscle. The extraordinary thing was that this man had worked at a manual occupation for no fewer than eight months after the incident in which he suffered this penetrating stab wound to his chest, which transfixed his heart.

Still another icepick case I mention elsewhere in this book was one in which a fellow was struck in one ear with a pick which traversed the base of his brain, punctured the central stem of the brain, and ended up in the ear region of the opposite side.

This museum is a fascinating place, even though the collection will never be complete, as each month brings something new. Cataloguing was never finished during my tenure and may never be completed now, but it remains a mecca for physicians, pathologists, and law-enforcement authorities.

On the sixth floor is another innovation, the Milton Helpern Library of Legal Medicine—but I'll get around to talking about that later on. There is also a double classroom accommodating up to 100 people, with facilities for slide projection used for lectures and training of staff.

These are the main physical features of the Office of Chief Medical Examiner. Since we opened there on First Avenue back in 1961, it has served as the center for all departmental operations. The plans and specifications of this new building have provided a model which many directors of medico-legal institutes throughout the world have studied and adopted for incorporation in their structural designs.

Persons in the community, including officials in other government agencies, are often very hazy as to exactly what we do in this busy building. Principally, our statutory duty is to stay open twenty-four hours a day to investigate the circumstances and determine the cause of death in that 30 percent of the 90,000 annual deaths in New York City that cannot be certified by a physician because the death was medically unattended, sudden, suspicious, violent, or traumatic. The violent deaths include suicide, homicide, and accident, including poisoning and death in prison or legal custody. Unusual deaths include those that occur while a patient is in a hospital and had undergone therapy, surgery, or diagnostic or therapeutic procedures. The Office is also required to scrutinize all cases in which cremation is requested, for the obvious reason that disposal of a body by this means irrevocably prevents any future satisfactory investigation of the death. Thus, quite a handful of responsibilities have been thrust on the Medical Examiner's Office, the scope of which encompasses virtually every type of death other than that in which the clinician is satisfied that a patient under his care died naturally from some well-diagnosed and potentially lethal disease. The responsibilities of the chief medical examiner are spelled out clearly in the law of 1915, which, as I have said, is a model piece of legislative drafting and actually has been incorporated verbatim into the legislation of other jurisdictions adopting a medical examiner system.

The law requires that the Office be notified by a police officer who learns that a body is lying dead in any of the circumstances mentioned earlier. The chief medical examiner or one of his deputies, associates, assistants, or medical investigators must immediately "go to the scene and take charge of the body." He must fully investigate the essential facts concerning the circumstances of the death; take names and addresses of any witnesses; and before leaving the premises, file an initial written report in the Medical Examiner's Office. He also has the duty to take possession of any objects at the scene or on the deceased which he thinks may be useful in establishing the cause of death and hand them over to the police, except suicide notes, which are retained by the chief medical examiner.

If the medical examiner or medical investigator can establish the cause of death with reasonable certainty from the investigation of the circumstances and examination of the body (and if there are no obvious legal implications), he shall so report it, but if an autopsy is indicated as part of the post-mortem investigation, such autopsy shall be performed by a medical examiner and the written report filed in the Office.

I have always insisted that these procedures be carried out to the letter. Only on rare occasions in my forty-two years in the Office did the system fail, because one of my medical staff did not fully comply with the required method of working. Like all systems, there are occasions when technical hitches occur, but considering that we were processing over 30,000 cases a year, our lapses have been few indeed! Unfortunately, the very nature of our work has made us at times vulnerable to criticism, and sometimes vituperative repercussions occurred when things went wrong. An unexpected death often makes bereaved relatives very sensitive, and understandably, sometimes resentful of mishaps. Due to budget limitations, we had no public relations staff, but the news media reported our activities and gave a great deal of space to many of our cases. Our Office has always been "news," and the one great concern I always had was preventing my staff from "leaking" or distorting confidential case reports. I have always felt that the district attorney should decide what could be public information in reporting homicides, so as not to interfere with the proper prosecution of a case. The hospitals and health service office should not be denied an opportunity to be apprised of autopsy findings relating to their cases before the public is made aware of such findings via the news media.

To get back to the way the Medical Examiner's Office functioned in practical terms during my administration, let us imagine a typical night at the big building down at 520 First

Avenue. It is late evening, and even some of the conscientious chemists and keen technicians in the upstairs laboratories have gone home.

The building is empty of anyone except the night staff manning our centralized communications center. They are receiving calls from the various police precincts and hospitals located in all five boroughs constituting the City of New York reporting deaths which need to be investigated by my Office. The night staff downstairs in the mortuary office are waiting to receive bodies.

A phone call is received from a local police precinct, say in the Murray Hill area of Manhattan, not too far from the Office. The body of a person has been found on a stairway landing in an apartment house, having already been pronounced dead by an ambulance attendant called to the scene.

The communications clerk fills out a form with the essential details and gives it to a medical investigator who is scheduled for the tour of duty that night.

The investigator, who is known as the "tour doctor," visits the scene immediately in one of the department vehicles, often a black station wagon with the Office insignia on the side.

When he reaches the apartment house, he carefully inspects the immediate scene of the death and then examines the body itself to see if there is anything inconsistent with the apparent facts of the case. He looks especially for anything that will lead him to suspect that the death was anything other than perfectly natural. He talks to the family—and neighbors if need be—and uses this information as an indispensable part of the investigation. A brother might tell him, "He was getting bad chest pains all day, Doctor". The son may say, "He was getting treatment from Dr. Smith for angina."

It may transpire that the deceased man had a coronary attack a considerable time ago, so the tour doctor will call the family physician on the telephone and be advised that Dr. Smith last attended his late patient some two months previous and confirms that he had long-standing coronary artery disease with an abnormal electrocardiogram. For some reason, the physician had not seen the dead man for several months, and since death occurred under unexpected and unusual circumstances, the deceased having collapsed and died on a stairway landing, Dr.

Smith could not, under the Medical Examiner Law, issue a certificate of death.

Armed with this knowledge and satisfied that the body shows no external signs to arouse the slightest suspicion, the tour doctor calls the communications center of the Office and orders the body to be removed by the mortuary hearse to one of the 128 refrigerated storage chambers of the Office basement.

The following morning, a medical examiner—a skilled pathologist this time—reads the night report of the medical investigator and re-examines the body, this time under more favorable conditions of lighting and environment compared with the darkened stairway where the body was found.

Seeing no signs of injury or even any subtle indications of trauma, and in view of the history obtained from the family and his physician, the experienced medical examiner might well sign the case out without autopsy as "coronary arterial disease." He would then issue a certificate and release the body to a funeral director engaged by the family.

However, while this procedure might be followed in a similar situation in which such an individual dies at his desk without reasonable possibility of injury, the fact that he was found on the landing brings up a real possibility that he might have fallen down the stairs and broken his neck. This would only be revealed by a searching autopsy, including a careful dissection of the neck area. An alert, well-trained medical examiner would never certify this case without autopsy.

In all boroughs, in addition to tour doctors scheduled for duty at all hours of the day and night, there are medical examiners who are skilled forensic pathologists scheduled around the clock for obvious homicidal death investigations. These medical examiners are transported to death scenes by the police patrol vehicles.

A couple of minutes after the incident on the stairway, another call comes in to say that a man has been found dead behind a derelict warehouse over on the waterfront of the Lower West Side. Although there were no witnesses, the patrolman who found the body is quite sure that the decedent had been shot. The medical examiner on duty for homicides is notified, and the police pick him up and drive him across Manhattan to the scene. This time it is out of doors, and several police cars, some with their roof flashers still operating, cluster around the location. Flashes of man-made lightning cut through the night, as the police photographic squad records everything on film. Detectives as well as uniformed police are there, and someone from the police forensic laboratory may also be on the scene.

The medical examiner threads his way through the throng of busy investigating officers and takes command of the investigation. Maybe tonight the victim is a man shot through the head with a handgun. The medical examiner checks to determine whether anything has been moved from the scene since the victim was found, then carefully studies the general position and condition of the body and the ground around it. The scene may be harshly lighted by portable lamps provided by the police, or sometimes by the headlights and spotlights of their vehicles. The doctor may be of the opinion that the man was killed where he lay, rather than having been dumped there after being slain somewhere else. He might deduce this from the fact that blood splatters from the head wound are radiating out for a couple of feet—maybe on the warehouse wall immediately above the man's head, where there are blood splashes shaped like printed exclamation points, with the little dot always in front of the direction of travel. The decedent has been shot in the front of the forehead, and even at that early stage, the medical examiner notes that the entrance wound, with some scorched skin and shrivelled hairs around it, is jagged and gaping. These facts immediately tell him that the gun was discharged at very close range, perhaps almost in contact with the head, although the firearms examiners in the criminalistics' laboratory may do a lot more work on the powder residues and other non-medical aspects to confirm this impression.

The bullet has come out through the back of the head via a great jagged wound, bursting through the skull and scalp, blowing tissue and blood with it, soiling the wall behind. The body is slumped against the foot of the wall, and the medical examiner intuitively begins to reconstruct in his mind what has happened.

The victim must have been standing up, close to the wall, when his assailant fired a weapon at his head from pointblank range, because the main soiling of the warehouse wall is at head height. The body then slid down to the sitting position in which it now lies. Finding the bullet is a job for the police and their laboratory crews; after hitting a brick wall, it is likely to be very much distorted, but they may still be able to observe sufficient rifling impressions on its base to match it with any suspect's weapon that may come their way.

The medical examiner next looks at the body to see if there is any clue as to when this murder took place. There were no witnesses to either sight or sound of the incident, so the time of death is wide open. He gently feels the limbs and jaw muscles; they are fairly still, so rigor mortis is present. This comes on within a few hours and lasts anywhere from one and a half to two days, although the variation is enormous. It depends on many internal factors, such as muscular activity before or at the time of death and other external conditions, especially the temperature of the surroundings. The medical examiner feels the skin of the man's neck, and although it's cool, its temperature is definitely above that of the chilly air on the riverfront.

Now he knows that the incomplete rigor is coming on, rather than passing off. A body in average circumstances feels cold to the touch in perhaps twelve hours, so he must make a rough estimate that the man has been dead long enough to have stiffened so appreciably, but not long enough to be cold. As a rough guess, he thinks between six and twelve hours ago, although he is not going to be held too rigidly to that by the detectives until an autopsy has been done. Experience tells him that estimating time of death is a chancey business, full of gross inaccuracies.

There seem to be no other injuries on the body, so no fight was likely. He has a quick look at the fingernails and sees no blood or suspicion of skin under them, so it was hardly likely that the victim managed to scratch his adversary in any attempt at defense.

The police have already lifted a wallet from the man's pocket and know who he is, so identification is no problem. The medical examiner can do no more at the scene. As soon as the photographers have finished, he writes a note on what he has observed so far and calls the Office. He wants an autopsy, and he intends to do it himself. The police already have a suspect in custody and want to get on with the case. It will be autopsied early the next morning, as part of the day's routine work.

In our hypothetical homicide, the body is brought to the Office from the scene by the mortuary vehicle. If it arrives in the morning at the unloading bay on the basement level, the staff in the mortuary bring it straight into one of the three autopsy rooms which are placed like an elongated island in the center of the wide circulating corridor that runs around the lower level. There is one large autopsy room and three smaller ones for special cases, including those of a decomposing or infective nature.

Before the examination begins, the medical examiner asks for the head to be radiographed; although it is obvious that much of the bullet had burst out of the back of the head, there still might be fragments of metal inside the skull. This is done quickly on the up-to-date X-ray equipment housed next to the autopsy room, and the wet plates are ready for inspection in a few minutes. As it happens, they show no dense metallic shadows, but at least the doctor now knows that he does not have to go searching for missile fragments.

The autopsy proceeds, and everything is dictated to a stenographer or into the microphone that is installed at each table. The recorded autopsy findings will be typed up by transcribing typists and checked carefully by the forensic pathologist before he signs the report. The law now requires that in every autopsy where there is suspicion of criminal violence, the procedure must be witnessed by at least one other medical examiner, who must also sign the report.

The entire body is examined, not just the area of obvious injury in the head. This is important, because all manner of things are frequently found, from advanced natural diseases to drug intoxication and other injuries unsuspected at the time. The actual examination is done with meticulous care and skill, after which the body is reconstituted by expert mortuary technicians working under the supervision of the medical examiner so that there will not be any disfigurement to distress the relatives. If need be, we can perform a full autopsy on the body of a woman and leave the cadaver in such good cosmetic condition that it could be dressed in an off-the-shoulder gown for viewing by the family and friends at the funeral services.

In a case of undoubted homicide like this one, the police criminalistics laboratory and our own laboratories in the building might be sent additional material for examination. Blood samples would be taken for human and animal *percipitir* tests and for grouping tests to compare with any stains found on the alleged or suspected perpetrator. Fingernail scrapings might be examined and hairs removed from the victim for comparison tests with any found on the suspect—these might include scalp, eyebrows, beard, and even—in appropriate circumstances— pubic hair. Included in such studies would be extraneous animal hairs and cloth fibers.

If the victim was a woman or an overt male homosexual, samples of lipstick, fingernail polish, and face makeup might be retained for comparison purposes—here the old gag about a man having facepowder on his suit collar might have more sinister implications.

Blood, urine, and stomach contents are very frequently kept for analysis for alcohol and a whole variety of drugs, again depending on what kind of case is involved. In a shooting, the ballistics laboratory may take skin scrapings or even skin samples to identify the type of propellant from the cartridge shell or primer, from which they can identify the manufacture and narrow down the search for ammunition by this means. These criminalistics aspects are not directly the concern of the medical examiner, but we naturally cooperate fully in providing samples and facilities for our colleagues in the law enforcement professions.

Once everything has been done that can and should be done, the body is stored away in one of the refrigerator units to await final disposal, though in a criminal case this may be delayed until it is certain that no additional examinations are needed, either by the medical examiner or, rarely, by another doctor retained by the defense attorney of an accused suspect. Such requests are cleared through the district attorney, who may acquiesce or require a court order.

These are typical examples of the initial handling of reportable deaths by the medical investigator and medical examiner. In the evident homicide, whenever possible a medical examiner is immediately dispatched to the scene of death and with firsthand knowledge of the circumstance is in a better position to perform the autopsy. Actually, at any one time in each of the five boroughs, there are two qualified physicians on duty: one a medical investigator for the ordinary, apparently non-suspicious cases and the other a medical examiner who is a forensic pathologist for the suspicious or apparently homicidal deaths. This arrangement, where it can be carried out, provides the best coverage for effective investigation of the deaths requiring visits to the scene.

During my administration, the examiners' and investigators' day in Manhattan was divided from 8:00 a.m. to 4:00 p.m. and from 4:00 p.m. to midnight. Double tours were frowned on in that they encouraged corner-cutting, and as a result, some scenes which should have been visited were not. Each tour doctor might have as many as twelve cases to visit. In the other boroughs the case load was lighter, and the tour doctor could take on a larger tour.

The medical investigators, who are all physicians, have had varied experience before coming to work in the Medical Examiner's Office. A few are salaried; most are paid on a per diem basis, including a group who are available for work between 12:00 p.m. and 8:00 a.m. Some are employed as resident physicians and interns; others are physicians in practice: all have a genuine interest in the work of the Office. Thus, the use of lay investigators has not worked out, but the idea has not been given up.

As chief medical examiner, I trained many young men who left the Office to take on greater responsibilities with higher remuneration. I was sorry to see so many promising assistants move on to greener pastures, but in other ways this metastasizing of the staff into positions of leadership and importance elsewhere in the country gave me a great sense of accomplishment. It was gratifying to know that these well-trained, dependable, and resourceful men and women would transplant our system and serve as ambassadors from New York to improve the system of official medico-legal investigation of deaths in other states and counties, especially where the old system of elected lay coroners was being abandoned and replaced by the medical examiner system.

Chapter 4

Nothing But the Truth– The Art of Being an Expert Witness

The early years of the Medical Examiner's Office, between World Wars I and II, threw up many an extraordinary case, a number of which are recorded in this book. Many of the major homicides were dealt with by Dr. Norris or Dr. Gonzales during their tenures as chief, but I saw many of them from my position first as an assistant, then as a deputy chief medical examiner.

I recall the notorious Easter Sunday killings in 1937 that filled the newspapers. They involved a 28-year-old talented, but quite crazy, sculptor named Robert Irwin and took place in Manhattan in the East Fifties. Here, in a walk-up flat in a row of six-story neighboring buildings, lived the Gedeon family— mother, father, and two daughters. One of the sisters was Veronica Gedeon, a very beautiful girl who posed as a model. The other, Ethel, was rather plain—and a friend of the artistic Irwin. He was quite attracted to her, but she jilted him and married another fellow. Irwin became miffed at this and, under the delusion that Ethel still lived with her parents, came around to the house on Easter Sunday to quarrel with her. The only persons at home were the mother and a boarder, who was very deaf and had a room in the apartment.

Mrs. Gedeon had a heated argument with Irwin and told him not to annoy her daughter any more now that she was married to someone else. Irwin got mad and strangled her, but she managed to scratch his face in the process. I don't recall where the father was while all this was going on, but Irwin then hid in the dark bathroom to wait until his former girlfriend got home. But it was Veronica who came in next; she went into the bathroom and undressed—and also was strangled by the distraught and unbalanced sculptor. Irwin left, but then he remembered the boarder, who, being deaf, was probably unaware of the double homicide already committed. Irwin, nonetheless went into the bedroom and stabbed him dead with an icepick from ear to ear, the track penetrating the brainstem.

Irwin then vanished into the neighborhood, and when the three bodies were found, all hell broke loose. Dr. Gonzales was called out to see the massacre. When the police arrived, they found the father sitting calmly on the step of the house, apparently indifferent to all the goings-on. The police immediately suspected him because of his attitude, but it turned out that he had always been a quiet, colorless fellow, who never showed any emotion.

Fortunately for Mr. Gedeon, someone remembered that Irwin had been there that day, and he was found afterward in a highly disturbed state. The homicide squad—real pros—did an excellent police job and discovered the scratches on Irwin's face.

Dr. Gonzales took scrapings from under the fingernails of the dead Mrs. Gedeon and found the best shaved hair I've ever seen, which had come from Irwin's stubble when she scratched his face. You can do this examination hundreds of times and come up with nothing, but this one was a real classic. (In fact, the photograph of that hair was used as an illustration by Gonzales in our textbook.) Well, Irwin was indicted for the three murders, but strangely enough was never tried.

Dr. Frederick Wertham, a distinguished forensic psychiatrist at Bellevue Hospital, had treated Irwin and had him transferred on three occasions from Bellevue Hospital to various mental hospitals in New York State from which he was released—all this before he had committed the triple homicide in the Gedeon apartment! Dr. Wertham has informed me that Irwin was never actually tried but pleaded guilty to homicide, of which there was never any question. On the basis of his guilty plea, he received an enormous prison sentence totalling 120 years. After he was first imprisoned in Sing Sing for a period of ten days, that prison asked for him to be sent elsewhere because they did not have facilities with which to treat him, and he was then transferred to Dannemora prison, like any hardened convicted criminal. Before Irwin died (only recently, from cancer, at the age of sixty-seven), he had been transferred to the Mattewan State Hospital for the Criminally Insane. In his book entitled *The Show of Violence*, published several years ago by Doubleday, Dr. Wertham devoted a chapter to the Irwin case entitled "Manhattan Tragedy."

Another old case, dating back to November 1935, was one in which I was personally involved—in fact, one of the first cases in which I received much newspaper attention, a situation which became embarrassingly more frequent as the years rolled on. This was the celebrated killing by Vera Stretz of Fritz Gebhardt, her paramour, in his room in the Beekman Towers hotel. He was a German national, described as a "travelling industrialist," who had been estranged from his non-Aryan wife and mother of his two children when the Nazis were coming into power. There were indications that he was tiring of Vera Stretz, the daughter of a musician in the symphony orchestra. Vera occupied a room on the nineteenth floor of the Towers, and the indications were that after midnight she went to Gebhardt's room on the twenty-first floor. Shots were heard on the floor and reported to the manager, who went to investigate and summoned the police. Vera was found seated on a bench in the hall on the third floor, and she admitted shooting the deceased with a double action .32 caliber Colt revolver which was in her bag, all of the cartridges in the cylinder discharged. The victim was dressed in a night shirt and was found on the floor at the side of the bed, dead from multiple gunshot wounds, which at autopsy were easily traced.

Eminent defense counsel, none other than the celebrated Sam Leibowitz, was retained for the defendant, who was indicted for homicide. Her defense was that Gebhardt insisted on having unnatural sex relations with her, but that she resisted and finally took her pistol and shot him dead.

I was looking at old news clippings quite recently and read rather wistfully about the "thirty-four-year-old assistant medical examiner, Dr. Milton Helpern," who was described as "a rotund witness with a mellow voice." In the newspapers were

artist's sketches of me demonstrating in court the tracks of the
bullets through Gebhardt's body. The text went on to say,
"Although called by the State, Doctor Helpern failed to go as far
as the prosecution wished—he refused to commit himself... the
witness was a young man who looked as if he had forgotten to
brush his hair."

Not particularly flattering, but I wasn't there to show off my
hair style—nor was I there to be a "yes man" to any attorney,
whether he was prosecutor or defender. I was on oath to tell the
truth, the whole truth, and nothing but the truth, and this first
report of my alleged stubbornness in refusing to go a bit further
in my testimony or to commit myself when I didn't wish to be
committed on a particular point has stayed with me—I hope—
from then until the present day.

People often don't appreciate that an expert witness—or any
witness, for that matter—isn't called to the stand to root for any
particular side in the case. He's there to describe what he found
and to offer his conclusions and interpretations based on *all* of
those findings, whatever they may be. He is *not* there to win the
case for one side or the other. If his conclusions were adverse to
the prosecution or the defense, they would not have put him on
the stand to testify in the first place—and if his medical opinion
was all that adverse to the prosecution, then the case should
never have got as far as trial.

So the medical witness shouldn't be outrageously partisan,
whatever side he's called for. We are sometimes accused of
getting up there on the stand and saying only whatever happens
to suit the party that calls us—but people don't see us on the
occasions when we've told our clients that what we have to say
won't do them a damn bit of good—and maybe *will* do them a lot
of harm; they don't see us then, because we don't get put on any
stand.

It annoys me when the attorney for the "other side" slips in
that frequent snide question, "How much are you getting for a
fee in this case, Dr. Helpern?", the insinuation clearly being that
I'm up there talking to order, at so many dollars a word. I usually
parry this below-the-belt attack by saying, "I expect to receive a
reasonable fee for my time and expenses," or sometimes, tell the
questioner that I haven't even discussed a fee, but that it will be a
reasonable one. When I have been called to testify in a case which
was handled in my official capacity, such testimony is part of my

official responsibility, and no fee can be charged. I remember that in an Oklahoma brain hemmorhage case the opposition counsel hit me with the question of my fee, and I told him truthfully that I'd come there to testify out of my interest in that type of case. But always there is the insinuation that your opinion is being bought by the highest bidder—and I must say that this is not an unknown phenomenon in medical and scientific testimony.

There is a very fine quotation in an old book by Dr. P.C.H. Brouardel, a famous late nineteenth-century French medico-legalist. He said something which is as true now as when he wrote it, if not more so: "If the law has made you a witness, remain a man of science. You have no victim to avenge, no guilty or innocent person to convict or save—you must bear testimony within the limits of science." I think that quotation should be framed and hung in every forensic pathologist's office, as well as over the witness stand in every court.

Chapter 5

An Epidemic of Sorts

Many people believe that "medical detective work" revolves entirely around homicide, but this is far from the truth. Even in a city like New York, with a population of about eight million and a worldwide notoriety for its murder rate, only about 3 percent of the cases are homicidal. Much of the work of a medical examiner's office is in connection with far less violent but often equally dramatic matters.

One of my favorite memories in this respect—and though early in my career, one which I still recollect with some pride—was my investigation into the deaths of certain drug addicts in 1933. I had then been in the Medical Examiner's Office for only two years—it was in the days of Dr. Charles Norris, the first chief medical examiner of New York City.

One day, a man was brought into one of the medical wards of the Second Division of Bellevue Hospital. He had a fever and was unconscious, and one of the tentative diagnoses was encephalitis, a brain infection. He died soon after admission, and because he was an intravenous heroin addict and no cause of death had been determined, his body was sent over to us as a medical examiner's case.

I noticed that it was heavily tattooed, consistent with his being a seaman. The history reported that he was addicted to heroin, and perhaps if it hadn't been a slack day that October 12— Columbus Day, I recall it distinctly—the death might have been signed out rather perfunctorily as one from addiction, although such cases were uncommon then. But one of the interns was interested enough to come over from the medical ward and ask me to autopsy the case, because they had not made any firm diagnosis. Partly out of curiosity and because I had been an intern on the same ward not long before, I agreed.

The preliminary findings didn't make much of an impression on me. The spleen was slightly enlarged, and it was an odd slate color. The lungs were congested, as they often are in acute deaths, which didn't mean much, but the brain was most peculiar. There was a remarkable purpura of the white matter— hundreds of tiny dot-like hemorrhages peppering the substance. At the time, I didn't appreciate the orange color of the organ and had no idea what I was dealing with. There was nothing else in the autopsy, apart from the slate-grey color of the liver. I then put through some sections of tissue for microscopic examination but didn't have the sense to make a quick smear of the brain which would have given me the answer straight away. Though to be fair, why should I have thought of it? It's so much easier to be wise after the event.

When I got the sections back from processing, I sat down at the microscope and almost fell off my stool when I saw the red blood cells heavily infested with malarial parasites blocking the tiny congested capillary blood vessels in the brain! This was the most intriguing problem I had ever come up against. I thought this fellow, being a seafarer, had come up from the tropics and brought his disease with him—it was malignant tertian malaria, the estivo-autumnal variety, due to *plasmodium falciparum*. I didn't recognize it at the time, as the only malaria I had ever encountered was on prepared slides when I was a medical student at Cornell. The last time a paper had been written on the subject in New York was in 1898, when Dr. James Ewing reported on fatalities from malaria at Camp Wyckoff on Long Island, of military personnel who had returned from Cuba after the Spanish-American War.

I did learn, on looking the subject up, that there had been small outbreaks of malaria among addicts reported in other parts of the United States—New Orleans, Fort Leavenworth, San Francisco—but these were "benign tertian", not "falciparum". Then we had another fatal case with cerebral localization of the malarial parasites—and another—and another! They were all intravenous heroin addicts with tell-tale needle puncture scars over the veins in the folds of the elbows, and they were dropping like flies in Manhattan.

An addict would fall ill, and while he was being transferred because of his fever from one hospital to another (usually a marine hospital because he was a seaman), by the time he got there he would be either unconscious or dead, so rapidly did the infection progress. Nobody quite knew what was happening—a few victims who were still conscious when diagnosed were caught in time and rapidly cured by the administration of quinine intravenously, but not if coma had already set in. The cause of these deaths was first recognized and called attention to by the Medical Examiner's Office. I figured that if all these addicts with malaria were succumbing to the disease, there must be less advanced cases walking around, awaiting discovery and diagnosis.

Now, where would one find heroin addicts who might have malaria? Well, down in the city prison known as "the Tombs," at Leonard and Centre Streets, where they were brought after arrest. This prison, since torn down, was described by Charles Dickens during his visit to New York in 1847. My chief, Dr. Norris, got permission from the Commissioner of Correction to go down to the Tombs and take blood smears of all the addicts they had there. The permission from Commissioner Tudor also enabled me to visit the correction hospital on Welfare Island, in New York's East River, and examine the addict inmates there. It was not a very pleasant job, not only because of the dismal surroundings and pathetic characters I had to observe and test, but because the warders at first were far from cooperative. They were suspicious of me: it was hard to get through to them, to reassure them that I was not there to spy on them or to throw a monkey wrench in their routine. I finally convinced them that I was not snooping, and then they cooperated and were most helpful.

In a short time, I managed to get blood smears from no fewer than 110 addicts using heroin. Among these I found eleven cases of estivo-autumnal malaria! They were sick and febrile, but their complaints had been erroneously attributed to drug withdrawal.

I began questioning the live addicts, who were promptly treated with quinine as soon as I reported their blood smears. I asked them if they knew any of the dead victims. "Aw, yeah, sure we knew them," they replied, "We used to shoot up with them poor guys," meaning that they used to share their injection equipment. I think it should be pointed out in passing that many of these addicts were homosexuals and possessed "stage names" by which they liked to be known, and when these were found out, it was possible to obtain their cooperation and information about sharing of syringes. Names such as "Lady Astor," assumed by a large, heavy-set black man; "Panama Flo," for a slightly-built white addict, are just a few examples. Had I not found out these names, I would not have been able to obtain this information.

In the gregarious way that addicts have, they would congregate in lavatories and flophouses, making communal use of the crude injection apparatus. One addict would "shoot" his heroin mixture after dissolving it in water in a spoon heated over a match and filtered through a piece of absorbent cotton. The spoons were most often taken from the Automat restaurants and carried the H & H monogram. After injecting the heroin into an arm vein, the addict would hand the works over to be used by one or more of his pals. A minute drop of malarious blood would be sucked back through the needle into the medicine dropper and become mixed with the next shot of drug, so the malarial parasites had a free ride into the succeeding man without having to rely on the salivary glands of the female anopheles mosquito.

One man died in the city unrecognized as an addict, and the death had been signed out as "pneumonia," but the drug addict fraternity told me that "he was one of us—he used to shoot with us," and the real diagnosis was falciparum malaria.

I traced one such undiagnosed addict to the anatomy department of Columbia University Medical School, where, as an unclaimed person, his body had been donated for dissection by the students. I obtained permission to go up to Columbia and found that the body was still in the refrigerator. The intravenous injection scars were immediately evident in the elbow folds. The brain vessels were filled with parasites of falciparum malaria.

Thus, I determined the correct cause of death from the embalmed, frozen cadaver, months after death, on a tip from several of his addict friends.

This epidemic of artifically acquired malaria began abruptly in 1933, and as far as I could tell, we had got in on the start of the affair, as nothing even suspiciously like it had been seen in the city before that date. It rumbled on for ten years, and in the period from 1933 through 1943 there were no fewer than 168 fatal cases of malignant tertian malaria in drug addicts in New York City, all of which I autopsied while I was an assistant medical examiner. Then the cases vanished as mysteriously as they had come. We never found out who had introduced the first case into the addict community, but in 1943—during World War II—they abruptly disappeared, never to return. I sometimes think that all the infected addicts went off to the South Pacific theater of operations and took the "Manhattan strain" of malaria with them to infect the Oceanic mosquitoes! There have been a few natural falciparum malaria cases here since 1943, but none due to artificial transmission via the syringes of addicts.

The filler or dilutent for the illegal heroin sold on the street used to be lactose or mannitol, but later the dealers began adding quinine to the mixtures, and I like to believe that this practice began because addicts and their suppliers discovered that it prevented the development of malaria—a sort of built-in prophylactic. Maybe I'm wrong, but since the last death in 1943—a Chinese who had lived in New York all of his life—addiction malaria has vanished here.

This exciting bit of medical detective work was the basis of one of my first published scientific articles. I read a paper on it in 1934 at a meeting of the American Medical Association in Cleveland, and it was published in *Public Health Reports* and also, in greater detail, in the *American Journal of Surgery*. The title of the paper in *Public Health Reports* was "Malaria Among Drug Addicts in New York City—An epidemic of estivo-autumnal and quartian malaria among drug addicts in New York City, transmitted by the use of contaminated hypodermic syringes."

The reason I am including all the details of publication is because the *Public Health Reports* article was reprinted in the September-October 1976 issue, forty-two years after it first appeared, in commemoration of the Bicentennial of the United

States, as an article of historic significance to public health. Recalling that the distinguished chairman of the 1934 American Medical Association session on legal medicine was annoyed with Dr. Norris and Dr. Martland for placing my paper on the program because he didn't think it was sufficiently medico-legal, I am indeed very happy and honored that *Public Health Reports* has thought fit to reprint it after so many years had elapsed since it was first published.

The malaria episode was an interesting aspect of the drug situation in New York, but at the time it began, back in 1933, the whole narcotics problem had not assumed anything like the overwhelming, almost epidemic proportions that it assumed in the sixties and early seventies.

Thankfully, though the situation is still very serious, it seems to have levelled off and even declined a little, so that in the last year or so of my term at the Medical Examiner's Office we had somewhat less of a problem than in the years before.

Maybe my experiences with the malaria phenomenon gave me an added interest in this matter, which is part public health, part legal medicine, and part sociology. No one could go around the Corrections Hospital and "the Tombs" back in 1933, nor visit scores of sordid squalid scenes of death, without being profoundly impressed by the misery and degradation that so often accompanies this desperate craving for heroin, morphine, cocaine, and other drugs of dependence.

In this period between the two world wars, the method of use of these drugs by narcotic addicts underwent a profound change. Originally, drug addiction was either a habit of seafarers in maritime cities like New York, New Orleans, and San Francisco, or was a localized problem among physicians and nursing staff, born of their proximity to addictive drugs intended for therapy.

Then the habit began escaping into the general population, especially the underprivileged section. Increasingly, as time went on, it flourished among the younger age groups, until it attained the almost explosive increase of the past couple of decades.

The change in actual usage began between the wars, as administration by inhaling, swallowing, or introducing the drugs through injection under the skin gave way more and more to the direct injection into a vein.

Instead of these people sniffing dry mixtures of heroin or

cocaine or "skin-popping," they began "mainlining" crudely-prepared substances directly into their blood vessels. The drug, mixed with inert filling agents such as milk-sugar or mannitol (and after the malaria, often quinine), was dissolved in a teaspoon or bottlecap of tap water heated by means of a match flame. The injection equipment was usually a glass medicine dropper with a rubber teat onto which was fixed a hypodermic needle. A flange of rolled-up paper around the glasstip and inserted into the needle hub made a firm, airtight junction. The apparatus was known as "the works"—part of the whole language of idioms that characterizes the twilight world of junkies.

Strangely enough, even when regular medical syringes were available, the addicts often preferred their crude equipment, mainly because it could be manipulated with one hand. A normal syringe with a plunger was more difficult to control.

By means of "the works", the crude solution that had been heated in a spoon or small bottlecap was sucked up through a pledget of absorbent cotton to filter out the solids, and the liquid was injected directly into the much-abused veins in the arms. To start with, the prominent veins in the crook of the elbow were used, but as repeated injections and sometimes infections progressively blocked up the blood-channels, the addict had to range further afield, down the forearm and onto the back of the hand, to find veins that were still open.

The radical change in the method of taking heroin from sniffing to the intravenous route, seems to have originated on a large scale in the Middle East in the 1920's. It was in Cairo, Egypt, that the mainlining habit really took root. The local addicts there, who already had the Eastern habit of sniffing heroin, saw how effective the intravenous route was in the medical treatment for bilharzia, a parasitic disease common there. They copied the idea as a more rapid method of getting the drug into their bloodstream. Seamen coming to the United States spread the habit, and the new method was first seen in New York around 1926.

All along the seaports, heroin was used more and more often intravenously by syringe instead of by sniffing, and it was this change that before long was followed by the outbreaks of malaria in the thirties. The intravenous method of injecting heroin soon became the method of choice everywhere for the administration of this narcotic among addicts.

Before 1943 there were not many deaths from overdoses of these drugs. Apart from the malarial deaths I've already described, there were a certain number at all times from infection due to unsterile, unhygienic equipment. Large abscesses under the skin, bacterial endocarditis due to infection of heart valves from septicemia, septic thrombosis in the maltreated veins, and even some tetanus infections were regularly seen, but not in great numbers. Oddly enough, many women developed these infectic, septic conditions, mainly because they preferred to use the "skin-popping" technique rather than "shooting" into a vein.

During World War II, heroin virtually vanished from the streets of New York and the other great cities of the United States. Addicts turned to other drugs, and this led to a greatly increased illegal traffic in barbiturates and amphetamines. There were still some deaths from septic injection sites with these other drugs, but, by and large, the Medical Examiner's Office had a quiet time from drug deaths during the war years.

But as soon as peace returned, so did the hard drugs. And now the trouble really became a massive problem, worsening each year until the peak years around 1970-72. The trafficking in heroin and morphine became a huge business enterprise, and though they had always been available, apart from the war years, the quantities became enormous.

There are no precise statistics for dependence upon these hard drugs, and estimates vary. But there is plenty of evidence from law-enforcement, social welfare, health, hospital, and voluntary agencies that it steadily increased during those years, despite the concerted efforts of those groups to combat the menace.

We saw more than our share of the problem in the M.E's Office. As chief medical examiner of the city with undoubtedly the greatest drug problem in the whole world, I took a particular interest in the one reliable index of the size of the problem— namely, the death rate associated with drug addiction.

There was a rapid, steady increase in this death rate in the twenty years preceding 1972, but this increase was caused by acute deaths from narcotism rather than the well-established complications from infection.

In 1959 there was a dramatic upturn in the fatal graph, which was maintained for a number of years thereafter. In the early sixties there were about 300 deaths a year and in the ten years

1950-59, there were just over 1,000 deaths. In the next decade to 1970, there were no less than 4,254 deaths from narcotism.

To compare single years, in 1959 there were 215 deaths, whereas in 1969 there were over 900.

The breakdown within the population is interesting, as well as the overall numbers. The ratio of deaths among blacks compared to whites was 12 to 1—and of the whites, 34 percent of the males were Puerto Rican.

The age incidence has been coming down to the younger people over the years, too. About 12 percent occur in teenagers and over a quarter in the under twenty-five group.

The relatively lower incidence of drug deaths outside New York City always strikes me as being very suspect. It may be at least in part due to the reluctance of the coroner or medical examiner to record a death as being due to narcotism if there is no confirming laboratory analysis. In my opinion—and that of those who worked with me in the New York Office during this epidemic of addiction—a diagnosis of death due to narcotism is more reliably arrived at from the investigation of the *circumstances* under which is body is found and the findings of a complete autopsy than from toxicologic analysis, which in our experience has been unhelpful in more than half the cases.

The giveaway features at the scene of a narcotic death fall into a pattern which the seasoned medical examiner can recognize and even sense by an intuitive feeling.

The premises where the death occurs may be very significant. Usually the addict chooses a place where there is some privacy for his shooting-up, unless he is indulging in a group-activity situation with other addicts sharing the equipment—the very thing that leads to cross infection with viruses and, in the old days, even malaria. The location of a corpse on a roof, an elevator, a hallway, or a vacant lot does not mean that death actually took place there, and the examiner must always be mindful of the possibility of the person having been moved, either before or after death, from the place where the fatal injection was given. We have seen cases where the bodies of dead addicts have been transported for miles to other jurisdictions to conceal the original circumstances.

Quite often the works—improvised syringes, needles, bottle-caps, spoons, heroin packets, and tourniquets—have been found alongside the body. Not infrequently, death has taken place so rapidly that the syringe is actually still in place in the arm, hanging by the needle point from the vein, the apparatus half filled with blood.

Conversely, other cases have been concealed, in that all the paraphernalia of injection has been hidden away and the body arranged to look like a natural death. In these, it needs the nose of an experienced investigator to ferret out the true nature of the case.

The actual causes of death cover a wide range, but the majority in recent years have been the "acute reaction" to heroin. The septic complications now give second place to the rapid extinction of life from a mechanism that is still improperly understood. This type of death forms an increasingly larger proportion of the total. From 1950-1961, the other complications made up 48 percent of the narcotic deaths in New York, but in latter years this has dropped markedly in favor of the acute mode of death.

As I say, there's a lot we don't understand about this reaction. Why should one addict drop dead after his injection, while another alongside him who is shooting-up exactly the same dose of the same batch of heroin suffers nothing other than the usual effect of the drug? Why does the same addict drop dead on that day, when he had been giving himself shots of the same substance for months without any sign of the adverse reaction?

In many cases, it's certainly not a simple overdose, but some unexpected sensitivity to the drug. This is where chemical analysis is often of little help. It may reveal only the usual dosage or sometimes even fail to demonstrate the presence of the drug at all—yet there is the corpse before us!

The main value of the autopsy in such cases is in confirming the presence of injection marks. All that is usually found internally is a frothy fluid in the air passages, due to sudden waterlogging of the lungs, and that itself is only a manifestation of sudden heart failure. It doesn't tell us what the basic mechanism was.

The veins in the arms may show all sorts of thickening, fibrosis, thrombosis, and sepsis. Recent puncture marks may be hard to find among all the old damage to the veins and skin, but a careful search usually reveals areas of fresh bleeding where the veins have leaked into the tissues at the site of the injection.

Older addicts—and especially women—may favor subcutaneous injection, and here completely unsterile methods may lead to all kinds of tissue damage. The injections might even be jabbed through the clothing into any part of the body—arms, chest, thighs, abdomen—anywhere. Scars of abscesses give the game away immediately.

It is these people who may die of septicemias—tetanus is much more common in women, and a likely explanation for this is that men have more frequently been immunized against this disease, either in the service or through industrial prophylactic programs. In New York City in recent years, deaths from tetanus—once common throughout the general population—are now confined almost exclusively to addicts.

The lengths to which an addict will go in order to introduce his drugs are extraordinary. Those who are unable to obtain hypodermic needles will sometimes jab a hole in their skin with a large hairpin, then force the tip of a medicine dropper into the wound, to squeeze the heroin directly into the tissues. No wonder that gross infection is the order of the day in such circumstances.

At the peak of the narcotic problem a couple of years ago, drug addiction was the greatest single cause of death in adolescents and young people in the fifteen to thirty-five-year age group in New York City. This exceeded deaths from accidents, suicides, homicides, or even natural disease.

Thankfully, the problem, if not actually declining in its social incidence, is at least altering direction since the introduction of methadone as a substitute to heroin.

Now the addict can take heroin or leave it alone, as he chooses, with the availability of methadone as an alternative which does not carry the same risk of sudden death.

If you look through the recent statistics of drug deaths with a little understanding, you can see that now 10 percent are due to heroin, another 10 percent to methadone, and the remaining 80 percent to all sorts of other drugs. The total death rate has been declining, albeit gradually, since about 1971. The other drugs consist of mixtures of everything under the sun, with barbiturates and amphetamines still well up the list.

The main decrease in the overall mortality is in the acute reaction to heroin—and this is good, because it also indicates a decrease in the usage of heroin. The heroin addict will steal, rob, mug, and kill to get his heroin, but now that he has so many alternatives, there is less pressure. It's good for law enforcement and for the community if he can choose something else that's easier and cheaper to obtain.

People have always made a great song and dance about the increasing quantity of heroin and morphine coming into the country. They talk about it "flooding in" from Turkey and Mexico and being dumped here deliberately from the Far East— but that's nonsense in the context of addiction. There has *always* been heroin available in the United States—plenty of it. The amount was controlled only by the demand—people get so steamed up on this topic—but now that addicts' habits have changed, so will the supply position.

I've lived through the rise of drug addiction in New York; I've seen the peak, and I hope I was in on the decline. I took a particular interest in the problem of these deaths, and in the first half of 1973, I made a close, detailed, personal study of them. Only 10 percent were due to acute heroin reactions, whereas in the decade 1960-69, the same figure was 80 percent.

This tremendous change in emphasis must mean something, and I fervently hope that it means that the problem is on the way to being licked.

Chapter 6

The Importance of First Impressions

So many times in the long years that I've been in legal medicine, I've seen cases ruined in the early stages, either by inexperience, sheer incompetence, or sometimes just an innocent lack of understanding.

What I've noticed in so many of these instances is that in the initial handling no one has had the ability to foresee what may come of his first opinions. These first steps are crucial in detemining whether or not a miscarriage of justice is going to take place subsequently.

The medical man who originally gets the case sometimes just doesn't sense what it's all about—and he may not take the trouble to find out. Once the investigation begins to run along certain lines, people seem to acquire mental blinkers that prevent them from getting out of that first rut—even if it's so obviously the wrong rut.

It may not altogether be the pathologist's fault. Often problems arise because some elected coroner wants to do the right thing. The coroner is told when he takes office, "Look, you have to get yourself a pathologist." Off he goes and makes an arrangement with someone who's got impressive qualifications:

a pillar of respectability, on the staff of some prestigious hospital, etc., or the pathologist may be an associate professor in a medical school who makes himself available to the coroner.

The coroner makes this arrangement, the pathologist is flattered, and all looks well. There's a beautiful laboratory, shining equipment, new scales in the autopsy room—the lot!

But what happens is that this poor guy waits and waits—and nobody ever calls him. The coroner makes all the decisions, and he forgets to call his pathologist on the very occasions when he can really do something. There's nothing in the law that says that the coroner *must* call the pathologist, so he doesn't get called. He loses interest and never gets the chance to accumulate the forensic experience he needs. The best clinical pathologist is still an amateur at medico-legal work if he hasn't got sufficient criminal autopsy and scene of crime experience under his belt.

When the coroner eventually does get around to calling him, he doesn't tell him enough about the case. "There's a body, son, just get on with an autopsy, and give me a report."

The doctor may be too busy or too discouraged to find out anything about the background for himself if there is no medical examiner system operating.

If a medical examiner doesn't dig up the facts, then he's responsible for the defects—even an M.E. system can fall down if he turns away a case. But under the coroner system, the poor pathologist is at the mercy of a lay official. If he isn't efficient and cooperative, then right from the start the whole investigation is built on shifting sands.

A case I was involved in down in Mississippi was one of those which was ruined right from the beginning. It involved the Biddy family, who lived in North Jackson.

Mr. Biddy was a consulting engineer who had made a very good thing of his profession, but he wasn't quite so efficient in his personal life. He had a red-haired secretary, Carolee, for whom he divorced his wife. Carolee already had two children, and Mr. Biddy had one five-year-old girl, Mona Lee, who was mentally retarded.

After the divorce, the father had the right to have Mona visit him and his pretty new wife. Mr. Biddy was very fond of Mona, but his ex-wife didn't think much of the new Mrs. Biddy and resented the court order which allowed Mona to spend weekends with her stepmother. Because of this antagonism, Carolee was even more anxious to do the right thing and make Mona welcome at their house, which was a big, rambling place.

Shortly before Christmas 1970, Mona went for one of her weekends with her father and stepmother. One afternoon, she was found crying by the other two kids, who ran in to report to Mom that Mona had got into the drain cleaner, an alkaline fluid used for cleaning out the sink pipes. This used to be a very strong caustic solution with about 40 percent lye, but due to protests of pediatricians and others, the Food and Drug Administration had made the manufacturers weaken it down to only about 6 percent.

The solicitous stepmother was worried out of her skull by the thought that anything might have happened to little Mona while she was in her care. She rushed out to see her and found that she had some reddening of the skin of the face where she had rubbed the irritated areas with her hands.

Carolee Biddy immediately called the doctor, who didn't come over but asked questions on the phone. Of course he couldn't have known about the reduction in strength of the drain cleaner and under the circumstances took proper action. He told the parents to look in the mouth and throat for signs of severe corrosion, consistent with the effects of the old type of liquid. They didn't see any, and the doctor was reassured. They told him that Mona was vomiting, so he told them to give her some Dramamine and put her to bed.

The new stepmother, anxious to do the right thing, followed the doctor's instructions and tucked Mona into bed. She was quiet apart from some whimpering, and Carolee left her to sleep. An hour later, she looked in on Mona—and saw no child in the bed!

Panic-stricken, she pulled back the bedclothes and found the little girl in a ball at the foot of the bed, quite dead.

Desperation swept over her. "My God, I know the child's mother didn't want me to have her over in the first place—she's going to blame me for this!"

Crazy with panic, she picked up the body and vanished into the darkness with it, taking it a mile or so to the Ross Barnett Reservoir on the Pearl River, where she left it face down in the sandy mud at the water's edge.

When she got home, she reported Mona missing, and a great hue and cry was raised. There was a great to-do, the town was called out, and the Boy Scouts roamed the countryside looking for Mona Biddy. Eventually, the body was discovered where it had been left, after a hunt which eventually made the whole town pretty mad at Carolee for making a fool of them.

Now in comes the coroner. He hears about marks on the face and gets the story, for by now Mrs. Biddy has admitted to her stupid action, which was born of panic.

The coroner calls his pathologist, an associate professor of pathology from the medical school, but apparently doesn't tell him a thing about the drain cleaner.

The pathologist, who naturally doesn't really understand the true issues at this stage, does an autopsy. The face was by then markedly discolored due to post-mortem hypostatis and the maceration caused by lying face down in wet sand and water.

Hypostasis—also known as post-mortem lividity—is the condition in which the skin of the lowest parts of the body are discolored due to blood sinking by gravity to the most dependent parts. If the body is moved after death, this settling of the blood can move to a new position, and in Mona's case, it had discolored the features, a condition made worse by the soaking effects of the water and the onset of post-mortem decomposition.

At the original autopsy, the throat organs were not taken out and the interior of the head was not examined, yet a cause of death of "suffocation" was firmly declared, even though in my opinion there were essentially no positive findings of any firm cause of death. No attention at all was directed to the possibility of the drain cleaner being a factor.

Now, to a lay person, "suffocation" means that someone must have applied mechanical asphyxia to the child—and the stepmother, Carolee Biddy, was charged with murder.

Next came a rather extraordinary thing. The defense lawyer quite rightly wanted another autopsy—but whom did they get to do it? The same pathologist who had done the first one!

This time he removes the throat organs, but by now the condition had deteriorated from the previous autopsy, embalming, burying, and exhumation. The original state of the organs was far from being well-preserved—the tissues were all dried out—for this second autopsy was weeks after the death.

As the same prosecution pathologist was doing the second autopsy, the family had another doctor there as an observer to represent them, but he didn't really know a lot about the issues involved. He reported that the larynx—the voice box—was normal. Yet, the epiglottis, which is the cartilage that stands up to protect the entrance to the windpipe from having pieces of food fall into it, was sticking up like a clotheshanger, with the mucous membrane—the lining of the larynx—draped all round it and drooping, like a dustsheet thrown over a narrow chair. No significance was attached to this by the defense doctor.

There were no additional findings at the second autopsy, and the indictment for murder went on to trial.

At the first trial in the following June, the thirty-two-year-old stepmother was neither convicted nor acquitted, as there was a hung jury; and the case had to go for retrial.

In Pascagoula, in Jackson County, Mississippi, the second trial came off in September. This time I was asked by the defense to go down to look the case over and give testimony if needed.

I didn't have time to see all the evidence before trial, and I was already on the witness stand giving evidence that the autopsy didn't prove any satisfactory cause of death at all, when a photograph was handed to me.

This was a picture of the larynx from the second autopsy. I took a quick look and saw with astonishment the draped folds of membrane hanging down over the epiglottis.

Now, no expert witness likes to be caught on one leg, with no opportunity to consider new evidence like that. I didn't want to shoot off my mouth without having time to study the thing, but I didn't get much choice. It was obvious that this was due to "laryngeal edema"—great swelling of the membrane at the entrance to the windpipe—from severe irritation by something. It's a classic cause of obstruction of the air passages and can happen in certain allergies, even an insect sting in the mouth. Or it can be due to certain virulent infections, or, as almost certainly it was in this case, to chemical irritation. Typical of that could be the weak lye in the drain cleaner. The stuff, in its recently diluted form, wasn't corrosive enough to burn the throat as the family doctor had thought when he asked Carolee Biddy to look for damage in the mouth—but it was certainly enough of an irritant to cause progressive swelling of the throat membranes over the ensuing few hours until it caused death from asphyxia.

I told the court this, and I explained that the marks on the face that the prosecution were getting so steamed up about could well be due to a combination of some weak lye, some post-mortem staining from lying face-down on the bank of the reservoir, and the macerating effect of the water in which she was lying.

But they didn't want to know about these alternative explanations, and at the second trial poor Carolee was convicted and sentenced to twenty years in the state penitentiary.

An appeal was turned down, and she is still in jail, though—as far as I know—there are further moves for a new appeal.

But I feel that this was one of those cases that went wrong right at the start. If the pathologist doesn't know all the facts before he does his autopsy, he just can't catch up later—once you get aimed down one particular pathway of opinion, it's hard to get yourself back onto a new track.

Similarly, great issues often rest on tiny foundations, and for an unfortunate supermarket owner in Tennessee, this was certainly a basic truth. I got involved in the Montesi case in Memphis in 1968, though the death concerned took place in November 1965. The legal processes dragged on until 1971, when they petered out due to sheer exhaustion on the part of the Tennessee prosecutors.

Louis Frank Montesi, a highly successful businessman of Italian origin, was about forty-six at the time of the tragedy. He lived in a large house in Memphis with his fifty-two-year-old wife, Evelyn, his teenage daughter Vicki, and his elderly mother.

On the night of November 2, 1965, his mother was in her own self-contained part of the house, and Vicki was in her room upstairs. Some married Montesi children, who had been over for the evening, had left just before nine o'clock. Louis Montesi went to bed to read the newspaper, but his wife stayed in the den.

At nine-forty p.m., the Memphis police had an urgent call from a neighbor to go to the Montesi house, because Mr. Montesi had appeared at his door in his pajamas in a state of great agitation, claiming that his house had been robbed.

A prowl car went there immediately and found Mrs. Montesi lying on the grass outside the patio with a gunshot wound through her right breast and a further injury to one of the fingers of her right hand, probably caused by the same bullet. She was alive when the police got to her but soon died without being able to tell them anything. She had bled profusely, and blood was spattered about in several parts of the house. Montesi himself had a cut on the back of his head, a wound on his forehead, and scratches on the right side of his neck.

At that stage, since there was no evidence—other than from Montesi himself—that any other person had been involved, the police were suspicious of him. Later, they did a paraffin test on his hands to detect any signs of nitrites, which would indicate that he had recently fired a hand gun, but the result was negative. Montesi produced a pistol and turned it over to the police, but subsequent ballistics tests showed that it was not the murder weapon.

Louis Montesi maintained from the beginning that he heard a disturbance when he was in bed and heard his wife screaming something that sounded like "Robbers, robbers." His bedroom was on the ground floor, and he ran through the hall into the dining room, where he saw Evelyn lying on the floor, a man standing over her. According to Montesi, the intruder then attacked him, and Montesi fled back through the dining area, throwing a heavy ashtray at his assailant as he went. The man caught him and inflicted the injuries to his neck and head. The prowler then ran out of the house, and Montesi, a heavy, fat man, tried to pursue him and ran out into the street in his pajamas and bathrobe.

The police found six revolver cartridges in the hall, one used, the rest unfired. The hall and dining room showed signs of a struggle and blood stains and disarrayed furniture.

Later, when the body was examined in the mortuary, a police officer noted that the fingernails of Mrs. Montesi's left hand were filled with some substance. It was alleged on subsequent microscopic examination that this was skin—but more about that later, since it was the crux of the whole circumstantial case against Louis Montesi.

What about the man who ran out of the house and vanished? Montesi maintained that he was a salesman from Massachusetts who some time previously had tried to sell Montesi customer carts for use in his chain of supermarkets. He had last seen the man a month before, when he came to the house to try to borrow money from Montesi. There had been some unpleasantness between them, because Louis Montesi declined to make the loan.

Now, on the night of the killing, Montesi did not know that the salesman was in Memphis until he saw him in his house, since there had been no contact between them for a month. When the police investigated, they found that the man was actually staying in a motel within four minutes' driving time of the scene of the killing.

No fingerprints were ever taken at the Montesi house, and the salesman was never asked to take a paraffin test to see if he had fired a gun. He flatly denied being at the Montesi house or knowing anything about the death of the wife. The character of the man was seriously attacked at the later trial, where it was shown that he was heavily in debt at the time of the shooting. He said that he had been in the motel all evening, except when he left to look for a place to buy a box of fried chicken. Several days after the homicide, a box of cartridges similar to the ones found in the Montesis' hall turned up near the fence of the backyard of the property adjoining the motel.

The other material witness was the daughter, Vicki Montesi. She was in her room upstairs. She heard the doorbell ring and thought she heard her mother going to the door and someone opening the door. Then she heard sounds of disorder below, as if furniture was being knocked over. She also heard screaming from her mother, which sounded like, "Don't kill me! Vicki, help, help!"

Returning to the scientific evidence, the material under the fingernails was stated to be human skin by the police laboratory, but they never identified it as belonging to Montesi; nor did they get a blood group on the fragments. Nevertheless, the prosecution maintained that the skin was under the fingernails of the wife's left hand and the accused had scratches on the right side of his neck; *ergo*, she must have scratched him. All this was completely circumstantial evidence, even assuming that the material under the nails *was* human skin—a fact that was later discredited.

This set of circumstances was put before a jury, and in spite of the alternative explanation concerning the intruder, they found Louis Montesi guilty of "voluntary manslaughter." This was the first trial, in April 1966, ending in a two to ten year sentence for voluntary manslaughter.

During the trial, a criminal court clerk was called to testify that an indictment had been sought against the salesman for first degree murder of Evelyn Montesi, but a grand jury had rejected it. In June 1967, the Tennessee Supreme Court reversed the decision and a retrial took place the following March.

It was at this stage that I was called to give an opinion, primarily on the fingernail scrapings. I brought in Dr. Robert Hausman, the medical examiner in San Antonio, Texas, to help, for he was an excellent microscopist and an expert on trace evidence.

The case came up for the second trial, and we looked at all the medical and scientific evidence. Considering that the first conviction hinged on those fingernail scrapings, it was a real travesty of science. The police had dug out a bit of material from under the nails after the autopsy—the hands had been contaminated with the wife's blood, for the bullet had gone through the finger as well. What little material they scraped out was then wrapped in tissue paper and sectioned for examination under the microscope. It was virtually worthless as evidence, since there was no reason at all to say it was skin, human or otherwise. It was just a lot of gunk. I looked on two occasions at all twelve slides they had prepared, and I said on the stand, "All I saw was a bit of nondescript material that you find under the fingernails of most people, with some variations."

There also appeared to be some plant tissue that looked as if it had been through the digestive tract and some partly-digested striated muscle fibers that came from some animal food material, I suppose, but there was no evidence at all for concluding that there was any skin—yet on the basis of this they had convicted him!

Bob Hausman gave more or less the same testimony—he suggested that the stuff could have come from some fried chicken that the Montesi family had eaten that evening.

After the first trial, the defense had found another witness, a Mrs. Dora Thomas, who had been changing a tire on her car in the street near the house at the time of the killing. She testified that she saw a man go to the front door of the Montesi house holding something in his hand, and a few moments later, he came running from the back of the house. He leaped into his car and took off so wildly that he almost hit her.

Then she saw a man "in an elephant suit," referring to the fat Mr. Montesi in pajamas and bathrobe, running across the street "yelling and hollering." She said she was too scared and worried to come forward at the first trial.

You would think that this should have just about wrapped it up in Montesi's favor, but the prosecution stuck to its guns, and this time Montesi was found guilty of a lesser offense, "involuntary manslaughter," and given one to three years!

In February 1970, the Court of Criminal Appeals reversed this second decision on grounds of insufficient evidence—which should have seemed obvious from the start. In 1971, the Supreme Court confirmed the quashing of the second trial, so Montesi was back where he started, liable to be tried all over again.

But to the best of my knowledge, the six-year marathon had worn down the persistence of the prosecutors sufficiently to discourage them from starting the whole roundabout going again.

The whole case points up a moral: that a bit of scientific mumbo jumbo, like a rash early opinion on fingernail scrapings, can lead to injustice and years of anguish, unless the poor fellow on the receiving end gets the chance to have this one-sided evidence challenged by experts acting on his behalf.

Below, coffined bodies at the morgue in nineteenth-century New York await the Coroner's attention. (*Helpern Collection*) Until 1960, the Manhattan mortuary, autopsy rooms and laboratories of the Medical Examiner's Office of New York City were located at Bellevue Hospital. The top picture on the facing page shows Dr. Helpern, far left, just prior to beginning an autopsy. At bottom, Dr. Helpern analyzes some findings. Both pictures date from the mid-1930s. (*Helpern Collection*)

On the facing page, Dr. Helpern holds bullet fragments from the skull shown in the background. (*Helpern Collection*)   Below, Dr. Helpern examines one of the exhibits of the Medical Examiner's Office's famous "Black Museum" that houses Dr. Helpern's collection of weapons and specimens from autopsies dating back more than forty-five years. (*Helpern Collection*)

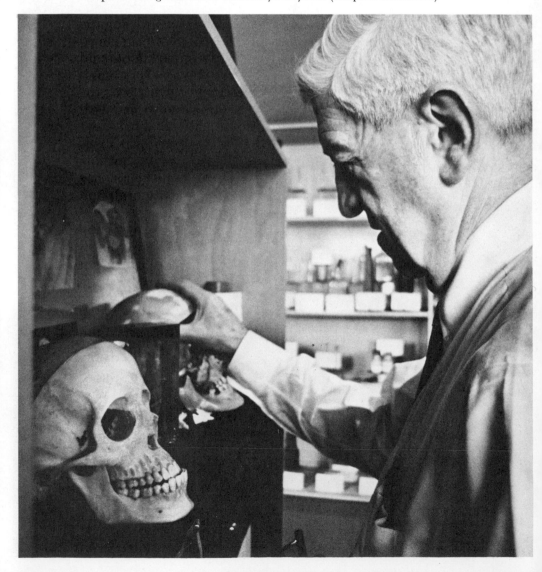

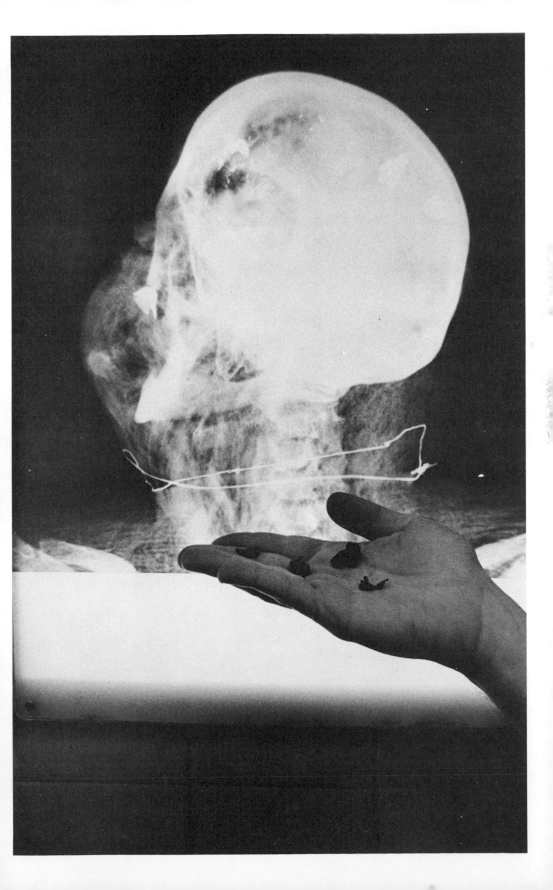

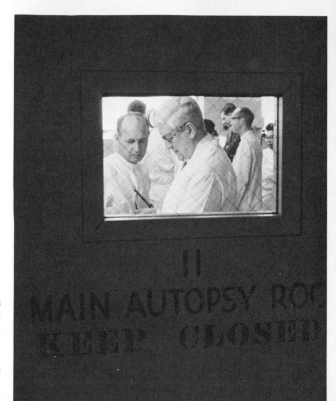

At right, Dr. Helpern discusses a case with colleagues at the Office. (*Helpern Collection*) At bottom, autopsy tables in the Medical Examiner's Office. Note the scales, used for weighing specimens upon removal from the body. (*Helpern Collection*)

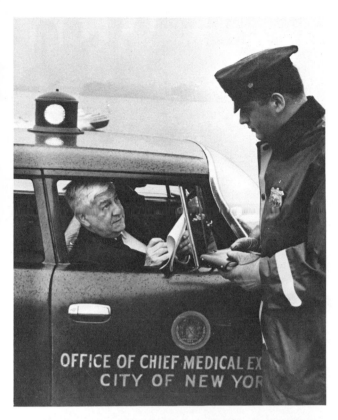

At left, Dr. Helpern visits the scene of a crime in his capacity as Chief Medical Examiner of New York City. (*Helpern Collection*) Below, refrigerated storage compartments holding bodies that come under the jurisdiction of the Medical Examiner's Office. (*Helpern Collection*)

Chapter 7

Writing the Book on Legal Medicine

Soon after I started as a young man in the Office of Chief Medical Examiner, I got mixed up in undergraduate teaching. Indirectly, this led to the establishment of what I think few will deny is the definitive American textbook on legal medicine.

This is the way it happened.

Around 1932, the students at Cornell were being given lectures on legal medicine by one Dr. Otto Shultz, but the poor fellow began to develop some acute mental troubles and had to be hospitalized.

Dr. DuBois, a senior physician at Bellevue, called me aside one morning after a clinical pathology conference and asked me if I would take over Dr. Shultz's lectures. I had only been working in legal medicine for about six months, and at that stage I wasn't too sure whether I really wanted to stick with this field. But rather fearfully I agreed, and I suppose, looking back, it was that meeting with Dr. DuBois that really sealed my fate for the rest of my life, as far as adhering to forensic pathology was concerned.

I started these lectures up at Cornell and joined in with the others at the Office, Dr. Vance and Dr. Gonzales, in lecturing at

Columbia, N.Y.U., Cornell, and the Police Academy. We did this for a year or so and then wondered if we couldn't put our combined notes together and make some sort of book.

We must have been pretty green then, and we didn't know a thing about what was involved in launching a book on the market. First of all we tried Hoeber, a New York publisher. They said yes, they were interested, but it would be very expensive, and they wanted five thousand dollars to get it going. Well, in those days that was more than a year's salary, so we gave up the idea until Appleton-Century-Crofts came to us. They were already doing a book on legal medicine, but the author had died and left them in midair with it: Appleton wanted to keep a foothold in the legal medicine market, so they asked us if we'd write a book to replace the one that had become defunct.

We got down to sorting out our lecture notes, amplifying them, and making up illustrations. We were so inexperienced that we didn't know that you had to leave places for the pictures—so when we got the galley proofs, they had to be altered to make room for the illustrations!

I did many of the pictures myself, as photography had been my hobby since I was a kid in East Harlem, when I used the bathroom for a darkroom. I had a lot of five-by-seven glass plates of all kinds of conditions I had seen in the autopsy room and mortuary. They were printed up by a good photographer I knew, who did them for thirty-five cents apiece. I've still got the original plates—over forty years old—in boxes somewhere. They still might come in useful, as I expect that the original printing blocks will by now have been destroyed or have deteriorated.

The book first came out in 1937, and was called *Legal Medicine and Toxicology*, by Gonzales, Vance, and Helpern. It was a big book in that first edition, over a thousand pages. The toxicology section in the original edition was written by Henry Sega, but by 1954, when the second edition appeared, Charles Umberger did the toxicology section, and his name was added to the authorship.

It was essentially a practical book, based on our experiences at the New York Office of the Chief Medical Examiner. It was a book for working pathologists—it didn't attempt to review all the world literature on every topic, as so many more academic texts would do. Almost all the illustrations were quite original and had never been published anywhere before. It got a very good reception and had wide appeal as an essentially practical volume that a medical examiner, pathologist, or lawyer could turn to and find what mattered in any particular situation.

After almost forty years on the shelves, it still remains a valuable guide to everyday practice in legal medicine. In spite of the many other books that have come along since, it still continues to sell and to be quoted in courtrooms, not only in North America but all over the world.

The last edition—the second—was in 1954, and the publishers have been petitioning me for years to update it and bring out a third edition. I've been working on it quietly but, in spite of their pleas, still haven't got round to finishing it. I don't plan on altering much at all, certainly not on lengthening it. It is basically as sound now as the day it was written, as it records and discusses the same medico-legal situations that existed in the 1930s. From the pathological point of view, a shooting or a traffic accident or a carbon monoxide death is pretty much the same today as it was before the war, so the book retains its usefulness for longer than a textbook on, say, internal medicine or therapeutics, some of which get outdated between the time of writing and the time of publication.

The names Gonzales, Vance, and Helpern on the spine of that book have gone around the world. It remains one of the things of which I am most proud. It certainly put the New York Office right on the international map as far as legal medicine was concerned.

And it all stemmed from that day back in 1932 when I was asked to give a few lectures at Cornell!

Chapter 8

New England Justice

I have always had the feeling that New England still lives in the past as far as crime and punishment are concerned. The atmosphere of the old Salem witch trials still persists—they're out to get you, and they're going to convict someone if it's the last thing they do!

I got mixed up in one such affair some years ago, and I think it was one of the most horrible cases I remember—not because there was anything revolting or horrific about the pathology, but because Boston was out to get this poor guy, come hell or high water.

My first knowledge of the case was a call from Doctor Isidor Snapper, a distinguished clinician and specialist in internal medicine, who was a friend of Mr. Kaumann, general counsel in New York for the Royal Dutch Steamship Company. He asked if I would meet with Mr. Kaumann, who asked me if I would advise him on some medico-legal matters in connection with the disappearance and death of a woman passenger from one of their ships—which was naturally bad business for a steamship line.

Bit by bit, the whole story unfolded. The Royal Dutch steamship—which was a freighter that carried nine passengers—

had arrived at the Commonwealth Pier, Boston, after a thirty-three day voyage from Singapore. Among the passengers was a vivacious divorcee named Lynn Kauffman, the twenty-three-year-old daughter of a well-to-do Chicago business man.

Lynn had been divorced three years earlier and since then had virtually moved into the home of her employer, Professor Stanley Spector, head of the Far Eastern affairs department of Washington University, St. Louis. Lynn Kauffman had enrolled in his department and, after her divorce, had lived with the professor, his wife Juanita, and their two children.

When the professor went on a sabbatical year to the Far East, Lynn joined the party as his secretary, interpreter, and research assistant. It might be relevant to what happened later that there was talk at that time of Lynn having to give up her room and her place in the Spector household.

In August 1959, Mrs. Juanita Spector, Lynn Kauffman, and the two children sailed from Singapore in the *Utrecht*; the professor left some days later by plane.

During the long voyage, Lynn was apparently the life and soul of the shipboard society—until they arrived at Boston on September 18. Then, so I was told, Lynn became morose and moody and refused to come out of her stateroom, even for meals. Mrs. Spector knocked on her door to call her to lunch, but she called that she didn't feel like having any. Willem van Rie, the ship's radio officer, also spoke to her through the porthole around noon, when the girl told him she felt "terrible."

No one saw her during the afternoon, and at six-fifteen, the ship began moving away from her berth for the short voyage down to New York. Just before seven, Mrs. Spector again tapped on Lynn's door to ask her if she was coming to dinner, but all she got was a mumbled answer that Lynn didn't want any dinner. A few moments later, a steward also knocked to announce dinner, and he also got a reply—"in a trembling voice"—that she didn't feel well enough to eat.

The ship cleared Boston harbor and speeded up to sixteen knots, heading toward the Cape Cod Canal.

During the evening, the company of the usually gregarious Lynn was missed in the lounge, and everyone was speculating on what was wrong. She'd never missed a meal before. About nine o'clock, the purser became worried and went to cabin seven, along with van Rie. The door was stuck but unlocked—they pushed their way inside and found it empty, with both portholes open. The cabin opened onto a companionway, not directly to the outside of the ship. There was a high rail on the opposite side of this gangway, so it would be virtually impossible for anyone to fall over accidentally.

Her dinner dress was hung on a hook, but there was no trace of Lynn Kauffman. Immediately, a hue and cry was set up for the popular girl. The ship was searched from stem to stern and an "Abandon ship" routine was called, which failed to flush her out of hiding.

At midnight, the captain accepted that she must have gone overboard, and he sent radio messages to the U.S. Coast Guard to keep a lookout for the missing passenger. He also had the cabin locked, as a safeguard for any later investigation.

The next day, the *Utrecht* berthed in Brooklyn, and by then, Lynn Kauffman had been found. Her body, dressed only in a pair of shorts and slippers, had been washed up on Spectacle Island, a small islet in Boston Harbor.

At this stage there were some rather wild theories about the possibility of Lynn having been murdered because she might have stumbled onto a drug-smuggling syndicate among the *Utrecht's* crew.

Joe Fallon, chief of the Boston Homicide Bureau, flew down to New York to confer with his Brooklyn police colleagues, who had been alerted when it was known that Mrs. Kauffman had been found dead. The cabin had been photographed and her luggage impounded, though there was no real evidence of any foul play. Captain Fallon made some inquiries, then flew back to Boston to report that he believed that Mrs. Kauffman had committed suicide. "She had received some distressing news that day, which would have affected her life profoundly," he said— and we can only guess that this was some development in her relations with the Spector family.

So far then, no great concern was being shown by the investigators; the young woman seemed to have been depressed, was acting oddly, and had vanished over the side of the ship.

But the whistle was blown soon after Fallon got back to Boston with his opinion that it was a suicide.

An autopsy had been done by Boston's Suffolk County Medical Examiner, Doctor Michael Luongo. Now he was a good pathologist—in fact one of the first eighteen experts to be board-certified in forensic pathology when it was recognized as a separate medical specialty the previous year.

He did a good autopsy and found undisputed signs of drowning, together with some small areas of hemorrhage on the membranes of the brain and a number of bruises on the body, virtually confined to the left side. But to the detective's surprise, Luongo then categorically said that death was due to "homicide." This is where I always fail to go along with people—when they take a set of pathological facts and add some attribute which cannot possibly be deduced from those facts. She was drowned— O.K.; she had a head injury—O.K.; she had widespread marks down her left side—O.K. But that doesn't tell anyone it's a homicide!

But Luongo said, "I'm not buying this suicide idea at all. This girl died of drowning after violence. She had been so badly kicked and pummelled that she was incapable of moving voluntarily into the water."

This put the Boston Homicide Bureau on the spot. The police commissioner and Francis Hennessy, his superintendent, had faith in their bureau chief, Joe Fallon. If he was satisfied it was a suicide, they were willing to go along with him.

But Michael Luongo was adamant and appealed to the Suffolk County district attorney for support.

The ship was still in Brooklyn, and the police down here kept on the job. At first they were told that Lynn Kauffman was a model of respectable behavior aboard the *Utrecht*, but then the whisper got loose that she had in fact spent many a night in the radio operator's cabin since leaving Singapore.

The detectives ferreted around some more and dug up a few inconsistencies in Willem van Rie's statements. His weather report to the bridge had been late on the evening that Lynn vanished. His coat was found in her cabin. There were some inaccuracies in the radio log for that evening.

On September 30, just before the ship was due to sail for Philadelphia, the Brooklyn investigators telephoned Fallon, and he flew down again to interview van Rie, who seemed to have answers for all these minor inconsistencies. The ship's departure was delayed due to a hurricane warning, and the detectives worked on van Rie all through the night. Eventually, he gave in and admitted that he was having an affair with Lynn Kauffman, but he maintained that it was a pretty ordinary sort of shipboard romance. A few days out of Singapore, she had asked him if he liked sleeping alone. "Not necessarily," he replied, and from then on, they visited each other in their cabins.

"I don't go looking for romance," he explained, "but when it comes my way, I don't turn it down!"

It seemed a casual affair; neither of them meant anything to the other. Van Rie had been married only months before and had his wife's photograph in his cabin, so there was no question (as was suggested later) that Lynn suddenly discovered that she wasn't the only woman in his life.

At six in the morning of that long night of interrogation, van Rie suddenly made a "confession," but he later withdrew it and angrily maintained that it had been dragged out of him after his questioners had trapped him into making it. The statement said that about seven o'clock on the evening that Lynn vanished, he went to her cabin to ask why she was sick.

"Are you pregnant?" he asked.

"What would you care if I were?" she is supposed to have replied, and this rather mild dispute is supposed to have led to a violent quarrel, during which he beat her until she fell to the floor.

He then left and went to dinner!

Van Rie was arrested and a Suffolk County grand jury indicted him for murder. The trial began in February 1960 and caused international interest because of the classic situation of a shipboard affair.

Boston seemed outraged at such immoral goings-on, and Massachusetts Assistant D.A. John MacAuliffe pulled out all the stops to get a conviction for first degree murder.

The evidence was all circumstantial, and its main prop was Dr. Luongo's immovable conviction that Lynn Kauffman had been murdered.

When the Royal Dutch Steamship Company's counsel, Mr. Kaumann, came to see me, he asked, "How can you decide on homicide merely from the autopsy?", and this was the central point of the whole case.

You don't always go solely on autopsy evidence; as I've said repeatedly, the autopsy is only *part* of the whole investigation. Maybe somebody saw van Rie throw her overboard—then O.K. But just from the autopsy appearances, all we can tell is that a drowned person has fallen from a height.

This case meant a great deal to the steamship line. The accused was one of their employees, and a conviction would mean bad business. They were concerned about a subsequent civil suit, so I went up to Boston to look over the autopsy exhibits. Luongo had taken fifty color pictures of the body. It was a good autopsy, but I think he went too far—an arbitrary conclusion had been drawn from undisputed facts.

There were superficial abrasions and bruises from head to toe, but virtually confined to the left side. There were contusions on the left forehead, left cheek, left eyelid, and chin. On the left shoulder, chest, inner and outer left thigh, and shin there were more surface marks. Under the covering of the brain, there were two smallish patches of hemorrhage—again on the left side— with a smaller one on the right. The lungs showed some deep injuries of a "comprehensive" nature. Now, when a person is assaulted to the degree alleged by the prosecution, the injuries don't just fall all on one side like that.

Now the girl had fallen from a deck some forty feet above the water of a freighter that was pushing along at sixteen knots. Even apart from the speed of the ship, by the time a body hit the water from that height, it would be moving at between thirty and thirty-five miles per hour—and water can be mighty hard material at that speed. There was a folded gangplank hanging down the ship's side at that point—an additional hazard—and I was convinced that all the injuries could have been caused by the body hitting either this or the ship's side and the water. The fact that virtually all the injuries were on one side fit in well with this idea; as did the conviction that no injuries from a beating are confined to one side of the body.

But Luongo stoutly maintained that the bruises and abrasions were consistent with the theory that the body had been pushed through the porthole and fallen to the deck outside. He said that all these injuries were caused before the brain hemorrhages led to death—though what evidence he had for that statement, I could never understand.

To back him up the prosecution kept promising that Dr. Alan Moritz, the great expert from Harvard, was coming. He was coming to clear the whole matter up for the court—he was coming by airplane—he was coming on horseback—always coming—always coming—but he never showed up! I suspect that he never *was* coming, but they used him as a psychological booster for their case.

So Michael Luongo testified about his autopsy and did it well. If he had confined his testimony to his autopsy, good! If someone had seen van Rie throw Lynn overboard, good! But Luongo testified that the injuries were inflicted *in the cabin*, and that she was assaulted *in the cabin*, and that she was rendered unconscious *in the cabin;* she would have had to have been carried and thrown overboard.

This sort of testimony scared the hell out of me; it showed me how a person can be trapped. As Moritz never showed up, they brought in another pathologist, Arthur O'Dea, who used to be medical examiner of Rhode Island. He supported Luongo, insisting that she must have been kicked, stomped on, rendered unconscious, couldn't possibly have moved after the assault, and must have been thrown overboard. I couldn't understand how in blazes they could tell that from an autopsy.

I got up and testified. I said simply that it was perfectly possible for this woman to have fallen or jumped overboard herself.

They asked me, "Could she have been pushed?" I said, "Yes, sure she could—but you have to *prove* that some other way; you can't tell that from an autopsy."

This woman came forty feet down the side of a ship going at the better part of twenty miles an hour—that alone could have caused all sorts of marks. Then she was washed round Boston Harbor all night and was ultimately washed back and forth among the rocks on Spectacle Island. I wasn't at all sure whether the sub-arachnoid bleeding over the brain had occurred before or after death. The whole picture was far more consistent with a fall from a height than with an assault.

The Massachusetts D.A. got real nasty with me; he wanted a conviction, and he was out to get one. The way he saw it, this rotten guy van Rie had been having immoral relations with this girl—in Boston, the affair was tantamount to evidence of guilt—so I got a hard time on that witness stand. The assistant D.A., this belligerent fellow MacAuliffe, asked me sarcastically "whether her head would have been bruised if her foot had been stepped on." I replied, "Well, I think that sort of question already contains the answer."

He tried to pick me off piecemeal by going through each of the bruises individually and asking whether it could have been caused by a blow from a fist or a kick. Naturally, each one could, but I'd been around too long to be cornered into that sort of advocacy.

"If you've ever seen a body falling," I told him, "you'll know there's a lot of action. It doesn't fall like a statue. A body falling forty feet is going over thirty miles an hour. The body is folded, the limbs are flexed, the head is moving. The impact is not single, it's composite. As soon as it strikes, it gets thrashed about. Anyone who has fallen off a boat or water skis knows what sort of impact occurs."

It's always hard to know what a jury makes of conflicting medical testimony. It has been said that in those circumstances the jury reckons that the doctors cancel each other out and ignores the testimony of both of them!

Whatever happened in the jury room in Boston that February, they came out March 2 and acquitted Willem van Rie, much to the delight of his plump wife, who had come over from Holland to stand by him.

He renounced the sea after that, "swallowed the anchor," and went home to Utrecht to work for a publisher.

But it was a case that left a bad taste in the mouth, the bitter flavor of old New England vengeance.

Another unusual case that took place in New England was the Massachusetts affair of John Franklin Noxon, Jr. This one occurred during World War II. As the van Rie case demonstrates, New Englanders tend to get pretty worked up about their homicides, and the involvement of a retarded infant in the Noxon case didn't make for cooler heads up there.

Mr. Noxon was an extremely successful, forty-eight-year-old lawyer, who was counsel to the General Electric Corporation—a very responsible job. He had an excellent military record in World War I, in which he had served in Europe with Patton. On leaving the service, he studied law and rose rapidly in his profession. He was married and had a fine house with a big garden on a lake in Pittsfield, Massachusetts.

The Noxons had one boy, who was about twelve at the time of this trouble. Then, rather late in their married life, they had a second child. It was six months before they began to realize that the baby wasn't all it should have been; in fact, it was a mongoloid. They took the infant to an eminent pediatrician in Boston, Dr. Hunt, who confirmed the diagnosis. He talked to them about the possibilities of putting the child into an institution, but he also assured them that mongoloids were easy to look after and, on the whole, were usually quite lovable children. They couldn't make up their minds what to do, whether to have it institutionalized or not, as the baby was otherwise physically perfect.

This was the situation in the household in 1943 when Mr. Noxon came home early one afternoon. He had been in court, and the case he was arguing had been unexpectedly adjourned, so he decided to make it an early day. He began to tinker with the radio, a large, console-type of instrument located in the lounge. Noxon started to change the tubes; his wife was in some other part of the house; and the cook was in the very next room, within earshot, preparing dinner. Eventually, his wife came into the room and placed the infant on a large, chromium-plated tray, which they used to prevent soiling of the furniture by wet diapers.

Mrs. Noxon wanted to go into the garden to pick some fresh vegetables and asked her husband to mind the baby while she was gone. The tray with the infant on it was placed near where Noxon was puttering about with the radio, and the wife left. After a while, he needed some new tubes and went out to the shed to get them. He was gone five, six, possibly ten minutes—he couldn't remember how long.

But when he came back into the room, he smelled something burning. Immediately, he went to the baby and found that its arm was wrapped in the electric cord of an extension lamp he had been using to see inside the radio set; it was a sort of "trouble cord", a length of flexible, fabric-covered wire with a socket and lamp on one end. The covering was old and frayed, so that the insulation was faulty in places. The cord was wrapped around the lower part of the child's forearm, just above the wrist.

The child had an obvious electrical burn in that region and was dead, but the cook, just in the next room, had not heard a sound. The Noxons were in terrible distress and immediately called their doctor. He was a physician who was also one of the Massachusetts medical examiners—not a pathologist, but one of the "discreet physicians" who are involved in the sort of half-

M.E., half-coroner system they have in the commonwealth there. He came to the house and pronounced that life was extinct in the infant. At that time, he was quite satisfied with the Noxons' account of the tragedy. He issued a certificate of death by electrocution and departed.

Noxon, distressed though he is, now assumes that the investigation is completed. The medical examiner had been there and issued a death certificate; what else should he believe? He immediately throws the faulty extension cord into the incinerator for safety's sake. (Later he would be accused of disposing of the evidence.)

The medical examiner has left; the body of the baby is taken to the funeral parlor and is embalmed in preparation for burial. Then, having released the case, the doctor has some kind of brainstorm and stops in to talk to the chief of police about it. Now the police chief doesn't like Noxon, on general grounds. He has always thought him snobbish and standoffish, a view shared by many other people. One reason for this dislike was that Noxon, who had contracted polio after leaving the army, wore leg braces, and if someone offered him a seat on the trolley, he would decline it to avoid having to unlock the braces to lower himself into the seat. But people thought he was being aloof; thus, he was unpopular in Pittsfield.

Anyway, when the police chief heard about the death from the medical examiner, he questioned Noxon. He also had an autopsy done by Dr. Alan R. Moritz, who had come to Harvard in 1932 as professor of legal medicine and consultant to the Massachusetts state police. Although he was an excellent academic pathologist and a protégé of Professor Howard T. Karsner of Western Reserve University, Moritz didn't have a great deal of practical experience at that time and had never had to run a high pressure, high workload medical examiner's office. In preparation for his professorship, he had been to Vienna for a time and studied the collection in Jellinek's museum laboratory on electropathology, but in those days his knowledge was more academic than practical.

Now Moritz examined the Noxon infant and found the big electrical burn on the forearm. No one ever denied that it was an electrical lesion or that it was not the sole cause of death. That never was the issue in the case; though to hear Alan Moritz later, you'd think that proving this obvious point was a most difficult job. The electrical burn was photographed with black and white film, and the pictures were perfectly adequate, showing the mark on the forearm for what it really was.

Noxon began to realize that he was under suspicion. He was an experienced lawyer but didn't seem to handle the matter too well for himself. He wrote some notes about what had happened, then changed his mind and threw them into the wastebasket. They were retrieved and used against him at the trial.

The whole setup was ludicrous. Here was a respectable lawyer, who knew his way about the world; if he had wanted to kill a six-month-old mongoloid, he would hardly have done it by electrocution, like some gangster, especially not with the cook only a few feet away.

Now for some reason, before the trial got underway, Alan Moritz called in a talented medical artist from Harvard, Miss Angela Piotti, who drew a lurid picture of the electrical burn in full color. She copied it from the good black and white photograph and Moritz's *memory* of the colors of the burn.

Why the prosecution should want to labor this point was always beyond my understanding. Sure it was an electrical burn; nobody ever suggested it wasn't. So why go to all this trouble to paint a garish impression? The black and white photographs showed perfectly well what the wound looked like—who cared, anyway? The debatable point was *how* the child came by this electrical burn, not what it looked like. But it seems the prosecution wanted a color picture to impress the jury with what a terrible thing Noxon had done. Yet Miss Piotti drew from memory—and from someone else's memory at that. It wasn't a color *photograph*; it was an artist's impression, a drawing for the purpose of illustration. As you might have guessed, I got pretty angry about that picture.

Well, they indicted Noxon, and I was called by his counsel, Mr. Walter J. Donovan, to see if there was anything in the medical aspect of the case that could help the defense. The principal attorney for the defense was Joseph B. Ely, a former governor of Massachusetts, which I think was a tactical error because when people—including a jury—see some unusually prominent name appearing for the accused man, they tend to think that he must be guilty or he wouldn't have gone to these extreme lengths to get the best defense attorney—almost an admission of guilt in their eyes.

The trial judge in the Noxon case was a worse mistake than the defense counsel. He was a Boston man, Abraham E. Pinanski, a fussy, pedantic, fuddy-duddy who could never make up his mind about anything. What they needed for a case like this was a down-to-earth jurist with plenty of experience, like Judge Donellan or Judge Jonah Goldstein of the Court of General Sessions in New York, who could cut through all the game-playing that went on there. But Pinanski was overawed by all the Harvard atmosphere. The district attorney was a Harvard man, the defendant himself was a Harvard man, Alan Moritz was a Harvard professor, and the defense counsel was an ex-governor—so Pinanski was all a-twitter even before they got started.

The prosecution wanted to produce that lurid picture in evidence, which was very much out of order. It would only inflame the jury, and it didn't mean anything as nobody was denying the existence and nature of the burn. What mattered was whether the electric cord was deliberately wrapped around the child's arm, or whether it just became looped around the wrist as the infant waved its arm around and came into contact with the cord—the picture didn't tell anyone anything about that vital point.

The prosecution put the artist, Miss Piotti, on the stand in an attempt to introduce the color picture as evidence. Mr. Ely, the attorney for the defense, was objecting to it as inflammatory. I remember this incident vividly. How the judge flapped about! Instead of just saying either "Objection sustained" or "Objection denied," he seemed thrown into a panic of indecision. "Oh, oh, oh," he cried, "I have to keep it out, I must keep it out!" Then he went on to make a long speech in praise of the artist and medical art. You would have thought he was working up to asking her out for the evening. "The medical artist has done such a wonderful job—an excellent picture," and so on. Why was that necessary? The issue was very simple—was the picture admissable or wasn't it? By the time the judge finally decided not to admit the picture, the jury had begun to believe it was significant to the case and felt cheated by the defense counsel's objection to its admission.

Judge Pinanski was like this all through the trial; he was impossible. When the jury returned their verdict, "guilty of murder in the first degree," he was so shocked that he nearly fell off the bench. Well, if you're in charge of a case, act like a judge, not a bystander. Pinanski was completely overwhelmed by the personalities there.

It was a long time ago, the Noxon trial, but it really sticks in my memory. The courthouse in Pittsfield was a primitive place. The prisoner sat in the back of the court in a kind of box or cage. The atmosphere was positively medieval.

I testified to the effect that it was equally possible for the child to have sustained this electrical burn in an accidental way as in a homicidal way. There was nothing inherent in the autopsy or the appearance of the burn on the forearm that helped to decide this either way—you just couldn't tell the difference. But the community was after Noxon. They didn't like him and were out to get him, a phenomenon I'd witnessed in New England before.

Like the judge, Alan Moritz was aghast at the guilty verdict. He had gone there armed to the teeth with evidence to substantiate the homicide allegation—colored painting and all. He was a most impressive witness, with prestigious qualifications. Yet afterward, he asked, "How could they convict him? I don't think the jury should have believed only my testimony, even though I believed it implicitly, and ignored that for the defense." But a jury has that prerogative in arriving at a verdict, and the jurors exercised it in the Noxon conviction. Nevertheless, Moritz was distressed by the verdict and wrote letters to Governor Saltonstall of Massachusetts and then to his successor, Governor Tobin, asking for clemency.

Noxon himself, a lawyer, drafted three bills while in jail, dealing with the question of evidence in criminal trials. The poor man had been convicted and sentenced to death, as at that time first degree murder in Massachusetts carried the capital penalty.

After the trial I approached Mr. Ely, the former governor, and Mr. Donovan, the defense counsel, to see what I could do, for I was convinced that no one should have been convicted on the evidence presented at that trial. It could quite as easily have been an accident as a homicide, especially if one considers the utter incongruity of an intelligent, educated lawyer using such an absurd method to kill an infant within sound and almost sight of his wife and the cook. On the one hand, the prosecution tried to suggest a motive for a mercy killing because the child had been diagnosed as a mongoloid, and on the other, it depicted the crime as having been done with gangster cruelty. It just didn't add up.

Noxon was a personal friend of the governor of Massachusetts at that time, Mr. Saltonstall. I went with Ely and Donovan to see him at the Harvard Club in Boston. He said that it was a very sad and unfortunate case and implied that the higher up you are connected, the more difficult your chances of acquittal. The ordinary citizen will be treated like an ordinary citizen, but if you are someone of importance and standing in the community and get involved with the law, you are really in great peril.

Well, Noxon, whose death sentence was mandatory, was languishing in a condemned cell, awaiting execution. A great number of people, including Alan Moritz, made efforts to have him granted clemency. Eventually, Governor Tobin came to office. I still have a copy of a letter I wrote to him expressing my deep concern that Noxon should have been convicted on such misunderstood evidence.

Well, eventually common sense must have prevailed, because Noxon's sentence was commuted; furthermore, in two years' time he was paroled, a pretty sharp change from impending execution within such a short period!

But as in other New England cases with which I have been involved, a great deal of passion was aroused over the Noxon matter, and I feel that justice doesn't always exhibit the impartial blindness she is supposed to possess, especially up in that part of the nation.

Chapter 9

Some Reasons for Murder

Although I've made the point that homicide is by no means the *raison d'être* of a medical examiner, I'd be the first to admit that it forms an important part of our work. It must also be admitted that one of the primary reasons for the establishment of any examination system for deaths in the community was the detection of unsuspected homicide. We see this way back into medieval times with the English coroner and also in the systems derived from Roman law that were developed on the Continent. When the American colonies adopted the institution of coroner for themselves and later when medical examiner systems developed, one of the basic reasons was to have some filtration method for screening out suspicious deaths from among the natural, accidental, and suicidal fatalities.

In modern times, this basic function runs hand in hand with the need to collect statistical information on mortality. This is part of the comprehensive—almost compulsive—tendency of contemporary administrations to have everything neatly tabulated and even computerized. But apart from this statistical aspect, there is a very real practical value in knowing how and why our citizens die, for very often if we know why they die we

can do something about it. This may be a long term project, such
as the dietary prevention of coronary artery disease, or it can be
very immediate indeed, as we found in the carbon monoxide
poisoning epidemic that I'll mention later on.

However, leaving aside these vitally important public health
aspects for the moment, it must be agreed that the medical
examiner's office, like any other forensic pathological agency,
has a primary responsibility in the detection and interpretation
of criminal deaths. The fact that the role exists and is rigorously
pursued forms an integral part of our law enforcement system,
just as much as police patrol cars or fingerprint techniques.

It is the existence and the efficiency of our medico-legal
expertise in the field of homicide investigation that both helps to
bring the perpetrator to justice and, equally important, should
act as a deterrent. The near certainty that a homicidal death will
be rapidly detected must surely be some protection against the
uncontrolled escalation of the murder rate.

Even though the present United States homicide rate would
make it seem that no deterrent of any kind exists, we must first
remember that we do not know to what astronomic heights the
murder rate might rise if there were no efficient law enforcement
agencies—and these include legal medicine as well as criminal
investigation departments. We might be able to guess, however,
because the homicide rate of certain Central and South
American nations is some three times greater than that of the
United States.

Secondly, we cannot expect the deterrent power of a high
detection index to have the same impact in homicide as it has in
crimes against property. By and large, manslaughter and murder
are impulsive, often irrational acts, where the thought of
detection and penalty is temporarily driven from the miscreant's
mind by the emotions of the moment—a different situation from
a premeditated bank robbery or a mugging. That this is so is seen
in the very slight effect, if any, which the abolition of capital
punishment has made on the homicide rate both in Europe and
in the United States.

To get back to New York, I've said earlier that our city is
looked upon by foreign colleagues as the mecca for students of
homicide. This is rather unfair, for though our total numbers
are very high, the rate *per capita* of the population of this
gigantic metropolis is no greater than that of many other major

cities in the United States, and in fact is rather less than that of several others, such as Detroit.

But there is still an awful lot of killing in the five boroughs, sufficient on occasion to provide our large autopsy room down on First Avenue with a full house of homicide cases at any one time.

The peak was reached in 1972 and thankfully has fallen slightly since then, though the general trend throughout the United States keeps on rising. In 1975, there were over 21,000 homicides in the U.S.A., over 16,000 of them from gunshot. By comparison, in the same year in Britain, with over a quarter of the U.S. population, there were about 400 homicides, only about 40 of them from guns.

Why New York should have had such a bad year in 1972 was never really clear, other than it was an exceptionally hot summer, a factor that always seems to push up the incidence of violent crime.

The records of the Office of Chief Medical Examiner of New York for that year make grim reading.

In the week ending July 22, an all-time record was reached; no fewer than fifty-seven homicides were recorded in those seven days. The hot weather and the receipt of welfare checks were blamed, the latter meaning that more money was available for drinking sprees. Of the fifty-seven, there were twenty-six stabbings, an unusually high proportion, as firearms usually lead the field. This time there were only twenty-four shootings, five assaults, one murder by fire, and one baby deliberately thrown from a window.

Most of the victims were between twenty and twenty-nine years of age, but they ranged from a baby of eighteen months to a man of eighty-five, who was stabbed to death by his son. Six were teenagers; five were over seventy; ten were heroin addicts; two were girls of fifteen and seventeen, who were shot by a man in a bar. Three of the addicts were taken to an abandoned apartment on West Ninetieth Street and shot, after being tied up. Three of the killings appeared to be assassinations in that black week, including Thomas Eboli, reported by the press to be a Mafia chieftain, who was killed on a dark street in Brooklyn.

The next month provided another record, this time for the highest daily total. In a twenty-four hour period over August 21-22, 1972, there were fourteen homicides. This time, the methods were more typical in that twelve of the fourteen were shootings; the other two were stabbings.

This wild period in New York crime history naturally struck the media at the time, and I was interviewed repeatedly about the epidemic of killings. There was a complaint in the *New York Times* in September about the situation in the city, linking the great number of homicides with the availability of firearms. No less than 65 percent of the killings were with firearms, 51 percent of them handguns.

By the end of that August in 1972, there had been 1,155 homicides and the total by the end of the year was 1,800 such deaths. Of the 1,155 killings in the first part of the year, 638 were by gunshot, a heavy responsibility on those who have persistently opposed and sabotaged legislation for effective gun control. The growing carnage that year was the direct result of unlimited access to firearms, and the gun lobby brazenly distorted the facts. Congress lacked the courage to oppose the highly vocal foes of meaningful curbs on guns. That the availability of weapons was a direct cause of this bloody year could be proved by looking at the proportion of the total homicide rate that was due to shootings and at the vastly lower rates all over Europe, especially in Britain, where strict legislation on guns, especially rifled weapons such as pistols, made homicide by shooting a comparative rarity.

I feel very strongly about this crazy notion that all Americans must have the sacred freedom to carry guns. We are not pioneering across the West now, and the freedom to carry a gun is all too often equivalent to the freedom to blast some fellow citizen into a bloody mess. Those men who see political advantage in supporting the gun lobby ought to come down to the autopsy room now and then and have a look at the result of their insensitive indifference to what is happening. Maybe it would give them something to think about instead of shouting about the right of one man to have on his belt the means of killing another man in a particularly mutilating way.

The pattern of homicide in New York is fairly constant in other respects. For example, the victims are predominantly black. In that year of 1972, during the first seven months, 552 blacks were murdered, compared with 237 whites. In addition, there were 191 Hispanics (mainly Puerto Rican) and ten Orientals. The predominant age was between twenty and thirty-four years, a quite understandable range covering the aggressive, drug-taking, often alcoholic young men.

The distribution over the various parts of New York City was also fairly regular, and Manhattan naturally provided most of the cases, as it always has and still does. Of the 1,155 deaths, 452 were in Manhattan; 342 in Brooklyn; 262 in The Bronx; 97 in Queens; and 2 on Staten Island.

I looked through our records for all the figures which the newspapers used at the time to emphasize their concern about the city situation—the records also showed that since 1962, certain police precincts, four in number, had dominated in homicide incidence, thus pinpointing the most dangerous areas. These were the twenty-eighth and thirty-second in Harlem, the twenty-fifth in East Harlem; and the forty-fifth precinct in the South Bronx. But we were getting them from all over the city; there were quite a few from the East Village.

If only someone had the sense to take to heart the fact that these expanding homicide figures could have been abated by a national gun control law. It mystified me to think that people were so shut off from logical thinking that they continued to oppose such commonsense controls. There was—and still is—a regular slaughter among the population, which could be dramatically reduced by positive measures. It's like smoking and lung cancer—the proof is there, but personal prejudice and personal advantage for some influential sections of the community block logical avenues to prevention. This epidemic in the early seventies was not confined to New York, of course— it happened in most other big cities, like Cleveland, Detroit, Denver, and Houston.

My many years as a medical examiner have shown me that another factor other than guns is related to homicide—that factor is, of course, alcohol. It relaxes inhibitions and allows a person to commit acts that he never would otherwise. The same factor is frequently related to accidents, suicide, and even natural deaths, though the mortality statistics usually fail to record this, as it never gets entered on the death certificate. You sometimes have to read between the lines of a medical history to determine that alcohol actually played a part in the causation of a death. We know that in the United States, 98 percent of cases of cirrhosis of the liver are alcohol-related, yet death certificates often give a remote cause, other than alcoholism. I said some years ago that the medical profession in New York covered up these deaths by inaccurate certification, and I called upon physicians to stop camouflaging one of the city's and the country's biggest public health problems. This is again an example of the way in which an agency such as the medical examiner's office can contribute to the good of the community in ways other than mere retrospective death investigation. Where the results of a large autopsy and case-recording system reveal facts that affect the well-being of living people, it can be seen that our Office is a lot more than just a retrospective diagnostic establishment.

I think the reason that many doctors fall over backwards to avoid certifying alcoholism is that there is still a stigma attached to the condition that the families wish to circumvent. The doctors claim that they are protecting the relatives, yet they are really perpetuating the stigma. I used to urge all doctors to treat alcoholism as the disease it really is and to confront the patient and his family with the seriousness of addictive drinking. The alcoholic deserves the same professional consideration that is given to any other sick person. There are far more alcoholics than there are drug addicts, and they are much more prone to commit crimes than is someone under the influence of narcotics, especially since the introduction of methadone has allowed the heroin addict to ease off on his desperate need to obtain heroin by any means, including crime. The addict commits a crime in order to sustain his habit, but the alcoholic is usually intoxicated *before* he commits an offense.

Increasingly, alcohol is becoming the drug of choice among young people because it's legal, easily obtainable, and more socially acceptable.

All these factors make the battle against compulsive drinking more urgent, and it is folly to cover up the size of the problem in fatal cases by some subterfuge on the part of the certifying doctors.

Chapter 10

The Crimmins Case

New York, with its diverse ethnic communities, its drug addiction problems, the abundance of firearms and the generally violent society of which it forms a significant part, is a city where murder is commonplace. But among all those homicides, bizarre as some of them have been, there is little doubt as to which one has attracted the most attention during the past decade or so. It was a case in which none of the factors mentioned above played a role—no racial factor, no narcotic element, and no firearms were involved, and the violence, to the best of our knowledge, was confined to the immediate family. The killings were pathetic, but no more so than many others. Then why should these two deaths have received the doubtful honor of being among the most notorious since World War II, with continuous coverage by TV, radio, the press, and a number of authors?

I attribute the brouhaha to two causes. First, a young, very attractive woman was the center of attention and second, the case has gone from crisis to crisis in the courtrooms of New York for the past twelve years and may not be over yet!

Anyone who picks up a newspaper or switches on his television will already know, of course, that I'm talking about the case of Alice Crimmins.

"To begin at the beginning," to quote from Dylan Thomas's *Under Milk Wood* (I autopsied him, too, come to think of it), the story started in July 1965, when Mrs. Alice Crimmins was twenty-six. She lived in a ground floor apartment in Queens, New York, with her two small children, a girl and a boy. The lad was named after his father, Eddie Crimmins, and the girl after her mother, though she was always known as "Missy." Eddie Sr., an aircraft mechanic for T.W.A. at Kennedy Airport, was separated from Alice Crimmins and was living a few minutes' drive away.

Missy was four years old; her brother Eddie was five. They lived, together with the family dog, Brandy, in the Regal Garden Apartments, a large residential area near Queens College.

There was no denying—as the later trial evidence clearly revealed—that Alice Crimmins was a lively, attractive, promiscuous woman who had a number of men friends with whom she slept, both at her apartment and elsewhere. Her husband had tired of being persistently cuckolded and had left home. He was a handsome six-footer with fair hair, and they must originally have made an impressive pair. Alice was a striking beauty: shapely, red-haired, well groomed, and vivacious. Alice's outstanding sex appeal, coupled with an undercurrent of titillating love affairs, contributed to the great attraction that the Crimmins epic had for the news media.

In fact, in a book on the Alice Crimmins case written after two successive trials in which she had been twice found guilty, I was accused of having been pressured into changing my original opinion by a member of the district attorney's staff and of having done this in order to convict Alice Crimmins because I didn't like her morals! Nothing could be farther from the truth—a woman defendant can be a latter-day Lucrezia Borgia for all I care; it is none of my business. My only concern is for the medico-legal truths provided by circumstances and the autopsy. The medical examiner or forensic pathologist is not concerned with the guilt or innocence of the defendant, although his findings and interpretation and opinion are important and may help to establish the one or the other.

To get back to the events of that July 14, the Queens police headquarters in Jamaica had received a call from the father of the Crimmins children sometime after breakfast. He told them that the children had been missing overnight from their mother's apartment on Seventy-second Drive. A patrol car was sent to investigate, and the policemen found Eddie at Alice's place; she had telephoned him a short while earlier. Alice Crimmins had gone to the children's bedroom at about nine o'clock that morning and discovered that they were missing. She had rung up her estranged husband to see if he had taken them clandestinely—but he had no knowledge at all of their whereabouts. The reason this thought had occurred to her, she said, was that a custody hearing was due to come up in court in a few days' time. Eddie wanted to have the care of the children, as he did not consider their mother a fit person to look after them. Anyway, the children were gone, and both parents denied any knowledge of what had happened to them.

The police examined the bedroom and saw that the beds were rumpled. There was a chest of drawers with a lamp resting on it under the window. The window was open and the screen was leaning against the outside wall.

The policemen noticed a hook and eye latch screwed on the outside of the bedroom door, and Alice explained that it was to prevent little Eddie from getting out to raid the refrigerator during the night. She said the hook latch had been in place when she went into the room that morning.

The implication was that the two children had either left on their own—or had been spirited out—through the open window. The two patrolmen called in to their stationhouse, and Detective Piering and another detective came over to investigate. One of the patrolmen told Piering the story, adding that he thought there was something fishy about it, especially since the parents were involved in a custody fight.

Piering interviewed the mother and father himself and was disturbed by Alice's attitude—he thought she was taking the disappearance very coldly. The story she repeated to him—and to which she stuck through thick and thin for the next ten years or so—was that she had put the children to bed at nine the previous evening, checked on them at midnight when she latch-hooked the door, and entered the room at nine the next morning, after having taken Brandy, the dog, for a walk. Piering gave both parents the chance to let him know in private if either of them had a hand in the disappearance, as he felt that with the custody suit coming up the next week, one of them might have taken the children away to a hiding place to beat the court's decision. They both strongly denied this, and with some misgivings, the police launched into a full-scale missing persons routine.

Meanwhile, Piering was nosing around the bedroom again. He found that when he attempted to reach the metal casement window to try to open it wider, the chest of drawers was in his way. He removed the table lamp and noticed a significant thing—where the base of the lamp had rested, there was a clear circle where there was no dust. The remainder of the polished top was covered with a fine film of dust, and he could see no way in which anyone could have climbed out of that window without leaving some marks on the sensitive dust trap on the bureau. There was also dust on the windowsill, again without any trace of disturbance.

Alice Crimmins had firmly stated that the latch hook was still locked in place on the outside of the bedroom door that morning and Piering began to wonder who was telling lies.

Mrs. Crimmins had also confirmed that the front door lock and a safety chain were in position when she got up that morning, so it seemed an impossibility that any intruder could have entered the apartment and left with the children through the bedroom door and the front door, replacing the chain behind him.

At this stage of the investigation, 150 policemen were drafted to search the neighborhood for two kidnapped children, but one detective was convinced that this was no kidnapping.

While the search went on, the detectives got further details from the parents. Alice Crimmins gave the following account of her movements the previous evening:

At five o'clock she had been riding with the children in her Mercury convertible and had stopped at a delicatessen for groceries, including frozen manicotti—the significance of which was to involve me deeply later.

At seven-thirty, she cooked the manicotti with string beans and fed the children. After that, she took them for a ride, got gas at a Gulf station in Flushing, and then tried to find the new apartment where her husband was living. It transpired that each of the Crimminses was trying to get evidence of the other's infidelity to use as ammunition in the custody hearing.

Mrs. Crimmins returned home at about nine o'clock and put the children to bed. During the afternoon and evening, she had telephoned Anthony Grace, a wealthy builder, who was her current boyfriend. At midnight, when she went in to see the children, she took Eddie to the bathroom and then returned him to his bed. She also tried to wake Missy to see if she wanted to go to the toilet, but the little girl just moaned that she didn't need to go, so Alice let her sleep. She hooked the bedroom door, took the dog for a short walk on the grass in front of the house, then returned to lie on her bed.

Her night routine seemed peculiar in that her husband rang to talk about the custody suit at three in the morning. She then took the dog out again, had a bath, and finally went to bed about four in the morning.

While the search went on, Piering and another detective, Martin, continued their investigation of the apartment. Another odd feature turned up—in the trash can in the kitchen were no less than thirty empty liquor bottles, but the refrigerator held only a leftover portion of manicotti, a half bottle of wine, and a jug of ice water. There was almost no food in any of the kitchen cupboards.

Piering linked the use of the hook on the door with three address books which he found, filled with the names of men. Piering suspected that the hook on the children's door was to stop them from wandering around the apartment at night, when Alice was entertaining in her bedroom.

In the early afternoon, a call came through to the Queens Communications Bureau of the New York Police Department that a patrolman had just found a body in a vacant lot on 162nd Street—it was that of a little girl. A nine-year-old boy had noticed it first and thought it was a doll. He told his mother, who came to look, and she immediately phoned the police.

Alice Crimmins was taken to the scene in a police car by Detective Piering, and she identified the body as that of Alice Marie—her "Missy." She seemed impassive about it, never shedding a tear or showing any emotion whatsoever. The detectives were at a loss as to whether this was because she was indifferent or because she was shocked by the revelation.

Back at the vacant lot there was great activity. One of the first persons to be called was one of my deputy chief medical examiners, Dr. Richard Grimes, who had almost thirty-five years of experience as a medical examiner, investigating and determining the causes of all types of violent death.

He came to look at the little corpse, which had lain

undisturbed since discovery. He found Missy bent up on her left side, wearing a white undershirt and yellow pants. Over the face was another yellow cloth (which turned out to be her pajama top), wrapped around the lower part of her face and held in place by the arms of the garment which were tied together in front of the face and neck.

The body was still warm, yet the muscles were already beginning to stiffen due to rigor mortis. The stiffening normally does not take place for six hours or so, though the time for this is very variable. The body seemed too warm for this length of time to have elapsed, yet this could be explained by the fact that it was a very hot July day, and the body was in the sun. Already there were signs of insect attack, as some flies had laid their eggs on the face. Grimes could see no obvious signs of injury and no external evidence of any sexual attack.

The time of death was to be the most vital aspect of the medical testimony in the Crimmins case, but there was little to go on, so far. Estimating the time of death is notoriously one of the most difficult and inaccurate techniques in forensic pathology—no one test is dependable, and all the possible evidence must be correlated to try to arrive at some sensible time bracket within which death could have occurred.

Within an hour, Dr. Grimes had the body moved to the mortuary in the Queens General Hospital in Jamaica, and he began a more detailed external examination. As soon as the cadaver had been shifted away from the sun-drenched vacant lot, he noticed a marked drop in the temperature of the body. This told him that the previous warmth had been only superficial, due to the warming effect of the sun's rays. The deeper tissues were already quite cool, which meant that death had occurred much earlier than he had previously surmised. Now he was convinced that the child had died not less than six to twelve hours previously, and perhaps even earlier than that. There was no direct way of making a more exact determination.

Richard Grimes did not carry out the internal autopsy himself. In view of the potential complexities of the case and the likelihood that the other child was now dead also, the body was ordered into Manhattan, because homicide autopsies were performed at the central building on First Avenue and the investigation was then carried on from there.

Dr. Grimes wisely did not commit himself to the cause of

death on external examination alone—though the presence of the pajama top knotted around the mouth and nostrils pointed strongly to some type of asphyxiation.

What he did do, however, before Dr. Benenson and I began the autopsy the next day, was to make a careful record of the slight external injuries that were present. "Missy" had a few scratches over the left side of her chest, some more small scratches on the back of her right leg, and some marks on the left side of her neck. There was another graze over the right collarbone, near the front of the shoulder. All these appeared to show a vital reaction, which meant that there was some reddening that indicated that the injuries had been inflicted before death. They might have been innocent, as many children have some bumps, scars, and grazes on them from the normal rough and tumble of play. But these were in odd places, and at the time, Grimes thought some of them might have been scratches in response to insect bites.

My assistant, Dr. Benenson, and I performed the autopsy the next day, on July 15, 1965, on the body identified by the father as that of Alice Marie Crimmins. It appeared to be about the stated age of four and a half years and was three feet five inches long and weighed thirty-five pounds. She was blonde and blue-eyed and was dressed in the previously mentioned white undershirt and yellow pants. Around her face and neck was the top of a yellow pajama suit, reaching up to the level of the nose. There was a knot on the right side of the pajama top, but the whole thing was not very tight at the time I saw it. There were fly eggs over the eyes and on the left side of the head, but none were hatched into maggots. There was little, if any, decomposition of the body.

On the neck there were two abrasions, one on each side. In the eyelids, there were many small petechial hemorrhages—tiny blood flecks suggesting asphyxia. These were also found in the larynx when it was examined.

There was a compression mark around the neck, suggestive of a ligature, though we could not tell if the asphyxiation was due to this alone or to manual strangulation (suggested by the marks on the neck).

The lungs were congested but revealed no evidence of natural disease; nor was there any sign of disease anywhere in the entire body.

With regard to the gastrointestinal tract, the stomach was

filled with a large amount of recently ingested food, extending from its upper end to its lower opening. In other words, the stomach was full, not empty or partly empty. It was my opinion that the finding of that much food in this case was indicative of a post-ingestion period (the time after the last food was ingested) of fewer than two hours before death.

The same problem arose in the similarly notorious Truscott case, in Canada, in which I had testified at the hearing before the Supreme Court of Canada. Death was caused by strangulation, and the same relationship of the time of death and the last ingestion of food was an important issue. (The Truscott case is discussed elsewhere in this book.)

In most homicides the cause of death is obvious, but important issues arise out of other findings in the autopsy. Let's get the facts right in the Crimmins case. Freshly eaten food material containing manicotti and string beans was found in the stomach, food which Alice Crimmins, on questioning, told the police had been given to Missy and her brother Eddie by her at about 7:30 p.m. that evening. Later, she altered her story to say that she had fed them veal cutlets, but we found that the food was indeed manicotti and string beans.

Our expert microscopist in the Chief Medical Examiner's Office, Al Stoholski, reported to me and testified to finding pasta noodles in the stomach, confirming what I saw with my naked eye when the full stomach was opened. He did not find anything looking like veal in the contents.

We were able to be very definite about the food because it was so fresh-looking. It was virtually undigested, as if it had just been swallowed. Stoholski, in systematically examining the stomach contents, also found a wad of swallowed chewing gum.

If a person eats a meal and lives on quite normally, the rate of digestion and emptying of the stomach (depending on the kind of food ingested) progresses in a fairly regular manner. Usually within two hours—especially in healthy children, who digest and move food along rapidly out of the stomach—the chewed, swallowed food is softened and propelled out of the stomach into the duodenum, the first part of the intestine, where a different kind of digestive process begins.

I will be the first to admit that if any physical or even mental disturbance occurs soon after the food is swallowed, the whole digestive process can be drastically altered. For example, if a person is assaulted, or frightened, or taken ill, or knocked unconscious half an hour after a meal, the digestive process can either stop entirely or proceed very slowly or irregularly. The most obvious and a very common occurrence is that the stomach rebels against its contents and expels them by vomiting. This may relate to a primitive protective process, whereby the possibility of some kind of poisoning is countered by unloading the suspect food.

In any case, a disturbance of the normal process may grossly alter the schedule of the digestive timetable, and the possibility of timing the ingestion of food in relation to the time of death is completely unreliable. It still may be helpful in trying to estimate the approximate time of death if the nature of the food in the stomach is distinctive and recognizable. For example, if a person is found dead and his stomach contains curry, then if it is known that he ate a curry at a certain time, it can be said that death occurred after that curry and before the next meal, but no closer than that. If a man has had some injury and lives for a time, then the state of his stomach contents at death is of no use in timing the death, other than in the curry situation. I have seen, as every pathologist has seen, a death in say, a traffic accident victim, who may have lived three, four, or even more days after a fractured skull and then died. At autopsy, the contents of his stomach may be easily recognizable, though we know beyond a doubt that his last meal was half a week before. The head and brain injury had signalled his stomach to stop digestion and to stop emptying into the duodenum, so the finding of recognizable food would not permit any valid conclusion as to a relationship between the time of the last meal and the time of death.

But now let's go back to Missy Crimmins. It was clear that she was strangled and suffered a rapidly acute asphyxial death. This tragic dying process could not have taken long—I was actually asked about this on the stand at the Crimmins trial and said that it could have taken either more or less than a minute. Whatever it was, it was very rapid and not sufficient to alter the digestive schedule, except to stop it completely. There was no disputing Missy's rapid death, and she had not undergone a prolonged period of unconsciousness or any kind of lingering dying process. Thus, the amount and state of her stomach contents would represent the usual degrees of digestion and emptying to within a moment or two of her death.

Now then, a stomach jammed full of virtually undigested food in a previously healthy young child means, without any shadow of doubt, that the food was swallowed not more than two hours before death.

But Alice Crimmins said that she fed the children manicotti and string beans at 7:30 o'clock that evening—and that she later saw them alive just before midnight, when she took Eddie to the bathroom and Missy sleepily said she didn't want to go and remained in her bed.

But that was four hours later, and Alice said she didn't go to bed herself until four in the morning, implying that anyone who broke in to abduct the children must have done so after that, when she was asleep.

Impossible—just impossible. If she said she saw them alive before midnight, how could the stomach of Missy show that she must have died within two hours of taking a meal at 7:30 o'clock? It is patently absurd to think that death might have occurred in the pre-dawn hours after her mother had gone to bed.

Based on the results of Missy's autopsy, it was evident to me that somebody was lying—and the only one it could be, by her own answers, was Alice Crimmins.

The essence of my conclusion and opinion, arrived at at the time of the autopsy, was fairly simple and straightforward and has never changed.

The autopsy, at which I was present as a participant throughout, was performed before I knew who was involved or even who Alice Crimmins was. Yet one misguided writer has accused me in his book of changing my opinion with regard to the stomach contents and their significance and of having been pressured by an assistant district attorney months after the autopsy, and has also announced on television and radio that I was not even present at the autopsy—because I'd heard that the defendant was an ex-cocktail waitress with a penchant for multiple boy friends! What nonsense!—compared to some of the defendants I've seen in my decades of medico-legal work, Alice was like Snow White! It was ludicrous to defame me with a crazy accusation like that. The facts are that, as I say, my observations and interpretations were made during the autopsy, and my opinion never changed for any reason. Actually, I examined the body prior to the arrival of the medical examiner, Dr. William Benenson, who came from Queens to Manhattan to perform and describe the autopsy. I was present during the entire autopsy and never left that room. I photographed the body, the asphyxial hemorrhages in the eyelids, and the ligature around the neck and pointed out why the stomach full of recently ingested food was important in indicating that the victim had eaten shortly before being killed. The fact that death clearly resulted from ligature strangulation, a rapid type of death, provided a basis for the reasonable conclusion that the last meal was ingested shortly before death. This was said without my being able to pinpoint the precise time that death occurred. However, the significance of the large amount of food in the stomach (with none of it having moved into the intestine), in a child dying rapidly from strangulation, was an obvious clue to guide further investigation of the death.

Alice and her husband were interrogated both at home and at the police station until late that night, but no more progress was made. Alice stuck to her original story, and Eddie Crimmins gave a fairly straightforward account of his movements the previous evening and night. He admitted driving past his wife's apartment at about midnight because he was keeping tabs on her movements and activities (as she was on his), hoping to get evidence to use against her character when the custody suit would be heard. He said he saw that the lights were on in the living room and in her bedroom, but that the children's room was in darkness. He then drove home and phoned her— corroborating what she had said earlier. The call was about some back wages that they owed a former maid. He then went to bed and slept until he was awakened by the phone the next morning, when Alice called to tell him the children were missing.

The case hung fire—everyone knew in his heart that little Eddie was also dead. Only the discovery of the body remained. The massive police hunt continued throughout Queens for five days and even included the use of helicopters.

But it was not the police who found the little boy, but a father and son out walking on a scrubby embankment about a mile from the Crimmins home. This was an unused area of barren ground alongside the Van Wyck Expressway, which runs toward Kennedy International Airport. The body was found near the site of the World's Fair, which was in full swing at that time.

This time, after almost a week in the hot summer weather, the body was in a very different state from that of Missy. It was lying amid some tattered vegetation, under a grey blanket, and the smell of decay was revolting. When the medical examiner arrived (not Dr. Grimes this time but Dr. Benenson), the decomposition was so advanced that at first he was unable even to determine whether it was a boy or a girl.

The body was beyond any recognition, but the blanket was identified as a plaid bedspread that Alice Crimmins had reported as missing from the children's bedroom. The white undershirt and shorts also tallied with the description of the clothes that Eddie had been wearing, so no one doubted for a moment that the search was over.

Eventually, this identification was confirmed by fingerprinting the tips of the fingers, which were not so badly decomposed. They matched prints lifted by the police experts from toys and furniture in Eddie's bedroom.

Dr. Benenson conducted an autopsy in my presence, but with such an advanced state of putrefaction it was an unrewarding and highly unpleasant task. The findings were essentially negative, and the cause of death could not be determined. I could not say that there had been any injuries, fatal or otherwise; but by the same token one could not say that any natural disease process had caused death. These findings of July 1965 were eventually to be used, but a long, long time in the future.

There was now a period during which the detectives and the district attorney worked away like beavers at assembling the evidence. The father, Eddie Crimmins, readily agreed to a lie detector test and passed with flying colors. He had originally been one of the prime suspects, but both the intuition of the investigators and the mass of evidence that slowly accumulated excluded him from any part in the killings.

Though he had been estranged from Alice before these tragic days, their troubles seemed to push them together for quite some time; eventually, however, they got divorced.

Eddie was in the clear, and by implication, the onus of suspicion fell even more heavily on the attractive redheaded mother, deepened by her refusal to continue with the lie detector test after barely ten minutes of questioning. Neither the police nor Eddie Crimmins was able to influence her at all, and with every new turn in the investigation, Detective Piering and his colleagues felt more convinced that she either was totally guilty or at the very least knew far more about the children's deaths than she would admit.

A considerable part of the laborious investigative work that the detectives were doing involved following up the list of Alice Crimmins's men friends, and a few of them turned out to be quite deeply involved with her. She had gone off on the spur of the moment on a sea cruise with wealthy fifty-one-year-old Anthony Grace. She claimed that the ship had sailed without her being aware of it, while she was at a party on board. Either way, her husband claimed that she had left the two children without any food in the house, and he had taken them to Alice's mother, whose sympathies seemed to be with her son-in-law. The grandmother kept the children until Alice returned. It was after that incident that Eddie began his legal action to get the children back, on the grounds that the mother was unfit to care for them. In order to gather evidence in his favor, he took to snooping on Alice to watch her affairs with other men—even hiding in the basement of the apartment house to listen to the goings-on in the bedroom above his head.

Another man who figured largely in her escapades was Joseph Rorech, a successful building contractor from Long Island, who would be one of the most damaging witnesses against her. He told the police that once, when he was discussing the deaths with Alice, she had told him that the children had gone out through the front door, not the window. This was contrary to the story that she had always told to the police. Far more damaging was Rorech's testimony that Alice had actually confessed to the killings during one of their frequent night trysts at a motel.

The police also made exhaustive enquiries in a wide area around the Queens apartment house—they questioned hundreds of neighbors and checked up on known perverts and men with records of sexual crimes, but nothing new turned up.

The list of male consorts in the Alice Crimmins sexual escapades became longer; some of the facts bordered on the outrageous and no doubt added to the unprecedented interest the media took in the case. There was still nothing in the way of evidence strong enough to enable the police to charge Alice with murder, even after Dr. Benenson made a personal phone call to the police giving his opinion that the little girl must have died in her bedroom, since Missy must have been dead at least ten and probably nearer eighteen hours when she was found. This put the time of death back in the previous evening, Alice Crimmins having said she had seen the girl alive in bed before midnight.

The detective team was strengthened by the addition of John Kelly from Brooklyn Homicide North and Walter Anderson of Queens. Yet the whole investigation, after the mass of information turned up in its earlier stages, began to stagnate as 1965 began to pass.

The telephone in the new apartment that Alice and Eddie— now living together again—had rented in another part of Queens was bugged, and relays of police listened in on every call. They did this for an incredible three years but never once picked up anything of value, though the content of the conversations that Alice had with her men friends made the listening duty a favorite chore with the detectives!

During these first months Nathaniel Hentel, temporarily appointed Queens district attorney, was keen to clear up the Crimmins affair. He was also keen to be established in the D.A.'s office on a permanent basis in the November elections. At this stage, three bits of evidence that pointed to Alice's guilt (or at least involvement) were all he had to go on. First, the ring in the dust on the chest of drawers, showing that the children must have gone out the door; second, the autopsy evidence indicating the time of death; and third, the evidence of two gas station attendants who said that Alice had called at their Gulf station in Queens with the children at about five-thirty that evening, although she maintained it had been nine o'clock.

None of this was sufficient for a grand jury indictment, but as Election Day approached, Hentel saw his Democratic opponent, Thomas Mackell, promising a new initiative in the Crimmins case as part of his election platform. Hentel convened a grand jury, and all the detectives on the case did their best with the evidence they had accumulated over the past year and more. The jurors deliberated for over a month to consider their answer. Hentel even subpoenaed Alice and Eddie to appear before the grand jury, but they pleaded the Fifth Amendment and refused to say anything. In any case, nothing came of it.

Tom Mackell won the election for district attorney and took office on January 1, 1967, almost a year and a half after the murders, the investigation of which seemed by now to have run dry.

A new face soon cropped up on the scene, however, as the new district attorney borrowed from the Manhattan prosecutor's office a man named James Mosely, who had an impressive record as a homicide investigator. He was put in charge of the Queens Homicide Bureau and took over the Crimmins case.

Within a very short time, something broke that was to change the course of all the legal battles to come. Among the papers left behind by the previous district attorney was an anonymous letter alleging that the writer had seen some suspicious goings-on in the vicinity of the Crimmins home at 2:00 a.m. on the morning of the day that the children were reported missing. Unable to sleep, the unidentified informant had gone to the window and had seen a man and woman carrying a bundle of blankets and leading a small boy by the hand. They were walking down the road to the car; when they reached it, the man threw the bundle into the back seat. They all got in and drove away.

Who was the person who had written the letter? He or she had said in the note that these persons had walked "down the street towards Seventy-Second Road" and had mentioned seeing the faces clearly because of the street lights; so by painstaking and very intelligent investigative work, Mosely and his detectives narrowed the search down to a few houses. They then reduced these to a possible thirty-nine apartments, because an air conditioner had been mentioned in the letter. The final elimination was done by comparing the handwriting in the letter with samples of signatures and complaint letters obtained from the management officers of the apartments.

The investigators finally tracked down Mrs. Sophie Earomirski, who was to be the most colorful witness in the several subsequent trials. She admitted writing the letter, but though initially she didn't want to get involved, she was persuaded to testify if necessary, and her evidence got the whole case off the ground.

She amplified the facts in her letter, and when another grand jury was convened on September 1, 1967, she told the jurors that the man she saw and heard in the street had told the woman to hurry up. The woman had shushed him, saying, "Be quiet or someone will see us." The man took the bundle from the woman and threw it in the car, and the woman said, "My God, don't throw her like that." Then Mrs. Earomirski started to close the casement window, but the rusty hinge squeaked, and the man and woman looked up and said, "Somebody's seen us."

Mrs. Earomirski identified the woman in the street as Alice Crimmins, which was all that was needed at that point for an indictment for first degree murder.

It was now September 11, twenty-six months after the deaths of Missy and Eddie Crimmins. On the next day, Detectives Piering and Byrnes arrested Alice as she was going to work. A crowd of reporters was awaiting their arrival at the police station, and all that day the media reported the event. Eddie managed to raise bail of $25,000 for his wife, and later in the day she went home with him.

Now there was another long delay before the trial began. In fact, Alice's lawyers sought to have the indictment dismissed because of the length of time that elapsed. The selection of a jury began on May 8, 1968, in the Queens courthouse, before Judge Peter Farrell. The drama began even before the trial, when detectives arrested a private investigator in the courthouse corridor and charged him with the larceny of lists of residents in Regal Gardens Apartments. The prosecution was keeping Mrs. Earomirski under tight wraps.

Alice Crimmins appeared in court looking her usual glamorous self. The selection of the jury took the rest of the week, and the evidence was not presented until the following Monday, May 13.

Alice was represented by attorneys Martin Baron and Harold Harrison, and the prosecutors were Assistant D.A.s James Mosely and Anthony Lombardino.

The words of the indictment asserted that "Alice Crimmins willfully, with design, and feloniously, and with malice aforethought, did kill Alice Marie Crimmins, by choking, strangling, and asphyxiating her with her hands or by ligature."

She was not being tried for the death of little Eddie, and it became difficult for the prosecutors to avoid even breathing his name during the proceedings, which might have meant a mistrial. Indeed, the defense more than once moved for a mistrial on these grounds.

After some technical witnesses, Eddie Crimmins went on the stand as a prosecution witness, but he valiantly stuck up for his wife.

During the testimony of Detective Piering, a matter was broached that was vitally related to my later medical evidence. This was the nature of the food that Alice had given the children on the evening before their disappearance. Piering said that she had told him it was frozen manicotti—pasta with soft cheese— and he related that he had found a portion left in the refrigerator and an empty carton in the kitchen garbage can.

But later, Alice was to swear that she had given her children not manicotti, but frozen veal cutlets. Unfortunately, Piering had understandably not saved the empty packet from the garbage can as evidence, but there seemed no reason not to believe his version of what she had originally told him and what he had himself discovered in the kitchen.

Then Detective Kelly came to the stand and related the discrepancy about the time that Alice went to the gas station with the children. All through the trial—and the subsequent trial—the prosecution and defense counsel cut and thrust continuously. Every point was fought and objections were flung about the court like confetti at a wedding. Several times during the trials, the mercurial Alice was unable to restrain herself, and when Mrs. Earomirski and Joseph Rorech gave particularly damaging testimony against her, she began screaming abuse at them, causing an uproar in the court.

Eventually, the prosecution got to the medical evidence in this extraordinary case.

The first doctor called was Richard Grimes, a veteran and deputy chief medical examiner in Queens. When he began describing the position in which little Missy's body had been found and the clothing she was wearing, Alice Crimmins suddenly broke into hysterical sobs. Judge Farrell had to adjourn the proceedings so that defense counsel could enable her to get a grip on herself again.

Dr. Grimes resumed his testimony, telling the court that after the body was removed from the sun where he first examined it to the Queens mortuary, he felt the temperature drop, that he saw various marks on the body, and that, in his opinion, the child could have been dead from anywhere between six and twenty-four hours by the time he arrived at that vacant lot in the early afternoon of July 14, almost three years before.

He did not venture to give any cause of death, as he had not performed the autopsy, which was not done until the next day.

When I was called as a witness, the defense attorney, Martin Baron, appealed to the judge to allow Alice to leave the courtroom during my testimony because of its possibly distressing nature, but Judge Farrell firmly ruled that the law required the defendant to be present during the whole of the proceedings.

I explained on that afternoon of May 15 the detailed findings of the autopsy, which I described earlier in this chapter, and Baron and Harrison hammered at me for the rest of that day and the entire morning session of the next day. Most of the cross-examination was conducted by Baron, who tried to trip me up time and time again. But my evidence was quite straightforward, and I had no cause to waver from my scientific findings and conclusions.

As the case continued, things got tough for Mrs. Crimmins. Joe Rorech, one of her steady men friends, dropped her right into the swamp by saying that she had told him that she would rather see the children dead than let Eddie get custody of them. He then testified that she had told him the kids went out the front door, not the window, contradicting everything she had told the police. But he really hurt her when he said that when they were spending a night at a motel in Plainview, in 1966, she started crying and said, "Joseph, please forgive me. I killed her...."

The court erupted into confusion at this. Alice Crimmins jumped to her feet and began hollering at Rorech, the spectators were in an uproar, and the judge nearly went berserk trying to keep order. The court reporters started a stampede to the telephones, but Judge Farrell made them sit down until he recessed the court.

Further witnesses came along afterward, and one of them was Dr. Rocco Bevilacqua, a physician from Great Neck, called to support my evidence about the stomach. He was a radiologist who had spent his working life looking at X-rays of stomachs coated with barium in suspected ulcer patients. He said that food cannot stay in a normal person's stomach for more than two hours—if it does, it must be assumed that the person is suffering from some pathological condition. Of course there was nothing at all to suggest that Missy Crimmins was not a perfectly healthy, normal young child.

The last and strongest weapon of the prosecution was their "mystery witness," Mrs. Sophie Earomirski. She had been under police guard for weeks, with a policewoman as her constant companion to keep the defense away from her.

Mrs. Earomirski was a plump, middleaged blonde, and though she had originally been reluctant to come forward, she soon compensated for this initial reticence.

Before her testimony, the prosecution complained to the judge about the strenuous efforts that the defense had made in trying to contact Mrs. Earomirski after finding her name on the records of the grand jury. The judge was very angry and gave stern warnings about what would happen if there were any more such attempts.

The essence of Mrs. Earomirski's evidence remained the same, though she tended to embroider it. She again told of the man "with the big nose," the woman with the bundle, and the child. This time she added a dog on a leash—"the dog seemed to be pregnant." In fact, Brandy, the Crimmins' dog, did have pups a week after the death.

When the man threw the bundle into the car, the woman said "My God, don't do that to her," and the man said, "Now you're sorry?" The little boy climbed into the front seat of the car; at this point, Mrs. Earomirski started to close the squeaky window, and the man and woman looked up at her on the second floor.

So far, the court had listened with rapt attention to this star witness, but the climax was reached when Mosely asked her if she recognized the woman with the bundle as anyone in the courtroom.

Sophie Earomirski looked around for a moment. Then she pointed an accusing finger at Alice Crimmins, sitting at the defense counsel table.

"That's the woman."

Immediately, as with Joe Rorech, Alice leaped up and began screaming at the witness, calling her "liar" repeatedly.

The whole court fell into confusion until the judge got an assurance from the defense counsel that they would control their client.

Sophie was given a hard time by the defense in cross-examination, both as to her evidence and her personal history, but she stuck to her story throughout. As she left the stand, the spectators applauded her, and she gave a boxer's triumphal salute with her clenched fists.

This terminated the prosecution's case. The defense began by calling a babysitter, who said that she heard the children saying their prayers at about eight-thirty that night—which didn't seem to add anything to what was already known—the babysitter was followed by a string of witnesses dealing with the quality of street lighting, in the vicinity of Kew Gardens, the clothes that Alice Crimmins had worn that day, and so on.

Then the defense called Alice herself, which caused a great buzz of excitement in the courtroom.

After a short time, during which she answered fairly routine questions about her background, Alice started to quake, and the judge again granted a recess for her to compose herself. By the next day, he had had the public works department install a microphone, since Alice spoke in such a soft voice that the court couldn't hear her. Her counsel went on to ask her about her sudden boat trip to the Bahamas with Anthony Grace, and she denied leaving the children without any money in the house. Then the examination came to details of the fateful evening of July 13, 1965, the one in which the children were last seen alive. She repeated her story, saying that she fed the children at 7:30 p.m., took the dog for a walk, took Eddie to the bathroom, latched the hook on the bedroom door, and had a call from her husband at three a.m., before finally going to bed at four o'clock in the morning.

She vehemently denied ever telling Joe Rorech that she had killed the little girl.

The cross-examination was given to Tony Lombardino, a really tough attorney. He tore into Alice and spent a long time emphasizing her varied and flagrant affairs with so many men. She admitted that once her husband had chased a man, Carl Andrade, out of the house and into the street in "a state of undress," after Eddie had caught them *in flagrante delicto*. Lombardino brought to light other sexual adventures, including an occasion when Alice let a barber named Pasquale Picasso make love to her in the back of his car. There were descriptions of nude bathing in Rorech's swimming pool, and at one stage, defense counsel appealed to the judge to stop the audience from "oohing and aahing."

The prosecution hammered at Alice about all the details of the last evening, but she was unshakable; she insisted that it was not manicotti but veal parmigiana that she fed the children.

The evidence had taken the better part of two weeks, and the summations began on Friday, May 24, 1968. The defense line was that most of the prosecution witnesses were against Alice because of her morals and that the evidence was nothing but circumstantial surmise. Baron and Harrison were particularly scathing about Sophie Earomirski and Rorech. After two hours Harrison finished by saying, "We can't bring back this innocent child, but as God Almighty knows, Alice didn't do it."

Lombardino summed up for the prosecution. On the following Monday, Judge Farrell summed up, in a sober and quite impartial way, as should be done. He cautioned, "We are not trying Mrs. Crimmins's morals. We are trying a homicide."

The jury retired and after a couple of hours sent a request for copies of the autopsy report and that of Dr. Grimes, together with some other documents.

All evening, everyone waited, the press seething with impatience. Alice and her counsel waited in a cocktail lounge opposite the court, and there they had champagne ready to celebrate her acquittal. It was almost midnight when the news came that the jury was coming back into court. It was a false alarm, as the jurors only announced that they were unable to agree.

The judge told them to go back, and at one-fifteen in the morning they again came back, to have the charges redefined for them.

At last, at two o'clock in the morning, under conditions of great tension and excitement, everyone filed back into court, and the foreman of the jury announced the verdict—"Guilty of first degree manslaughter."

There was pandemonium in the courtroom, and Alice slumped, racked with tears. The judge remanded her for sentencing, and she was taken off by a matron from the Department of Corrections.

Three weeks later, on June 18, the defense attorneys made an application to set aside the verdict—of course, the sentence had not yet been announced, but Baron and Harrison were hot on the trail of anything they might use to have the verdict dismissed. They had unusually good grounds, too, compared with the usual scraping of the bottom of the legal barrel that goes on at this stage. Three of the jurors had made a private and unauthorized visit to the place outside Mrs. Earomirski's apartment where she said she had seen the man, woman, and child.

This was contrary to the judge's directions, but when the defense threw this at Judge Farrell, he dismissed it. He also dismissed an application for Alice to be released on bail pending sentence, though she had been at freedom for the past three years since the killings.

It was not until August 9, between two and three months after the trial, that Judge Farrell announced his sentence. He gave her not less than five and not more than twenty years detention at the New York State Prison for Women at Westfield State Farms.

Alice took it calmly, as it was the expected sentence for a first degree manslaughter, but she had something to say to Judge Farrell. "I am not guilty of this horrible charge. I did not do it, and Mosely, Lombardino, and Mackell are rotten through and through." Farrell angrily protested to Harrison about this personal tirade, but Alice hadn't finished. "You don't care who killed my children, you just want to close your books. You didn't give a damn."

So Alice went off to Westfield State Prison—but not for long. She ditched Baron and Harrison as her legal advisors and engaged Herbert Lyons, who took on the defense of Alice free of charge. Lyons was, of course, a noted criminal lawyer, and from then on, he took up a crusade on behalf of Alice.

Within a couple of weeks of the sentencing, Lyons applied to Queens County Supreme Court Judge Frank Samansky and obtained bail for Alice on the grounds that there was a reasonable doubt that the conviction should stand.

Twenty-four days after going off to prison, Alice was out on the street again, and she remained out for almost another three years. The three judges of the appellate court considered the appeal sixteen months after she was convicted, and they quashed the sentence on the grounds of the wrongful behavior of the three jurors who had visited the scene. They ordered a new trial.

As a last ditch stand, the district attorney took the case to the highest court possible, the New York State Court of Appeals in Albany, to try to get the dismissal reversed, but in April 1970, the court upheld the decision, and so District Attorney Mackell and his men were back where they started five years before—outside the Crimmins apartment, with two murders on their hands.

The next time I was personally involved in the Crimmins saga was in March 1971, when the retrial took place, but a lot of work had been done by the D.A.'s office before that came about. One of the new developments was the follow-up of a possible lead on the man who had accompanied Alice Crimmins on her two a.m. walk with the dog and little Eddie, which had caught the attention of Sophie Earomirski. A prisoner in "the Tombs," New York's prison, had claimed long before that he knew the "inside story" of the Crimmins affair. Though his name was not properly known, the detectives worked on the matter and came up with Vincent Colabella, awaiting sentence for a payroll snatch.

But try as they would, Colabella wouldn't reveal anything. He got fifteen years for his robbery, and though the police from Queens went back to him time after time, he still refused to talk. At one stage, he agreed to take a lie detector test, but his lawyer forbade it.

So the Colabella angle was unprofitable as far as getting new material for the prosecution.

Rorech contributed a little more in that he told the detectives that Alice not only had told him about killing her daughter, but had also said that she had help in getting rid of little Eddie. He came up with the name "Carrabella" and said that Alice had shown him a picture of a dark, good-looking guy as the one who helped her that night. They immediately put ten photographs in front of Joe Rorech, and he unhesitatingly picked out the one of Colabella.

As the time came for the prosecution to get cracking on the second trial, they decided to have Alice indicted for both deaths, instead of just that of the little girl. This would free them from the inhibitions that they suffered during the first trial, when they could not use anything that touched on the death of little Eddie.

Lombardino had been appointed to a federal job as assistant U.S. attorney, and his place on the Crimmins team was taken by Thomas Demakos.

On July 13, 1973, five years to the day since the children were last seen alive, a grand jury returned indictments against Alice

Crimmins for first degree murder of her son Eddie and first degree manslaughter of her daughter Missy. Again the indictments referred to "choking, strangling and asphyxiating" the little girl but mentioned no mode of death for the boy, as I could not even hazard a guess as to what had killed him. I could only exclude gross injuries like a fractured skull or bullet wounds.

When Alice was arrested and taken for the routine fingerprinting at Fresh Meadows precinct house, the place was bursting with newsmen, T.V. cameras, and photographers. Again Mrs. Crimmins collapsed, and this time cracked her head on the floor. She was given bail for $15,000—rather extraordinary in that for that sum, she was now out on a first degree murder charge, whereas at the first trial, she had to put up $25,000 for a mere manslaughter charge.

The second trial began on March 15,1971, approaching six years after the deaths of Alice's children. She had spent only twenty-four days in prison in those six years.

By now, Eddie Crimmins had finally broken with Alice. They were divorced, and it was obvious that his attitude toward her had hardened since the first trial, when he was helping her in every way he could. Some of the other men in her life had changed their positions, too, partly as a result of the publicity. The new judge was George Balbach, but most of the witnesses were familiar faces from the previous trial, including me.

The medical evidence this time included the details of little Eddie's case, though there was not too much to be said because of the decomposition.

This time, the defense alleged that the children had been carried off by an intruder, fed a meal, sexually molested, and then killed. They had to build up this unlikely series of events to explain away the insurmountable discrepancy between the contents of Missy's stomach and the time that Alice had fed them, but as the prosecuting attorney pointed out, who ever heard of a homicidal sex pervert feeding his victims before murdering them? And how come the very food he gave them was the stuff that remained in Alice's refrigerator and of which there had been an empty carton in the garbage can?

The sexual aspect was precariously founded on some hairs that had been found inside Missy's pants, on her thighs. There were reddish-brown hairs, different from Missy's own blonde hair, and there were also some red threads.

At the trial, Al Stoholski, the criminalist-microscopist from our Medical Examiner's Office, showed that the hairs were identical to those from Brandy, the Crimmins dog, and that the red threads were indistinguishable from those in a red dress that Missy often wore.

This threw the sexual assault case out the window, as there were no signs whatever of any sexual assault or penetration, a fact to which I had testified at the 1968 trial and repeated again now. Dr. Richard Grimes was recalled from retirement to attend the second trial, and he, too, was subjected to a barrage of questions about the possibility of a sexual assault, the loophole on which the defense were hanging all bets.

Grimes repeated all his evidence from the previous trial. Then he gave a more detailed account of his examination of the genital areas of the little girl.

The discussion included the state of the girl's anus, as it had been described in the original autopsy report as gaping widely. Grimes explained that this relaxation is a common and well-recognized occurrence after death, due to loss of tone in the muscle of the sphincter. I can vouch for that, too—many a mistake has been made by an inexperienced doctor or pathologist who sees what is called a "patulous" anus and wrongly suspects that it is stretched because of some sodomistic assault. Only experience can teach one that the limits of normality are wide, as well as the actual orifice. As Grimes went on very lucidly to say, the absence of tears, abrasions, or lacerations was the thing that excluded any possibility of forceful penetration. Grimes also testified that the same lack of abnormality existed in the vulva and vaginal region. Nicolosi, the new prosecutor, repeated these questions so often (in order to make the jury well aware of the answers) that eventually the judge had to stop him on the grounds of tedious repetition.

In cross-examination, Lyons tried to make Grimes reverse what he had just said and admit that anal dilation must be the result of a sexual attack, but Grimes was too old a hand at court work to be twisted around and insisted repeatedly that any such penile penetration would cause detectable injury. When the counsel then tried to get him to agree that lubrication would make it possible, Grimes firmly denied the possibility of any sort of sexual abuse whatsoever.

After Grimes's testimony, the prosecution called Anthony Grace to the stand and established that Alice had gone on at least four boat cruises with him, two before and two after the deaths of her children. They tried to get Grace to say that he had sent a man over to help Alice after her 11:30 p.m. phone call to him, but he flatly denied it, and they were unable to take the matter further.

When Mrs. Earomirski was called there were real fireworks, as Alice again screamed a tirade of abuse at her and called her a liar. The judge, angry at the commotion in his court, called a recess so that Lyons could control Alice again. The defense made a great issue of the psychiatric history of Sophie Earomirski following a head injury she had suffered. Her testimony nevertheless carried great weight, and she remained the idol of the public gallery.

Al Stoholski preceded me on the stand and described the hairs and fibers I mentioned earlier. He also gave a detailed rundown of the stomach contents: "I found carrots, potatoes, a green-leafed vegetable such as spinach, parsley, lima or string beans. There was some fruit material, resembling peach. There were noodles, chewing gum, and some fruit seeds." Nicolosi specifically asked him if there was any meat. Stoholski said there was definitely none, so Alice's story of the veal parmigiana was not true. Al Stoholski had been with me for nine years, and what he couldn't recognize under a microscope doesn't exist on this earth. If he said there wasn't any meat, well, there wasn't any.

Then I was on the stand again and swore to tell the truth, the whole truth, and nothing but the truth—a task quite unaffected by Alice Crimmins's social habits, I might say.

I went through the whole of the 1968 evidence again, concerning the autopsy on the little girl.

I then came to the explanation of the findings on the remains of the little boy. "The direct identification of the body was not possible, due to the extensive post-mortem changes that had taken place. The soft tissues of the head, chest, and abdomen were for the most part destroyed by the activity of an enormous amount of maggots that hatched out of fly eggs. This prevented a direct identification of the body, which was done subsequently by fingerprints, which were obtained from the right hand. The right forearm and hand were preserved sufficiently for finger-printing."

Judge Balbach called another recess to let Alice Crimmins recover from the recital of the autopsy results, after which Nicolosi questioned me again.

"Would you say, Dr. Helpern, that the little boy died a natural death?"

This was the first time this question had been asked in public. Now, I had no evidence of a direct nature to answer that—the body was a mass of corruption and could give no clues, except to exclude massive violence to bones and tissues like an extensive fracture or a gunshot wound.

But I was a medical examiner, and my job was to assess deaths by a full consideration of what I knew about the whole case history. To focus narrowly on the autopsy table, like a horse with blinkers, would be pedantic and foolish. If you are searching the horizon, you don't look down the end of a fixed telescope. He asked me "Did he die a natural death?" and I knew, as the whole of New York and half the United States knew, that little Eddie had been in perfect health the night before he vanished. I knew that he had been found a mile and more from his home, hidden under scrub on a waste lot. I knew that his sister had vanished at the same time and had been found strangled. So what possible reason could I—or anyone else in my position—have for evading the issue? The boy had not died a natural death!

"I would not say that," I told Nicolosi, "and I base my opinion on the classification of the death, the circumstances of the death of the sister, the findings, and so on. It is a conclusion about the manner of death derived from knowledge of the circumstances and of the cause of death of the sister. I would say, in my opinion, that this was not a natural death."

I wasn't saying it was a homicide, though it could hardly have been an accident and certainly wasn't a suicide. I wasn't saying who was responsible—that was not my concern. Nevertheless, I was certainly justified in stating that it wasn't a natural death.

Herbert Lyons must have taken the point, as he never challenged me on it, rather to my surprise. In fact, he hardly challenged me on anything to do with the boy but returned to Missy's death, obsessed with the hopeless task of proving that this was sexual assault and murder. Like Richard Grimes, I adhered to the cast-iron facts of the external examination and the internal autopsy, which proved that there was not the slightest indication that any such molestation had taken place.

Round two of the Crimmins affair was over for me.

The second trial continued in full spate after the medical evidence. Journalist George Carpozi, in his excellent book *Ordeal by Trial*, had a chapter heading at this point entitled "Rorech Strikes Again," and this aptly describes the way in which Alice's friend once again helped in her conviction. He alleged that she said to him during an emotional outburst, "Joseph, please forgive me, I killed her," and later, "I didn't want him killed—I agreed. They'll understand, they'll know it was for the best."

At this, Alice Crimmins threw one of her tantrums in the courtroom, screaming "You miserable, lying worm!" at Rorech.

Rorech admitted that Alice had given him the name of the man who had helped her that night, a name given in the presence of her previous attorney, Harrison. This was Vinnie "Corrabella," and later he said that Alice had shown him pictures of a man, whom she said was "Corrabella," and said that he was the man who helped her that night.

Lyons took him apart in cross-examination, but the impact of his evidence had already been made on the jury.

Harrison was called to testify, and he said he obtained the name of Colabella (not Corrabella as Rorech had pronounced it) from contacts inside prison. A high point in his testimony came when it was learned that he had signed a contract with Alice Crimmins for the book and movie rights for her story!

The trial wore on into its fifth week, and the defense struck a hard blow with a new witness, Marvin Weinstein, who said that in the early hours of the fatal morning he had been on 153rd Street, within view of Mrs. Earomirski's windows, with his wife, small son and daughter, and their dog—a poodle. He claimed to have been carrying his daughter, aged two, in a blanket, just as Sophie Earomirski and a new witness the prosecution had found had described. They said that they had been visiting a friend named Anthony King in the neighborhood and were sure that the day in question was the correct one.

However, the prosecution later fetched Anthony King from vacation in Florida and used him to discredit the details of Weinstein's story.

Meanwhile, Colabella was called from a fifteen-year sentence in the Atlanta penitentiary—he had been successful in an appeal against New York State for his conviction for payroll robbery but had been sentenced again for dope peddling. Colabella bluntly denied any knowledge of Alice Crimmins, the children's deaths, and even Queens.

This time, Alice and her counsel decided she should not testify—after the massacre that had taken place during the first trial, there seemed nothing to gain and a lot to lose, if her multitude of amorous affairs were to be paraded before the jury again. The defense rested, and the usual summations and judge's charge to the jury took place.

For the defense, Lyons went for Mrs. Earomirski in a big way, taking her character and psychiatric condition to pieces in order to discredit her as a reliable witness.

Demakos, for the prosecution, managed to drive Alice into another frenzied outburst, when he challenged her to stand up and tell the truth about how she killed her children.

The jury went out during the mid-afternoon but at eight that night requested various photographs and documents and that some witnesses' testimony be reread. The jurors continued to deliberate until one-thirty in the morning, when they reported that, due to fatigue, they couldn't go on. The judge adjourned until ten the next morning and remanded Alice in custody—she had been out on bail until then. She went berserk and clung to her chair, and four court attendants had to drag her out to the car that was to take her to the Women's House of Detention in Manhattan for the rest of the night.

During the next day, the jurors requested the autopsy report and Al Stoholski's report on the stomach contents. The first jury, three years before, had also asked to review the medical aspects of the autopsy; it seemed to play a most significant part in their deliberations.

This was the last request, and it was almost six o'clock on the evening of Friday, April 23, 1971, that the verdict came in— nearly six years after the deaths of little Eddie and Missy Crimmins.

"Guilty of first degree murder—and guilty of first degree manslaughter," the jury foreman announced. In spite of the large number of policemen and court officials present, there was a near riot in the courtroom. Once again Alice was taken to detention to await sentencing by the court, which took place on May 13.

Before Judge Balbach passed sentence, Lyons made a motion, in which he complained about the detrimental effect of all the publicity on his client's case. He also said that the grounds on which Alice was convicted of the murder of Eddie were without proper foundation, as the only testimony which showed that the boy died violently was "a statement of speculation offered by the chief medical examiner, Dr. Milton Helpern." Yet when I made this statement on the stand, Lyons had not uttered a single word to refute my opinion.

The judge turned down all his motions and gave the sentence that everyone expected for first degree murder and manslaughter—life imprisonment for the one, and five to twenty years for the other.

Ironically, if Alice Crimmins had accepted the sentence in 1968, she could have been out on parole almost by the time of the second trial. She now received a life sentence, which meant at least another twenty-six years in prison, making her eligible for parole at the age of fifty-eight.

But this still wasn't the end of the Crimmins saga. Alice was sent upstate to Bedford Hills Correctional Facility and spent almost as many months in jail as she had spent days in 1968. After twenty-three months, the Appellate Division of the Supreme Court in Brooklyn reversed the conviction for Eddie's murder and ordered a new trial in the case of "Missy".

Alice Crimmins was released on bail in the summer of 1973, pending an appeal against this decision by the district attorney. Early in 1975, the New York State Court of Appeals upheld the dismissal of the charge that she murdered Eddie but returned her conviction for the manslaughter of Missy to the Appellate Division of the Supreme Court. This tortuous legal ricochet resulted in the latter court's upholding the conviction, so Alice was sent back to prison to await the next round of the contest between her attorneys and the prosecutors.

In January 1976, Mrs. Crimmins was transferred to a

residential work release facility in Harlem and has been working in a secretarial job in Queens. She still hopes for a parole that will set her free, but in the meantime, she commutes to work every day, compulsorily saving half her salary in expectation of the day she will be permanently released.

Chapter 11

The Career Girl Murders

Another celebrated case in which I was involved was notable not so much for the forensic medical aspects as for the alarm and indeed terror it aroused in certain sections of Manhattan, especially among career girls living on the Upper East Side. This was the notorious Wylie-Hoffert case, for which the wrong man was very nearly convicted.

It began in 1963, on the kind of hot August day that so often seems to push the murder rate up in New York. Three young women were sharing a very nice apartment on East Eighty-eighth Street in a good area of town between Madison and Park Avenue. They were intelligent and spirited, thrilled to be making their way in the bustle of New York.

Janice Wylie, a very pretty twenty-one-year-old, was a daughter of Max Wylie, an advertising executive and writer and also a niece of the well-known novelist, Philip Wylie, author of the 1942 best seller *Generation of Vipers*.

Her roomates were Patricia "Trix" Tolles, age twenty-three, the daughter of the dean of Hamilton College in Clinton, New York, and Emily Hoffert, also twenty-three, the daughter of a prominent physician in Minnesota, who had just become a schoolteacher. Upon these three very respectable and well-connected young women, tragedy fell.

Patricia Tolles, the lone survivor of the trio, must have had a terrible shock that August evening. She came home from her work at the book division of *Time*, Inc. about 6:30 p.m. and found signs that something was amiss. There was a raincoat belonging to Janice on the floor of the hallway, and on going further into the apartment, she found more disorder and some bloodstains in the bathroom. Afraid to go into the other rooms, although she did not see anything worse at that stage, she left to telephone Janice's father, who lived only a few blocks away. Max Wylie hurried over with his wife. He found the bodies of his daughter and Emily Hoffert in the main bedroom, covered with blood and horribly mutilated. Keeping his wife and Trix in the foyer, he called the police, who responded immediately.

When the homicide squad saw the scene, they notified the Office of the Chief Medical Examiner. Dr. Bela Der was on duty and responded to the call, but Mr. Wylie—whom I knew personally—asked him to call me, and I went over immediately. It was obvious from the outset that this was going to be a case of considerable public interest. The media labelled it "The Career Girls Slaying" and put the fear of God into thousands of young working women who lived in that area and elsewhere in Manhattan, for it seemed that some maniac was able to invade even the most secure and elegant apartment houses and wreak such savage mutilation.

Both victims were lying on the floor between the bloodstained bed and the window. Blood was everywhere, and even the first glance showed multiple stab wounds and lacerations on the bodies. Janice Wylie was nude, the other girl fully dressed, but the most bizarre thing was that they were trussed up with strips of bedsheet around their wrists and ankles, and both girls were tied together by the arms.

I didn't care to guess the precise time of death, as this is a notoriously inaccurate procedure, but it seemed probable that they had both been killed a number of hours before they were found, perhaps around noon. The electric clock had stopped because its plug was pulled from the wall—the hands were fixed at 10:37 a.m.

Two bloodstained carving knives were found in the bedroom and another in the bathroom. The blades of those in the bedroom were snapped in half. Two broken Coca-Cola bottles littered the room—these had obviously been used to batter the bodies.

Particia Tolles told the police that she had left the apartment to go to work at 9:30 that morning. Janice was still in bed, as she had the day off from her job at *Newsweek* magazine. Emily Hoffert had already gone, since she was moving to a new apartment on Park Avenue and was going there to clean it.

Later, the detectives surmised that Janice was surprised either while still in bed or after she had got up to answer the door, which might account for the raincoat in the foyer. Emily, who was due to return some time before noon, had possibly walked in on the killer, still in the apartment after having already murdered Janice.

The next morning, Dr. Der, as associate medical examiner, and I did complete autopsies on both bodies. Janice had been stabbed in the lower abdomen, the wounds causing partial evisceration, and also deeply through the left side of the chest. Much of the body was smeared with blood. The area between the legs was heavily coated with a greasy substance, and on the floor near the bodies was a jar of Noxzema cream with the lid removed, but there was no sign of rape. In contrast to the naked Janice, Emily Hoffert had all her clothes on, but her injuries were more numerous. She had stab wounds in the neck, and her hands showed many lacerations typical of "defense wounds," indicating that she had tried to ward off her attacker. Slivers of glass, which had come from the broken soda bottles were on the body. The arrangement of the bonds tying up the two girls was complicated, and the fabric was cut (rather than torn) from the bed sheets and a green bedcover. There was a Gillette razor blade lying on the floor near the bodies.

The medical evidence was clear cut and did not help much in the police investigation or the search for the perpetrator, but it re-emphasized the horrific and macabre nature of the killings. Later on, the detectives called in a psychiatrist-criminologist who claimed the ability to conjure up character pictures of the perpetrators of various crimes, but he was not at all successful in pinpointing this one.

Newsweek magazine, where Janice Wylie had worked, offered a $10,000 reward for information leading to the conviction of the murderer. The police conducted an intensive investigation over a period of months, interviewing over a thousand people. All sorts of leads were followed up—it was thought that perhaps the killer was known to the girls, as he had somehow gained access to the apartment. The service door to the kitchen was unlocked, though there were no indications that the murderer had left or entered by that route.

Another fact came to light—Janice, a beautiful girl who had ambitions of going onto the professional stage—had been receiving anonymous obscene phone calls in the weeks prior to her death. These came to her at her office. One time the caller had said, "Call this number back or your father won't be alive next week." She dialed the number but there was no answer. When her father urged her to go to the police, she laughed it off. The investigators spent a lot of effort on this angle, but it led nowhere.

A few months went by, with Manhattan still uneasy about the safety of lone career girls in the city. The detectives got no new leads. "We need a crystal ball on this one," one of them commented. A handyman in the apartment block was suspected at one point, as he had once assaulted a hospital clerk, but he was cleared of the killings.

Then, many months later, in April 1964, the whole case opened up again. A cleaning woman was stabbed to death in the backyard of a Brooklyn house, and almost two weeks later, a night nurse was followed and assaulted. A police officer fired at the assailant, which chased him away, and the nurse, Mrs. Borrero, later identified the young black man as George Whitmore, of Wildwood, New Jersey.

After a lot of interrogation (later termed "third degree" tactics), Whitmore confessed to the killing of the cleaning woman and to the attack on Mrs. Borrero. In his wallet he had a photograph of a young white girl, with "From Lucille to George" written across it. He alleged that he had picked it off a pile of junk in his father's scrapyard in Wildwood, but later, again after heavy interrogation, he said, "I got it from that building up on East Eighty-eighth Street."

The detectives naturally went to town on this. Although his first "confession" was full of discrepancies, Whitmore eventually made a statement. The police said it could only have been written by a man who had knowledge of the circumstances of the girl's killings, which had been kept secret. He was indicted on both the Brooklyn crimes and the Wylie-Hoffert murders and was committed for trial.

However, Whitmore, through his lawyer, withdrew all his confessions and said they were forced out of him by prolonged brutality on the part of the detectives. He found an alibi for the date of the Eighty-eighth Street killings—then the Wylie family said that the photograph was not that of Janice. A handwriting expert showed that the writing on the picture did not belong to Janice, and the prosecution case began to evaporate. The trial was delayed, further alibi witnesses were found to swear that Whitmore was in New Jersey at the time of the Manhattan deaths, and it was discovered that the photo was one of Arlene Franco, a Wildwood school girl, taken way back in 1956.

The case then took another abrupt turn-about. A New York drug addict, Nathan Delany, was arrested for stabbing a drug peddler to death. To make a deal with the police, he told them that he knew who had really done the Wylie-Hoffert killings. "You got the wrong guy in Whitmore," he said, "It was Ricky Robles."

Richard Robles was another drug addict and ex-convict. Delany said that twenty-two-year-old Robles had turned up at his apartment on August 28th, 1963 "looking like a wild man, with his clothes covered in blood." Robles badly needed a shot of heroin and said that he had "just iced two dames when I was robbing their apartment on East Eighty-eighth Street." According to Delany, Robles had told him that he got in through a service door and found a naked woman, covering herself with a sheet. She begged him to go away, but he wanted her more than he wanted to rob the place. While he was trying to rape her, another woman appeared. He tied them together, back to back, until he could decide what to do with them. The second girl had screamed, "I've seen you—you won't get away with this," so he got three knives and the soda bottles and stabbed and beat them both to death. The clothed girl died quickly; the other one took a long time.

Well, Delany could have fabricated all this from the stories that had been in the press, and in January 1965, when Robles was finally confronted by the police, he laughed the whole story off as the ramblings of a drug-fevered mind. But Robles had convictions for burglary and sex offences, and some of his victims had been tied up in the same fashion as the career girls.

The detectives continued to string Delany along, getting him released and bugging his flat with microphones. He even unknowingly carried a small recorder under his armpit on some occasions.

Although there was never any direct admission of guilt by Robles on the tapes, the police eventually put enough evidence together to have him convicted of the murders of Wylie and Hoffert. He was sent to prison for so long that it will be the year 2019 before he is eligible for parole.

George Whitmore was never tried for the same killings, but he had a number of trials and retrials for the two Brooklyn attacks. He came pretty close to a double murder conviction because of the confession extracted from him by an over-enthusiastic detective. It was a very tragic and peculiar case and is still remembered by the inhabitants of Manhattan's fashionable Upper East Side.

Chapter 12

The International Scene

The Truscott affair, in Canada, was widely publicized for several years and caused quite a stir on both sides of the Atlantic. The main reason was that the accused was a fourteen-year-old boy, who was convicted of rape and murder and actually sentenced to death by hanging.

In June 1959, a twelve-year-old-girl, Lynne Harper, was found strangled and sexually assaulted at the edge of a wood not far from a Royal Canadian Air Force base near Clinton, Ontario. There were any number of children in the neighborhood on that hot evening, all of them members of families of Air Force personnel at the base. One youth was Steven Truscott, who had been cycling with Lynne not long before she was last seen alive.

When Lynne failed to return home, a search was begun. Almost two days later, a line of R.C.A.F. men moved through the countryside and came across the body, already showing early signs of decomposition.

The autopsy was done by Dr. John Penistan, a British pathologist who had emigrated and now practiced in Huron County, Ontario. He was responsible for the medico-legal work in that area and was quite experienced.

The autopsy was done at the Royal Canadian Air Force Base, under admittedly poor conditions, in a small room lit only by a single electric bulb. A service doctor from the base assisted him, and Dr. Penistan did an excellent job, though later it became the subject of intense criticism and indeed almost abuse.

There were considerable similarities to the Alice Crimmins case, in that the central issue was the estimation of the time of death from the contents of the stomach.

Dr. Penistan found that the stomach was full of undigested and partly-digested food, with remnants of meat and other material consistent with the last meal that Lynne had eaten at home at 5:30 p.m. on the evening of her disappearance. From this, the pathologist gave his opinion that she must have died within two hours of the meal. She had been seen with Steven Truscott at about 7:00 p.m. to 7:15 p.m., going along the country road near where her body was later found, and the natural implication was that he had at least been in her vicinity at the time of death.

There were other factors which pointed to his guilt, though they also came under heavy fire later on. He had marked damage to the skin of his penis, and there was much dispute as to whether this was at least partly due to the sexual attack or whether it was a pre-existing skin condition. As in so many other cases, a confession (later retracted) was obtained after lengthy interrogation.

A trial was held at Clinton, and in view of the circumstantial and medical evidence, Steven Truscott was found guilty. As he had turned fourteen, he had to be sentenced to death according to Canadian law, and though this raised a shock wave of horror that reached overseas, it was upheld on appeal. The sentence stood for a considerable time, although everyone realized that it could never actually be carried out. It took a decision of the Canadian cabinet to commute the sentence to one of life imprisonment.

This was way back in 1958-59, but the Truscott affair still had a long way to run. It was revived in a most vigorous way in a book published by a Canadian woman journalist, who made the case her personal crusade. Mrs. Isabel LeBourdais published a book in England called *The Trial of Steven Truscott*, which, though well written and extremely persuasive, was entirely biased in favor of Truscott. All the evidence against him was denigrated and that in his favor was inflated, so that unless the reader had the trial transcripts in front of him, he might well be misled into taking all her strong arguments as gospel truth. The main theme of the book was that Dr. Penistan was utterly wrong both in his autopsy findings and in his testimony in court.

However, the book provoked a strong reaction in Canada as well as in Britain, where it was published. One of those who took an immediate interest in the case was my old friend and colleague, Dr. Francis Camps, one of the foremost forensic pathologists in London at the time. Francis frequently visited the United States (he died a couple of years ago); and I knew him quite well. He was one of those restless, enthusiastic men who sometimes stampede down the wrong track. He read the LeBourdais book and without checking on the facts, immediately began beating his breast in England about the enormity of the injustice that was being done to this poor boy in Canada.

Camps even wrote a letter about Truscott to the Lord Chancellor of England, the high government minister responsible for the courts and judges. Somehow this letter became known publicly, and Francis Camps appeared on television in England to talk about the miscarriage of justice that had taken place in Ontario. The substance of his complaint was that Penistan was utterly wrong in using stomach contents to calculate the time of death, and that he, Camps, thought Lynne had died ten hours after her meal.

Well, there was a very difficult legal situation in Canada. A strong public outcry had arisen as a result of the LeBourdais book, but for a time the authorities resisted it. There was no means of reopening the matter, as the appeal had been turned down, and at that time, further appeals could not be made from the province of Ontario to the federal courts in the capital, Ottawa.

Then some legislation took place, and the Canadian Parliament ordered that the case be brought before the nine judges of the Supreme Court of Canada to see if there were any grounds for a retrial.

The defense got Francis Camps over, together with Dr. Charles Petty who was then in Baltimore, though now he directs the Forensic Science Institute in Dallas, Texas.

As the defense had a famous London forensic pathologist and another from the United States, the crown evened up the score by asking Professor Keith Simpson over from London; Dr. Samuel Gerber, coroner of Cuyahoga County from Ohio; and me from New York. Keith Simpson was the doyen of British legal medicine; there was considerable rivalry between him and Francis Camps, though Simpson had much more experience and expertise and had taken over from that legendary pre-war figure, Sir Bernard Spilsbury. I knew Keith very well both as a close friend and a respected colleague and still have the pleasure of seeing him now and then. He has retired from his official position as Professor at Guy's Hospital at the University of London, but he remains as busy as ever.

Well, Keith Simpson and Francis Camps came over to Ottawa in October 1966, almost eight years after the death of the girl. Charles Petty, Sam Gerber, and I came up from the U.S.A., and Dr. Penistan and another forensic pathologist, Dr. Jaffe, from Toronto were there as well. So we had seven forensic pathologists ready to argue the case, about equally divided on each side.

During the hearing, Professor Simpson's polished manner in court rather caught the ear of the newspapers, especially when he astonished counsel by pointedly emphasizing that by 1966, he had personally performed no less than one hundred thousand autopsies! One of the Ottawa newspapers ran some very witty, accurate cartoons of Simpson and Camps. Francis Camps, a somewhat incoherent speaker became rather entangled in his testimony; his brain raced ahead of his tongue, as is sometimes the way with such dynamic men. Keith Simpson and I were independently quite in agreement about the medical aspects— upon which the whole case really rested, as the time of Lynne's death and the proximity of Truscott were the central issues.

I had recently been involved in the Crimmins case in New York, and the same argument applied there. If a victim is killed suddenly, as in an unexpected rape and strangulation, then there is none of the long-lasting emotional or physical stress that can alter or delay the processes of digestion and the emptying of the stomach. It would be a totally different matter if the victim had been set upon, bound and gagged, and left for some hours before being killed—then, the shock could quite well cause any sort of distortion of the normal emptying time of the stomach.

But in the Truscott case the circumstances made this impossible—the assault had been sudden, short, sharp, and fatal and the condition of the stomach and its contents reliably reflected the recency of ingestion of food at the time of death. Dr. Penistan's finding of a large volume of food material, with easily recognizable pieces of meat and other foods, indicated that death must have taken place no more than a couple of hours after the last meal.

But Camps and Petty would have none of this and argued that it was impossible to say anything about the time of death from the stomach's contents. (Camps estimated the time as "from one to ten hours.") But they were arguing without taking into account the premise I've just mentioned about the sudden nature of the assault and death. What Camps and Petty said might have been correct in other circumstances where I would wholehear- tedly agree with them—but that just wasn't the case here.

Simpson and I must have got our point across, for in the event, the Supreme Court issued a very short judgment which stated that there was nothing whatsoever in the evidence to suggest that the findings of the previous courts were in error, and it declined to recommend a new trial.

It was a case that received a great deal of publicity in the lay and medical press on both sides of the ocean. I felt sorry for Dr. Penistan, who had been given a really rough ride for a long time, during which his professional ability and integrity were called into question. I hope that the backing that Keith Simpson and I gave him in Ottawa helped to make up for some of the acrimony that he incurred during those intervening years.

I read in a newspaper only a couple of months ago that Steven Truscott is now out of prison and is living under a new name with his wife and children. Once again, I think about all the work, emotion, and ballyhoo that many of these well-known cases generate for a time; then, with the passage of more time, it seems as if they never even happened.

Another interesting case that necessitated my travelling abroad occurred in South Africa a few years ago. A medical acquaintance, Dr. Arthur Helfet, who divided his time and practice between New York and Cape Town, had given my name to the authorities there as a medico-legal consultant. The South African Consul General in New York, Mr. Owen Booysen, called on me one day to ask if I would go to Cape Town to advise the prosecution there in an unusual homicide. My expenses were to be paid, but no fee was discussed. I was intrigued by the case, and the opportunity of seeing South Africa during my vacation time induced me to accept the invitation.

As matters turned out, I never actually gave testimony, but I did do a lot of work behind the scenes in preparation for the trial during the three weeks I was there. I also had the opportunity to meet and make friends with many new professional colleagues and give some lectures to the police and to the Cape Town University Medical School faculty and students.

The case concerned an extremely well-to-do family, the Cohens. The father, Mr. Isidore Cohen, was a millionaire and was highly regarded in the community. He had a son, Ronald, about forty years of age, also successful and wealthy in his own right and married to a beautiful wife, Susan.

The younger Cohens lived lavishly in a large, modern Moorish-style mansion in Cape Town, and all seemed well until the night of Sunday, April 5, 1970, when Ronald, in a great state of agitation, called the police to say that his wife had been murdered by an intruder.

The police arrived to find Susan dead on the living room floor with obvious, severe head injuries, apparently inflicted with one of two modernistic statuettes. The statuettes, now lying on the floor, had been wedding presents; one was made of stone and weighed twenty pounds, the other, shaped like a ram's head, was made of bronze and weighed eight and a half pounds. The excited husband eventually explained that he had come back into the room, after having gone to the toilet, to see his wife struggling with and being assaulted by a man wielding a weapon. He said he rushed to her assistance, but the intruder then struck him a blow on the head that knocked him out. By the time he recovered consciousness, the assailant had disappeared, and his wife was lying dead on the floor.

Asked by the police for a description of the man, Cohen gave a clear and initially convincing account. From what was learned later, the person he described was an actual person about whom he had been told, a door-to-door salesman who had recently called there to sell books.

But there was one major flaw in his story, of which he was unaware because of his lack of medical knowledge. He told the police unhesitatingly that he remembered distinctly the impact of the blow he received when he was struck on the head and rendered unconscious. Now this is virtually impossible, and at the trial, a neurosurgeon called by the prosecution testified that in any head injury severe enough to cause even transient concussion with loss of consciousness, there is a loss of memory of the occurrence. This backward loss of recollection of the traumatic event is called "retrograde amnesia" and is related to the fact that there is a time-lag before sensory impressions are stored permanently in the brain. If the brain function is temporarily disrupted by an injury to the head causing unconsciousness, the impressions waiting to be stored in the memory fail to become imprinted. This well-known loss of ability to recall is a protective mechanism, designed to prevent anguish from repeated recollection of the pain and shock that naturally accompany such injuries.

Cohen unwittingly denied this vital attribute that would otherwise have made his story credible, and when the discrepancy was pointed out to them by one of their medical advisors, the police became suspicious. There were other circumstances that aroused their suspicion as well, but these did not touch on the medical aspects of the case.

Cohen had been quick-witted and clever, but he slipped up on this important point. He tried to retrieve the situation by some further quick thinking. During the time that he was out on bail awaiting trial, he visited his Malaysian tailor in Cape Town. In the middle of a fitting, while gazing out of the window, he suddenly gave a great shout and to the amazement of the tailor, rushed out into the street shouting, "There he is, that's the fellow who did it!"

He gave chase, later alleging that he'd lost the man in the street. He maintained that, through the window of the tailor's shop, he had seen the intruder who had killed his wife and had hit him.

At the trial, which lasted from August 25 to September 18, 1970, a large and impressive defense team appeared on the scene and attempted to crowd the prosecution off stage. They believed in offense as the best defense and began picking on and challenging each item of the prosecution's case. In effect, they were saying, "What's all this horrible nonsense that you are attributing to our client? You're trying to make him appear guilty of an obvious, crudely perpetrated homicide that the police won't take the trouble to track down. Our client has been trapped by circumstances!''

One of the main reasons the South African authorities called me into the picture was because of a language problem existing there. The police force was largely Afrikaans and they had a difficult time following the subtleties and nuances of English, and much of the forensic medical terminology was in that language. The trial itself was conducted bilingually in both English and Afrikaans, with simultaneous translation facilities in the court.

The autopsy on Mrs. Cohen was performed by a bright young pathologist, Dr. Deon Knobel, who is a member of the faculty at the medical school in Cape Town and senior government pathologist to the state health laboratories. He did an excellent job, carefully documenting the findings.

Although I never took the stand to testify, as young Knobel had done so well, I had done a lot of work both in and out of court during these weeks, going over the evidence with the police and the prosecutor and clarifying and interpreting the medical and scientific evidence. The newspapers speculated at length on who this white-haired doctor from New York was and what he was doing in court so often; I had the feeling that they thought I was some sort of secret weapon that the prosecution had up their sleeve.

The red-robed judge president, Mr. Justice A.J. Beyers, presided over the court with his two assistant judges (or assessors), in civilian attire. One of them, Mr. M.R. Hartogh, a former chief magistrate of Johannesburg, questioned the defendant as to precisely what had taken place when he returned to the library to find his wife being assaulted by the intruder. The judges had the case very well sized up. The evidence was effectively and fairly presented so that the prosecution did not need any secret weapon. The court found Cohen guilty of first degree murder, the penalty for which would be capital punishment.

Nevertheless, the court permitted the defense to present psychiatric evidence that the defendant was an obsessive, compulsive, perfectionist type of individual and that there were extenuating circumstances to justify a lesser sentence. The presiding justice accepted this argument and considered that the unusual method used by the defendant to kill his wife was an extenuating circumstance. He pointed out that a man who plans to murder his wife does not do it with two heavy ornaments. On that basis, the court sentenced the defendant to a term of twelve years in prison.

Mr. A.J. Lategan, the prosecutor, wrote to me in September 1973 that Ronald Cohen, while in jail, had confessed to the killing of his wife under the delusion that she was having unnatural relations with their children; Cohen also admitted having invented the story about the elusive stranger whom he saw in the house and outside the tailor shop. He had met his wife at the airport the night of the murder, drove her home, and started a quarrel about her alleged unsavory inclinations. He got mad at her, hit her over the head with the statuettes, and then fabricated the rest of the story.

It was a sad business and I felt particularly sorry for old Mr. Cohen.

In closing this chapter, I would be very remiss if I did not mention the many kindnesses that were extended to me by so many persons during my interesting stay in Capetown. I was pleased that I had an opportunity to see this part of South Africa. I came away very impressed by the country and its unusual legal system—and I also enjoyed making interesting new friends.

Chapter 13

Mercy Killings–
Euthanasia or Impatience?

I've remarked before that New England has produced some very unusual cases, many of which generated a lot of emotional heat—the Noxon case in Pittsfield, Massachusetts and the van Rie affair in Boston are prime examples. The extraordinary business of Doctor Hermann Sander, back in late 1949, was another.

I first became involved when the attorney general of the state of New Hampshire, William L. Phinney, and his deputy attorney general, Mr. William S. Green came down to New York to see me.

They had heard that our Medical Examiner's Office had a reputation for being interested in the phenomenon of embolism. This is a pathological condition in which some substance—a blood clot, fat, tissue (like bone marrow), or even air—gets into the bloodstream, circulates, and eventually becomes jammed in some vital area, where it may cause serious trouble, and even death.

Air, introduced into the body by injection into a vein and distributed as bubbles, can block the small blood vessels, especially of the heart and brain. An artifically produced air embolism was the central issue and source of trouble in the case in Manchester, New Hampshire. Phinney and Green told me the whole story and asked if I would go up there and help clarify the situation. It was January 1950, and the event they told me about had occurred over a month earlier. It was to cause a great hullaballoo about the subject of "mercy killing," but (as with other such cases that have come my way over the years) there didn't seem to me to be much mercy involved, as the patient hadn't been complaining.

Now, in Manchester, New Hampshire was a forty-one-year-old physician named Doctor Hermann Sander, and one of his patients in the hospital on December 4 was a fifty-nine-year-old woman named Mrs. Abbie Borroto. Some time previously Mrs. Borroto had undergone an operation for cancer of the bowel, but the cancer had recurred and had extensively invaded other organs, including the liver, so she was beyond any hope of survival. But though she was in an advanced stage of cancer, and the outlook was completely hopeless, she was not suffering a great deal. Pain-killing drugs were administered to her, and she lay quietly in bed, causing no trouble. Indeed she had her hair coiffured and her hands manicured regularly. There was certainly none of the agonizing business sometimes associated with the process of dying. As with many people with advanced carcinoma, she was in a sort of transcendental state; it was hardly a "kill me, do away with me, I can't stand it any longer" situation.

There she was, lying quietly in her bed in the hospital in Manchester, New Hampshire, in early December of 1949. Now the husband began to question the doctor, wanting to know more exact details of the prognosis. "When do you expect her to die, Doctor Sander?"

Mr. Borroto evinced a certain impatience—not that he wanted to hasten death in the slightest way—but he wanted to know what was likely to happen in order to plan. His wife had been ill a long time and everyone seemed to know she was dying—but when? That was the question.

Eventually, one night, according to testimony, Dr. Sander said to Mr. Borroto that he didn't expect her to live through the night.

That night, Dr. Sander prescribed a massive dose of narcotic drugs, the ones his patient was receiving for pain-suppression. He gave her a large amount of Pantopon and Demerol. These are powerful narcotics, but when you over-sedate a dying patient, you may slow down the life process and actually prolong life for a time; apparently this happened in the case of Mrs. Borroto. In the morning, according to Dr. Sander's own notes as revealed later in court, he went to the patient's room and discovered that she was still alive. The massive dose of medication had put her flat out, but she was still living, noted Dr. Sander, though he was later to assert that she had died before his subsequent ministrations. He turned to the nurse and said, "Get me a twenty cc. syringe and a tourniquet."

She didn't know what was happening but was trained to comply with the instructions of a doctor. According to her later testimony, this is what then occurred:

She went to the cupboard. "We don't have a twenty cc., Doctor." Sander then told her to get him a ten cc. syringe. Mystified, she did as he said, and flabbergasted, watched as he put the rubber tourniquet around the arm of the cancer patient and stuck the needle into a vein in the crook of the elbow—after taking out the plunger of the syringe!

Sander then put the plunger back into the syringe barrel and blew a syringe-full of air into the vein. He pulled the plunger out again and repeated the process—four times in all—pumping a total of forty cc. of air into the bloodstream of Mrs. Borroto. The nurse later testified that she heard the patient gasp as the air was injected.

Why four syringes-full? Well, apparently he was doing what is called a "minimum lethal dose" test. It just happened to be four because that was enough. He didn't say to himself, "I'm only going to give her four syringes-full and see what happens." He gave her air until, as the nurse testified, she gasped and died—it was as simple as that.

Did he know it was going to be four syringes-full? No, of course he didn't. I have to emphasize this because later, everyone suddenly became overnight experts on how much air was safe to inject and how much was lethal. I had doctors say to me, "How can forty cc. of air kill?" They'd start to roll up their sleeves and say, "Come on, Milt, I'll take forty cc. right now."

But, as I said to them, they missed the point of the whole thing! He didn't give four syringes-full out of design. It just happened that Mrs. Borroto, at that stage in her condition, evidently needed only four to achieve the desired effect. Some people just wouldn't see the point.

Well, the patient died. The husband was notified—what Dr. Sander said had come true: she died that day. He wasn't told what actually had happened, but he had been told the day before to make arrangements with a funeral director.

A death certificate was prepared which read "carcinoma of the large bowel with metastases." An autopsy was not requested. It was a perfectly innocent certificate, in keeping with what was well known from her clinical history. The husband then made the necessary arrangements with the funeral director, who embalmed the body, and within a few days it was buried. Nobody knew differently, yet. There were some unfair insinuations later on that the nurse had "snitched" on Dr. Hermann Sander because he wasn't very nice to her, didn't compliment her on her standards of work, etc., didn't make enough fuss over her. Pure press nonsense, to stir things up! The nurse had nothing at all to do with the case, except that, when they asked her later, she said, yes, she was there, she saw it and was frightened about the whole thing.

In mid-December, about ten days after the body had been buried, the hospital chart of Mrs. Abbie Borroto was, as is customary, delivered to the attending physician—Doctor Sander—for a final note before it would be filed away in the records department.

Sander knew that no autopsy had been done and that a certificate of death from natural causes had been issued. He also knew that the body had been embalmed and was already safely in the earth of the cemetery—no chance in a thousand years of finding any air embolism!

He then sat down and wrote a meticulous note in the chart describing exactly what he had done to Mrs. Borroto. He set it all down: the excessive drugs administered the night before and the forty cc. of air injected the following morning.

There it was, in black and white in the case record—his own voluntary statement. No one asked him to write it; he was under no coercion, no duress. He just did it.

But he didn't realize that proof may also include a voluntary admission. If someone accused him of doing what he said he did and he denied it, never in a million years could it be substantiated in a court of law, *unless he had voluntarily admitted it.*

After the chart was completed, the record room librarian read it and was alarmed by what he had written. She then showed it to the doctor in charge of medical records, who in turn brought it to the medical administrator of the French Hospital. Both of these physicians were very disturbed by this extraordinary admission and sent for Hermann Sander. "Doctor Sander," they asked, "Were you in your right mind when you wrote this?"

But the doctor refused to change his statement. And nothing they or anyone else could say would bring this unbending physician to recant this most damaging confession of murder in the chart.

Now, the newspapers got hold of the story, and Sander discussed the matter freely with them. He was undoubtedly a good doctor and a popular fellow—when he was indicted, thousands of dollars poured in to pay for his defense, and there was a rush of witnesses to testify to his excellence as a physician, in every sense of the word.

But he was proud and he was stubborn and he wouldn't take back what he had written. By the time it became public, it was too late. The papers were holding him up to be some kind of saint, and the word "euthanasia" was being bandied about.

When the medical administrator got hold of the chart, he felt obliged to call in the official physician, who in New Hampshire is called the medical referee, corresponding to a medical examiner in Massachusetts. The medical referee was Doctor Biron, not a forensic pathologist, but a physician—and a decent, straightforward person. Dr. Biron took the matter to the attorney general of New Hampshire, William Phinney, and there was nothing else for Phinney to do but to send the affair to a grand jury. All very unpleasant for the attorney general, but Sander had forced his hand.

Now the grand jury had no autopsy findings before them, because the body had been buried without one. They decided to waive an autopsy, reckoning that time, embalming, and burial would make it impossible to prove air embolism. They didn't seem to realize that proof is not only what you find in the body— but also what you cannot see in the body in the way of a competing cause of death. Plus, of course, the fact that proof includes the admission.

By now, Sander had obtained prestigious counsel to defend him. Counsel said, "We will do an autopsy," in which the state acquiesced. The state made a big mistake, right at the start, in allowing the initiative to pass out of its hands. You never relinquish the right to perform the autopsy, even if you are required to change your mind on the case. But the prosecutor allowed the defense to engage an expert to perform the autopsy—not appreciating what a tactical blunder this was to prove.

The person they called on was Dr. Richard Ford, at that time a relative newcomer to the field of forensic medicine. Dick Ford was a recent appointee in the Department of Legal Medicine at Harvard Medical School, an able pathologist, not long separated from the medical corps of the army. He was also serving as a medical examiner in one of the districts of Boston. When Attorney General Phinney and his assistant came down to see me, they wanted an expert to serve as observer at Richard Ford's autopsy, and asked if I would do this. I wasn't too happy about it and told them, "You know, you shouldn't have let this happen; you're at a serious disadvantage, with the prosecution there merely as observers, instead of being in charge of the procedure. You're abdicating your control of the situation."

But it was too late to alter the pattern, and I made the best of a lopsided arrangement, agreeing to represent them as an observer. Well, I went up there to Manchester on January 21, which was forty-eight days after Mrs. Borroto had died. The prosecution obtained the help of another pathologist as an observer, Dr. Ralph Miller, who was head of the New Hampshire Board of Health and also professor of pathology at the medical school at Dartmouth. He was an excellent pathologist, and we understood each other.

The three of us were there in the mortuary, with Richard Ford all geared up, full of crusading enthusiasm. He had an attractive personality and knew his pathology, but in this case he had no real insight into what the case was all about. When we got to the body, he got down to work, busy as a beaver, making notes of his own on some papers that he was carrying.

This was no good to me, and I said so straight away. "Look, Dick, if I'm to watch this autopsy, I want it all dictated loud and clear, so we won't have any dispute about the findings later. Otherwise, I want no part of it; I'm just going to go home."

This was fair enough, I felt. I wasn't going to compete with Ford on the descriptive aspects of the autopsy. We all had good eyes, and we all should be seeing the same things. It was no good going to court later and arguing about what each of us thought we saw. "I want a single autopsy protocol," I insisted, "Interpretation of what we see is a different matter and can come later, but at least let's all have the same set of findings as a baseline." The others agreed to that, because I told the attorney general that I wasn't prepared to stick around and then accept the notes that Ford was busy writing—how did I know what he was writing?

Anyway, we carried on amicably and got all through with the autopsy, including the removal of the veins from the arm. The veins showed plenty of connecting channels, a point which came up at the trial. The liver was full of cancer deposits; there was a thrombus—a blood-clot which had formed during life—in the main vein of the trunk—the inferior *vena cava*. This came almost up to the level of the heart, but there was no detachment or embolism of this clot, no fragments which might have broken off and suddenly caused death by being carried through the circulation to get stuck in the lungs. If that had happened, then we would have had to concede that tissue embolism was a possible cause of death, and that the injection of air was a coincidental event.

But there was nothing that had suddenly gone wrong—there might have been the next day, or the day after that, but there was nothing on that fatal day. As I testified, in my opinion there was no competing cause of death that might have made Mrs. Borroto suddenly expire that particular morning, had she not been injected with air. Of course, due to the embalming and exhumation delay, there was no hope of making a positive diagnosis of air embolism, which is not always easy even in a fresh body. Still, we had Sander's admission that he had injected her.

The trial came along at the end of February and lasted into March. What a circus it was—every press reporter in the country seemed to be there, and a number of foreign ones as well. The event had international notoriety, just like the van Rie case ten years later. It was billed as " 'The Mercy Killing Trial': test case for euthanasia," but it was nothing of the sort. Abbie Borroto never asked to be done away with; she lay quietly in her hospital bed, bothering no one. Yet the media turned the whole affair into a great debate about ethics versus the law. The courtroom was full of society women from New England and elsewhere—sitting there in their big hats, all agog for sensation. I spoke to Fanny Hurst, who was there with her quiet husband in tow. "You just don't understand the issues," I said, "This has nothing to do with euthanasia."

But by this time Sander had decided to change his story after all. He now claimed that Mrs. Borroto had been dead when he had put the needle into her arm. So apparently he was doing something idiotic, injecting air into a dead body! He explained this by saying he wanted to make sure she was dead, so she wouldn't wake up to any more pain.

Well then, the case came to trial. I was staying in a hotel in Manchester, waiting to testify. The place was swarming with newspapermen, all cracking bad jokes about the case. At breakfast, you could hear them ribbing each other. "Have you had your injection today, Joe?" . . . "Have you had your air this morning, Jack?" I kept very quiet. I didn't talk to anyone there, just sat and listened to all this hysteria that was sweeping the town. Ralph Miller, the pathologist at Dartmouth, and I understood the main issue well enough—if she had been alive, Sander had killed her; if she had already died, then he hadn't.

I took the stand for the prosecution, and on the hypothetical question I said, "If this woman was alive and Doctor Sander injected air into her veins—as he said he did—until she died, obviously the cause of death was air embolism, and nothing else in the autopsy provided a competitive cause of death against air embolism, which by exclusion would therefore have to be given precedence as the cause of death."

I had a blackboard in court and drew diagrams to explain air embolism to the jury. I told them air pushed into a vein in the arm can travel through the blood stream until it reached the right side of the heart, and then the pulmonary artery in the lung. At a certain critical volume of air—which is different for various people and in different circumstances—the injected air forms bubbles and froth in the heart which results in an air lock (the air also is suddenly released through the lungs to form bubbles in other vital organs, especially the brain). The press published dozens of sketches of the trial and the witnesses, as cameras were not permitted in the courtroom, and one drawing showed me at the blackboard.

In cross-examination, the defense asked me, "Doctor Helpern, if she was dead, then he couldn't have killed her, could he?"— which I had already admitted in direct testimony. Thus, the jury had the option of believing Sander's second story, which was put forth after he was indicted. I had already left them that option. I didn't want to try to prove to them that I could tell whether she was dead or alive—the only one who knew that was Dr. Sander. You couldn't tell from reading the chart whether or not she was dead, except for the admission which was retracted before the trial.

But when Ford got up to testify, he said he could tell that she was dead from the chart! Then we had a big dispute about the condition of the veins. Ford asserted that they were so blocked up with bloodclot that no air could have got through them. Phinney, the prosecution counsel, hammered at him for hours, and he weakened enough to admit that air could have pushed past the clots under pressure—which seemed pretty self-evident, considering the embalming fluid had got through quite successfully in preparation for the funeral.

Then we had a big argument about how much air was needed to kill a human being. Ford stated categorically that it required 200-300 cc. and went into long explanations about experiments on animals. I said honestly that I just didn't know—and I suspected that no one else knew either, because everyone was different and you couldn't lay down such rules like that. There was grave danger in trying to transfer animal results to the human situation, especially as dogs, rabbits, horses, and other animals are much more resistant to air than humans.

"How long would it take for death to ensue?" I was asked. [It would ensue] "very rapidly—maybe within seconds, or maybe a minute or two. In any event, it is a rapid type of death."

"Could forty cubic centimeters of air cause death?"

"Yes, in some persons, especially if it was injected rapidly."

"Is forty cubic centimeters a substantial amount in your opinion, Doctor Helpern?"

I said it was—and if Mrs. Borroto had been alive, then the proof of it having been a substantial amount is self-evident, for it had succeeded in killing her.

Sander was saying that he saw no sign of life in Abbie Borroto when he injected her—and he brought in another physician, Dr. Albert Snay, to back him up on this, though yet another doctor, Harold King, testified that Sander told him that "he had given heavy doses of drugs, followed half an hour later by injection of air."

I said in my testimony that these massive doses of Demerol and

Pantopon may well have depressed the patient's respiration and pulse to a point where she looked lifeless. I told them of my examination and dissection of the veins and subsequent microscopic examination, which showed that the veins were not so obstructed that an air embolus would not have passed through them—and that was really all I wanted to say for the benefit of the jury.

We had put before them the commonsense facts and the questions arising out of the facts. Was Mrs. Borroto alive at the time—did she coincidentally die of her long-standing cancer at that time—or did the air injection kill her?

Well, they brought in a verdict of "not guilty," and the court and the town of Manchester went wild for the heroic Hermann Sander, who no doubt was a good doctor and did a lot of good for his patients. The jury could have founded that verdict just as well on what I had said on the stand, for I made it clear that if she was dead, he had committed no crime. I never maintained anything to the contrary from the autopsy findings, but who in heaven's name really knew what happened except Dr. Sander himself? And he had written down on the chart what had happened, before he declared she was already dead, after he was indicted; yet they found him not guilty, which is the jury's right.

You should have seen the newspapers after the verdict. The Sander case is still referred to as an example of a "mercy killing," but as far as I'm concerned it was nothing of the kind.

It did a lot of harm, that trial. Our serologist at the Medical Examiner's Office, Dr. Al Wiener (just recently deceased) told me that some time after this, a woman was sent to his laboratory for a blood grouping test in a disputed paternity proceeding. When he approached her with the syringe to take the sample, she backed off in fear, crying, "You're not going to inject me with air, are you, Doctor?"

The subject of "mercy killings" reared its head more than once in my professional career. The next time I became involved was in 1972. As in the Sander case, a terminal cancer patient, a doctor, a nurse, and a syringe were all involved.

A fifty-nine-year-old patient, Eugene Bauer, was admitted for the second time to the Nassau County Medical Center in East Meadow, Long Island, with a malignant growth of the throat, which had extended to involve the adjacent structures, including a carotid artery. He was in the hospital just five days, and then he died. Mr. Bauer was undoubtedly in the terminal stages of his disease, moribund and unconscious. However, he was so comatose as to be unaware of anything at all, so his alleged disposal could again hardly be called a "mercy killing" in the accepted sense of the words.

On December 4 it was charged that another doctor, surgical resident Vincent Montemerano, put a syringe into a vein in the arm of Eugene Bauer and injected a solution of potassium chloride, a chemical which has a powerful and immediate action on the heart muscle. If a sufficient amount is given, the heart stops almost immediately.

Nothing further happened for six months; then Montemerano decided to tell his surgical chief, Dr. Anthony DiBenedetto, what he had done.

DiBenedetto later testified that Montemerano had told him that on the day of Bauer's death, he had injected him with 35 millilitres of potassium chloride solution, which is a large and lethal dose of potassium, and in my opinion, more than adequate to cause cardiac arrest and death. In the Medical Examiner's Office in New York City there are documented suicides in which this amount was self-injected.

Information reached the district attorney and a grand jury was convened, which indicted the resident for wilful murder. Again there was a great hue and cry in the press about "euthanasia" and "mercy killing," just as there had been when the Sander case broke.

Though the body had been buried for six months—much longer than Abbie Borroto in the Sander case—it was exhumed and an autopsy was carried out by the Nassau County medical examiner, Dr. Leslie Lukash. He found an extensive cancer of the mouth ulcerating through the skin of the neck, a terminal pneumonia, some arteriosclerosis, and a few small pulmonary emboli—blood clots in the vessels of the lungs. However, he didn't consider that these accounted for the sudden nature of the death, and with a history of an injection of 35 ml. of potassium chloride containing 70 milli-equivalents, he said that he believed that the injection was the immediate reason for the death.

The defense called Dr. Alfred Angrist, Chairman Emeritus of

Pathology at the Albert Einstein College of Medicine in New York City, who reviewed Lukash's autopsy and said that he believed that the cancer killed Eugene Bauer, not any injection of potassium.

So we had the familiar situation of one expert saying one thing and another expert saying the opposite. The prosecution then called me in to look over the autopsy findings and the general medical aspects of the case. The three pathologists— Leslie Lukash, Alfred Angrist, and myself—were all quite agreed on the physical findings of the autopsy, but it was in the interpretation that two of us differed from the third.

As I've said so often throughout these pages, you simply can't take the autopsy findings in isolation—they tell you just so much. The circumstances and every other little bit of surrounding information then become vital. As in the case of Hermann Sander, the fact that, according to testimony, the doctor *admitted* injecting something was central to the whole issue, and the autopsy was only of value in deciding the validity of the competing causes of death.

Yes, Bauer had an advanced disease which was going to kill him fairly soon anyway—but I couldn't as a medical expert get away from the fact that Dr. DiBenedetto had testified that Montemerano had admitted giving Bauer a large potassium injection. Now Dr. DiBenedetto was reluctant to testify against his resident, but he felt morally bound to do so. He said unequivocally that Montemerano had told him that he had given his patient 35 ml. of 70 milli-equivalents of potassium, a precise statement that seemed to be incontrovertible. Yet the practical nurse, Clara Miles, testified that she prepared a 5 ml. syringe of potassium solution for Dr. Montemerano and that she saw him inject this into veins at the crook of the elbow. She didn't seem too sure of the size of syringe, as far as I recollect, but the defense maintained it was 5 ml., even though the surgical resident himself evidently had told his boss that it was 35 ml.— seven times that amount!

Now Dr. Angrist, the retired pathologist, told the court that he believed that the pulmonary clots were the immediate cause of death, combined with the advanced cancer of the pharynx. He further maintained that neither 5 ml. nor 35 ml. of potassium chloride would have killed the patient, an opinion I found very hard to accept. Angrist further said that it would be unique and unusual if Montemerano had been able to find a vein in the arm to inject into, because they would all be collapsed due to low blood pressure.

Well, members of the jury have a perfect right to listen to all opinions and make their choice. I went on the stand and testified that if the injection *had been* 35 ml., then it would have been lethal and would have been the cause of death without any doubt, and that the other conditions found at the autopsy could not compete with it as the cause of death. As in the trial in New Hampshire years before, I said to the court, "You can't overlook what Dr. DiBenedetto said in his testimony. He was told by his resident that he injected 35 ml. Only Dr. Montemerano knew if the patient was alive or dead when he gave him that injection—and only he knew exactly what he injected into him." The point which I would like to make in this discussion is that the medical expert cannot, like the jury, exclude unequivocal evidence in arriving at an opinion. He is an advisor to the court and cannot select or discard what clearly is in evidence.

As in the case of Mrs. Borroto, if Bauer had been dead already, the injection couldn't have killed him—but in either case, what on earth was the point of injecting a *dead* person?

But as I said, it is entirely the prerogative of the members of the jury to think what they like of the evidence—and to draw another close parallel with the Sander case, they acquitted Dr. Montemerano without much hesitation, the main plank in the defense's case being the uncertain recollection of the practical nurse concerning the amount of the injection that was given. They concluded that the patient was already dead when the potassium was administered, which was a remarkable coincidence, I thought, just as it had been in New Hampshire twenty-two years earlier.

After the trial, chief defense counsel J. Russel Klune prevented Dr. Montemerano from answering a question at a press conference. "Dr. DiBenedetto must have been confused over my client's confession," he said, "We're not here to discuss the trial or euthanasia." I guess he was right there, for this wasn't euthanasia in any case, but DiBenedetto's testimony was not at all confused.

Euthanasia does occur now and then under diverse circumstances, but I have seen very few "mercy killings" that arose out of true compassion. For instance, I remember a middle-aged police officer who had an operable cancer of the large bowel that was resected in the hospital. He recovered from surgery and was sent home to convalesce. He had done reasonably well and had no complaints, yet his daughter got hold of his police service revolver and shot him dead while he lay in bed. She said she couldn't stand to see him suffer, but I felt that it was far more likely that she didn't look forward to nursing him for a long time ahead. She was never prosecuted, yet that case seemed to have far less basis for doubt than either the Sander or the Montemerano affairs.

The two cases I've described had marked similarities, but a much more recent case with similar overtones never came to trial, and I feel I was instrumental in keeping this from happening, by pointing out its uncertainties on medical grounds.

It all occurred very recently, just east of New York City in Nassau County, Long Island, where the Montemerano affair had taken place. The poor girl whose death was the central issue was sixteen-year-old Maryjane Dahl, an honors student at Newfield High School in Selden, Long Island, where she lived with her aunt, Mrs. Jane Sheehan.

On October 25, 1975, Maryjane was admitted to Nassau Hospital, seriously ill with Hodgkin's disease (a low-grade type of malignancy affecting the lymph glands), meningitis, and kidney failure. She was given dialysis for her kidney failure and placed on a mechanical respirator, her only means of breathing. On November 2, during the day, she suffered a cardiac arrest in the hospital's intensive care unit, and that night, at a quarter-past nine, she died. Thus far, there was nothing unusual or suspicious about these circumstances, and the entire story depicted the tragic decline of a young girl with an inevitably fatal outcome.

But—and it was a very disturbing "but" to the hospital—at 9:15 that night, just as visitors were leaving the intensive care unit, an alarm sounded that immediately alerted the medical and nursing staff that something was wrong with the mechanical respirator. When they hurried to the bedside, they found that the electric power that fed the machine—the only lifeline for Maryjane—had been switched off, and the electric cord-plug pulled from its socket on the wall. When they examined the girl, she was already dead, and their attempts to revive her were fruitless.

Now, moments before the alarm sounded, Maryjane's mother, Mrs. Janet Dahl Sarvent of Upper Nyack, New York, and the aunt, Mrs. Sheehan, had left the bedside after visiting the unconscious girl. In the circumstances, the hospital authorities had no choice but to report the matter to the police and the medical examiner. Dr. Leslie Lukash, the same person who had conducted the autopsy on the potassium chloride injection death in the Montemerano case, was again the medical examiner here. Dr. Lukash spent two weeks looking into the medical aspects of Maryjane Dahl's death and eventually arrived at the conclusion that she had died from "respiratory failure and cardiac arrest resulting from the disconnection of the respirator." He further classified the death as—*homicidal*.

The ball was now passed to Nassau County District Attorney Dennis Dillon. He was in the hot seat over the decision on whether or not to present the matter to a grand jury. The whole case rested entirely on the degree of medical certainty with which the classification and cause of death could be explained, and he wanted further opinions on the matter, rather than relying on the single positive declaration of the medical examiner, because the mother and aunt strenuously denied any tampering with the power supply.

Mr. Dillon asked me to come and give my views in this matter, and I went through all the material available to assist them in this difficult and delicate problem. Here were an apparently devoted mother and aunt stoutly denying any part in turning off the respirator. In addition, the emotional pressures on them must have been very punishing, for they had seen their girl hopelessly ill after suffering a heart attack earlier that same day.

Because of her condition, they had requested that Maryjane be taken off the artificial kidney. I told the district attorney this and went on to say in my report, "I note also that the relatives were opposed to any expansion of treatment of the patient." In other words, though they weren't advocating any active measures to terminate Maryjane's suffering, they did not want further treatment to pointlessly prolong the short time that was left of her life. As an ancient medical aphorism puts it, "That shalt not kill but thou needst not officiously strive to keep alive."

But *did* the power failure actually kill her? My report had to explore the options. It is perfectly *possible* that the turning off of the respirator and the pulling of the plug hastened the death of the deceased, but considering the nature of the girl's illnesses, one cannot exclude the other *possibility*: that the deceased could have died while in the respirator, even if the machine had not been turned off.

"In any case," I continued, "I would not be willing to state with certainty beyond a reasonable doubt, or even with reasonable certainty, that the turning off of the machine shortened the deceased's life."

I wasn't there as a witness for the prosecution or the defense, as there was no legal contest at that stage, so I wasn't in the slightest way biased toward any particular opinion. I try not to be prejudiced, even in the most contentious of criminal trials, but I want to emphasize that, in stating my opinion in the Maryjane Dahl death, I was absolutely neutral, subject to no outside pressure. The issue was the degree of certainty with which an opinion can be expressed; I just wanted to come as near to the truth as it was possible to come with the available facts.

The district attorney also asked the opinion of Dr. Francis Moore, former deputy medical examiner of Nassau County, and he said the same thing—that you couldn't tell one way or the other. There was no possibility of proving that she wouldn't have died at that time if the machine had continued working normally, keeping in mind that this was a dying girl, who at noon that same day had suffered a heart stoppage and was liable to have another at any time.

Well, Leslie Lukash was away at that time, but he made a statement. He said quite properly that he had carried out his duties and obligations as medical examiner and that his opinion was as stated previously—death was due to the power cut; therefore, if the power cut had been the deliberate act of a human being, it was homicide.

Dillon, the district attorney, held a news conference in his office in Mineola on November 28. The place was packed, as this kind of case is God-given copy to the media, as had been proved by both the Hermann Sander and the Montemerano cases.

Dillon told the reporters, "The investigation has been unable to provide adequate supportive evidence of the medical examiner's opinion, to establish beyond a reasonable doubt that the cause of death was the disconnecting of the respirator. The case is being closed because the evidence does not justify a presentation to a grand jury." As the mother afterward said publicly, "We are innocent, and now the whole world knows we're innocent. This was the passing away of my only child, and I'm glad that the district attorney found that we told the truth."

Chapter 14

Accidental Death

Much of a medical examiner's routine work is retrospective in nature—by that, I mean that he comes into the picture after a death has occurred. Often, the work he does assists law enforcement agencies in both the investigation and the prosecution of crime. Other times, it is his job to provide information to reconstruct some suicidal or accidental death. Yet on other occasions—and these are the most numerous—his function is to diagnose, in retrospect, the type of natural disease that killed a person. Quite often, it is not crime, but matters of compensation and insurance that require his expert delving into a case.

All these functions have sometimes made both laymen and other doctors think that a medical examiner or forensic pathologist is merely the man who comes along to clear up the mess after a fatality—a kind of medico-legal garbage disposal man.

This isn't really an accurate or fair picture of what our profession can—and does—do for the community.

During our work, we constantly come across facts and observations that are constructive, not retrospective, in terms of the public health—and I use the term public health in the broadest sense, for not only do we point out to the appropriate authority any disease hazard to the community, but we frequently are able to pinpoint areas of considerable danger both to specific groups of people and to the community at large.

There are many examples of this, widely diverse in nature. Take the malaria I came across in 1933, for instance. That had a very real relevance for a certain section of the public—for heroin addicts are part of the community and deserve protection. If that incipient epidemic had gone undiagnosed and unchecked, other states might have received a spillover into their communities that would not have amused them at all.

Another area that concerned us in the New York Chief Medical Examiner's Office was one that had the highly emotional aspect of accidental deaths in children as its basis. Back in 1959, I became very worried about the number of infants and small children who were said to have suffocated as a result of the thin plastic film of polyethylene bags being put over their faces. At that time, this new wrapping substance was really coming into extensive use and was suspected of constituting a new environmental hazard. We had a meeting of the Department of Health in New York City to discuss the matter with representatives of the plastics industry. A month later, I called a further meeting at our Office, to which a large number of medical examiners from all over the United States were invited by telegram to discuss the matter with health officials and with Mr. William T. Cruse, vice president of the Society of the Plastics Industry. As it turned out, the meeting, though agreeing that plastic bag deaths did occur, felt strongly that the accident was being heavily overdiagnosed and that the majority of the deaths were really "crib deaths" due to natural disease. The fact that a cover of polyethylene happened to be on the pillow or mattress was mistakenly being taken to mean that suffocation was the reason for the death. We produced a fifty-seven-page report of this meeting, but we had to make our recommendations carefully and decided that much of our discussion could not be generally released to the public. Although we felt that most of the so-called plastic film deaths were not genuine, we could not say so too loudly, as there were undoubtedly a number that *were* due to this substance, though usually in different circumstances, such as where a child out of the crib death age group might have pulled a bag down over its head.

The plastics industry and the various pediatric and public health agencies conducted an energetic campaign in the media to publicize the dangers. The medical examiners felt strongly that a number of homicides were being committed in this fashion, and we cautioned strongly that such deaths should be taken to be homicidal until proved to be otherwise. The discussion also increased the awareness of the intrinsic problems of the crib death syndrome, which in 1959 was only beginning to attract the interest that it now commands.

When talking of situations where a medical examiner has made some really worthwhile contribution to public safety, I think that the one that gave me the most personal satisfaction was the exposure of a dangerous problem in the fifties. It reached almost epidemic proportions in New York—and, as it turned out, in many other places as well.

One case can serve to illustrate this hazard, as the same circumstances were repeated time and time again. A well-to-do businesswoman from South America lived in an attractive apartment over on the West Side. It was a big flat, with large rooms and a foyer. She exported clothing to Venezuela and Colombia and spent part of her time in South America, the rest here in Manhattan.

One Saturday, she went out about noon. On the way out, she called on the superintendent of the apartments to say that her gas flame refrigerator seemed to have a funny odor and would he get it checked? Now that idiot, not realizing the urgent nature of such a complaint, merely rang up the repair company and did nothing more to check that they actually came to fix it. The woman arrived home at nine that evening; the elevator man let her off at the ninth floor. The next day some friends of hers failed to get any reply when they telephoned her, and eventually an alarm was raised. The police found her dead in bed, smeared with blood. Reasonably enough, they treated it as a homicide.

It was only when we came from the Medical Examiner's Office and examined the scene that the true nature of the case was discovered. The refrigerator had been giving off carbon monoxide, and the woman gradually became affected. The gas caused her to vomit and to be bowel-incontinent. She must have staggered to the bathroom to try to clean up, then fell with a glass pitcher in her hand and cut herself, bleeding profusely. Almost overcome, she managed to crawl back into bed to die. It was almost like a Greek tragedy—if someone had checked that the refrigerator repair men had come, or if someone had happened by and rescued her—but all these "ifs" just didn't happen—with fatal results.

This case was just one of a great number—many of them fatal and some pretty near misses. The whole danger arose from a variety of faulty domestic appliances utilizing either illuminating gas or bottled gas. The common factor was the production of deadly carbon monoxide gas fumes.

Normally, domestic gas appliances burn the fuel completely to produce carbon *dioxide*, as well as other end-products, but none of these is particularly dangerous unless there is absolutely no ventilation over a prolonged period. However, when a fuel is burnt improperly, then the incomplete combustion products will include carbon *monoxide*, which is very dangerous because it has the power to combine with the hemoglobin of the blood, thus preventing oxygen from being circulated to the tissues. This causes a progressive poisoning that will end in death if unchecked. Unfortunately, carbon monoxide has two hundred times the affinity for hemoglobin that oxygen possesses, so a relatively low concentration in the air can soon build up to fatal levels.

Raw illuminating gas, as piped by the gas company, has a variable amount of carbon monoxide already in it, less now than years ago, due to mixing it with and replacing it by natural gas, which does not contain carbon monoxide. Whatever fuel is used will produce carbon monoxide if the flame is incorrectly adjusted, if there is restriction of the supply of air, or if the flame impinges on a cold metal surface, which retards the full conversion of fuel to carbon dioxide.

In the Medical Examiner's Office, we started seeing deaths from this cause as far back as 1937. In that year there were two fatal incidents, both involving newly-married couples who were found dead in their bedrooms.

In the following years, the numbers began to increase. There were thirty-nine deaths in twenty-eight separate incidents in New York City between 1944 and 1950. There were far more non-fatal cases, which were the lucky ones in which faulty appliances were detected before fatal levels of carbon monoxide accumulated. In 1950, for instance, there were twenty-one incidents involving fifty people.

The same kind of trouble was being reported elsewhere throughout the country. In 1951, I became very concerned with the upward turn these deaths were taking and reported the matter urgently to the New York City Health Department. Assistant Commissioner Jerome B. Trichter, in charge of the Division of Environmental Sanitation, and I wrote some articles for the medical press on the matter, and the direct result of our combined representations to the city authorities was an ambitious program set in motion during 1951.

On the first day of May in that year, a Carbon Monoxide Inspection Program was launched by the Health Department. One hundred health inspectors were assigned to the project— each was given special training in the examination of gas appliances and in the use of instruments to detect the poisonous gas. They were equipped with a carbon monoxide indicator and other testing apparatus. The targets were ninety-four buildings, in each of which from two to six cases of accidental carbon monoxide poisoning had occurred; also, the half million gas-flame refrigerators in New York City were to be inspected, especially the 85,000 water-cooled models, which were particularly dangerous.

After four months of this program, 22,000 apartments had been visited and in them 11,000 faulty appliances found which were either leaking raw gas or had some other dangerous defect. In other words, one out of two apartments had a potentially lethal bit of equipment standing in the kitchen. There were 8,000 faulty gas cooking ranges and 2,140 defective refrigerators.

So bad were 1,087 pieces of equipment, that they had to be sealed off immediately in order to avert any possible hazard. A survey of another 1,075 gas-flame iceboxes showed that no less than 568—over half—were in bad repair and were generating carbon monoxide.

This program, initiated by the work of the Office of Chief Medical Examiner, achieved two things. First, within four months, defects in thousands of pieces of gas-burning equipment were eliminated, and second, a dangerous situation for the occupants of those apartments was averted. In many instances, the health inspectors actually came face to face with people suffering from carbon monoxide poisoning. When they knocked on the door and were admitted, not infrequently their training and experience led them to suspect that the occupants were already suffering the effects of the gas. In one instance, they actually took a blood sample from a woman and found that she already had 16 percent saturation of her blood with carbon monoxide, enough to give the early symptoms of headache, nausea, and sickness. She might have died if they had not come along, and this applied to a number of other cases.

I used to do autopsies not only on the victims of these deaths but on the iceboxes as well! I became quite proficient at taking them apart and demonstrating that they were defective. The gas flame often changed color when it was not burning properly, and one could then find that the flame was impinging on the edge of the flue, instead of being centered directly up the tube. Then the chimney might be blocked by heavy deposits of soot— this could block the flue and prevent proper burning—and sometimes a lump of soot would fall down the flue and partially block the gas jet. Restriction of access of air to the base of the box and falling gas pressure in the piped supply both contributed to this highly dangerous state. It was this sort of information and demonstration of the defect in actual equipment that enabled the Health Department to take such prompt and effective action. I feel that here was a major occasion when an agency such as our Office, mainly concerned with death, actually helped the living by pointing out a real hazard in the community. There are many citizens of New York alive today who would have died if our Office had not brought this matter to the attention of the proper authorities.

I strongly urged the authorities to get the manufacturers of these refrigerators to modify their design, as thousands of these models were being sold in the United States and many thousands more being exported all over the world—each one as potentially lethal as a bomb.

It's still happening, of course. In the summer of 1975, we read of a mysterious incident in France, where a whole family of four Britons was found dead in a Volkswagen camper vehicle. I had alerted my friends in the U.K. to the dangers of the refrigerators in closed spaces like campers, boats, and trailers and sure enough, a one-cubic foot icebox fueled with bottled butane turned out to be the culprit. The diagnosis of unlabeled cases of carbon monoxide poisoning is so often missed; the doctor, not thinking for a moment of carbon monoxide, comes up with the most way-out diagnoses, but rarely the correct one. The treatment is so simple: remove the victims from the atmosphere of the gas. Unfortunately, though, if a survivor has been exposed for a long time, there is the risk of permanent brain damage, with both nervous and psychological aftereffects.

By no means are all carbon monoxide poisonings due to faulty refrigerators or other gas appliances. Anything burning incompletely will generate this gas as in a house or room fire. It is not the reduced oxygen supply but the inhaled carbon monoxide that causes people to die in apartment house conflagrations.

A particular incident is vivid in my memory, mainly because it was an excellent example of how the whole thing can be missed, especially by doctors, who seem to prefer the more unlikely diagnoses to the obvious.

We had a case which involved the family of a woman, the mother of seven children, whose husband was in jail. She was Puerto Rican, in pretty poor circumstances, but she was good to her children and did all she could for them. She lived in a little tenement flat over on the Lower West Side, and she had a boyfriend who was enamored of her.

It was cold, and she kept the apartment warm for the children by heating up a lot of kettles on the stove. The trouble was that a gas flame impinging on a large relatively cold metal surface like the bottom of large kettles produces an appreciable quantity of carbon monoxide all the time.

At this time the woman was suffering badly from headaches during the daytime, which was quite understandable as this is the regular first symptom of carbon monoxide poisoning. She went to a clinic, where they told her she had sinusitis. They gave her a shot of penicillin and she set off for home, and as she had been out of the house for some time in the fresh air, her headache got better. In the afternoon she was back at home, and when the boyfriend came to visit, she told him she had her headache back again, and he said he would go to the store to get some more penicillin. But they told him he couldn't have any more without a prescription, and he took back a package of aspirin instead.

He left the tenement later, and the woman and her children went to bed, the kettles still on the stove for warmth.

She remembered later that one of the children woke her up

during the night and said, "Mama, I've got a terrible headache." The child was also nauseated, and the mother got out of bed to look after her. This was the last thing she remembered as she collapsed on the floor, the box of aspirin beside her.

If her boyfriend had not been so devoted, they would all have died. He returned in the morning to see how her "sinus headache" was, but when he reached the apartment door, he heard a lot of moaning from the inside.

He broke in immediately and found six children unconscious, one dead, and the mother lying on the floor.

He called an ambulance, and they were taken to the hospital. A rather obtuse ambulance doctor tested their necks and found them stiff—a constant sign in carbon monoxide poisoning, due to increased muscle reflexes. However, he diagnosed "meningitis"—though how the hell he could imagine eight simultaneous cases of meningitis in almost identical condition, I just don't know. The children were taken to one hospital and the mother to a different one, where she was diagnosed as having "attempted suicidal poisoning" after trying to kill all her children!

I was getting out of the shower after being in the autopsy room at the Office when a clerk said to me, "You know, Doctor Helpern, they just reported six cases of coma and one child dead—they're calling them meningitis, but don't you think this sounds like carbon monoxide?" Even the clerks in the M. E. Office had better intuition than the doctors. "Yes, it sounds as if you might be right," I answered, and I went right over to our mortuary where the dead child was taken, quite near the hospital which had admitted the other children. The body was a dusky pink, the child being a dark-skinned Puerto Rican, but the telltale color was easily apparent. We opened the body and a blood sample showed 40 percent carbon monoxide—this one had died because it had vomited and blocked its air passages.

I had a difficult time convincing the police about the rest of the family. They said, "If a clinician says it's meningitis, then it's meningitis."

"What the devil!" I said, "They're all carbon monoxide poisoning!" But if I had not had the dead baby to prove it, they wouldn't have believed me, and they would have waited for the mother to recover consciousness to slap a homicide charge on her.

Then I called up the hospital and spoke to a young woman resident. "Do me a favor," I said, "Tell me the diagnosis on those six children you've got there."

She replied, "Well, they came in with a diagnosis of meningitis, but now we think they're tuberculous meningitis!"

I nearly fell off my chair at this, but I managed to ask her, "Have you ever seen six or seven cases of tuberculous meningitis developing simultaneously overnight in one family?" I told her, facetiously, "If you report these, you'll get the Nobel Prize for medicine—you won't ever have to do anything else to become famous!" I called up another intern at the hospital to ask how the children were getting along. "Oh, they're getting better," she said. "Isn't that a little peculiar, if they're supposed to have tuberculous meningitis?" I asked. "If I were you—and I'm intruding, I know—I've got no authority over live patients—but do me a favor, stop doing lumbar taps, and get some blood for a carbon monoxide analysis, will you?" For this had never been done, in spite of the obvious indications.

The mother woke up in another hospital and told them what had happened. The boyfriend should have been awarded a Carnegie Medal, for he saved their lives. But it goes to show how lack of experience and common sense can lead one astray—they were all incorrectly diagnosed as "sinusitis," "meningitis," "tuberculosis," and then "attempted suicide," but nobody, except my clerk, had any idea as to the real answer.

Almost the same thing happened in Brooklyn, where a mother was found unconscious in a house, with one dead child and five other children in coma from "starvation." It was all over the newspapers for a day, and the mother would possibly have faced a homicide charge—until our Office discovered that they all had carbon monoxide poisoning from a broken flue backing monoxide into the apartment. These events were happening all the time—and not only in New York.

I remember the case of a Spanish-speaking woman down in Florida who was found unconscious in a wooden tenement flat. She was erroneously assumed to be a case of acute brain injury and promptly taken to surgery, where burr holes were drilled in her skull to look for a nonexistent blood clot. She died, and at autopsy the softening of the basal ganglia of the brain, typical of prolonged exposure to monoxide, was found. Only then was her refrigerator checked and found to be discharging a thousand parts per million of carbon monoxide into the atmosphere of the kitchen. The gas company denied all responsibility: they said it was working properly when they last checked it. The defects in these boxes were not always obvious, but we created such a fuss about this problem in the early fifties that the design was altered and the manufacturers withdrew the worst types. But cases still crop up, especially where the boxes are not maintained properly.

In the lobby of the new building for our Office of Chief Medical Examiner, I had the architect, Ben Moskowitz, place an inscription in Latin on the marble wall. It was given to me by my friend in Durban, South Africa, Dean Okkie Gordon of the medical school in Natal. Its origin is lost in the mists of time, but it says:

> TACEAT COLLOQUIA. EFFUGIAT RISUS.
> HIC LOCUS EST UBI MORS GAUDET
> SUCCURRERE VITAE.

Translated, this means, "Let conversation cease. Let laughter flee. This is the place where death delights to help the living." Legal medicine does just that—as it has in the case of the carbon monoxide deaths.

Below, Robert Irwin, in white, being led into police headquarters after the Easter Sunday slaying of his girl friend and her family in 1937. (*N.Y. Daily News Photo*) On the facing page, Massachusetts lawyer John Franklin Noxon, Jr., with cane, walks down steps of courthouse after his arrest for the slaying of his mongoloid child in 1943. (*N.Y. Daily News Photo*)

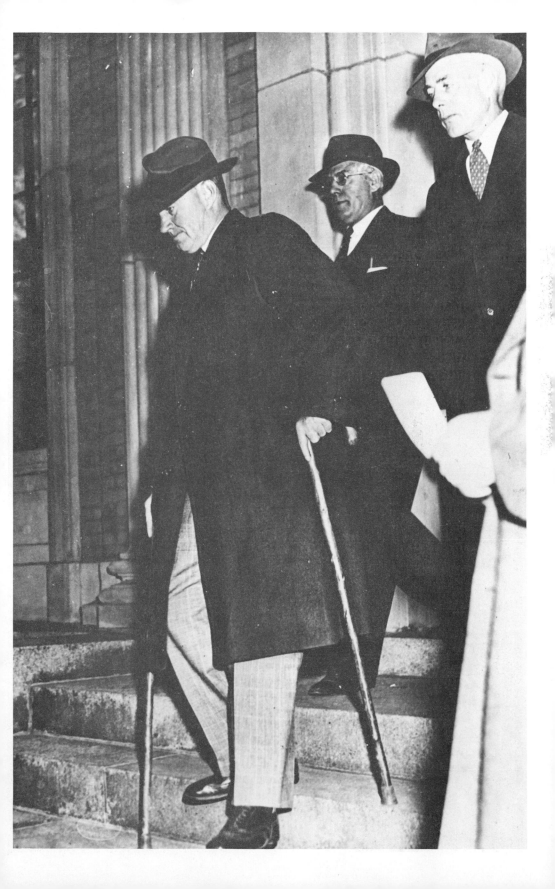

The mystery surrounding the death of Texas heiress Joan Robinson Hill has not yet been resolved.   Bottom, Joan Hill in 1961.   Facing page, top, Joan Hill with her father, oil millionaire Ash Robinson.   Facing page, bottom, Joan Hill with her husband, John. (*All Copyright © The Houston Post Company*)

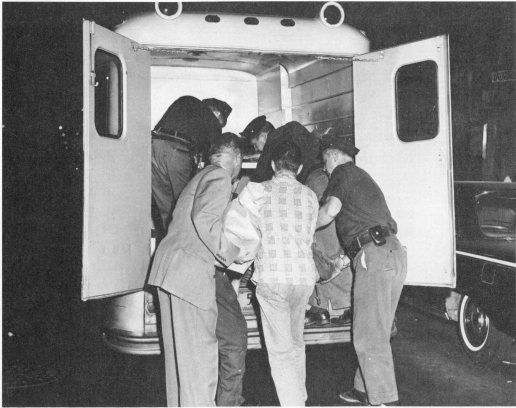

The Career Girls Murders created a furor on Manhattan's fashionable East Side. Facing page, top, the bloody bedroom of Janice Wiley. Facing page, bottom, police carry one of the murdered young women into an ambulance wagon. The two victims: above, Emily Hoffert; below, Janice Wylie. (*N.Y. Daily News Photos*)

CRIMMINS CRIES:
SHE DIDN'T DO IT

DA Hints at Custody Motive

**He Stands
At Wife's
Side . . .**

Edmund Crimmins escorts his wife into Queens Supreme Court for trial in which Mrs. Crimmins, a redhaired former cocktail waitress, is accused of killing her daughter, Alice Marie, 4. Crimmins took stand and denied that he or his wife killed Alice Marie or her brother, Edmund Jr. 5. Crimmins was asked: "Do you know anything about the death of your children?" "No," answered Crimmins. "Did you kill your children?" "No, sir, and neither did my wife."

Story on page 3

★

DAILY NEWS
NEW YORK'S PICTURE NEWSPAPER ®

10¢

Vol. 49. No. 280   New York, N.Y. 10017, Thursday, May 16, 1968*   WEATHER: Sunny, warm, more humid.

ALICE SOBS
AT DEATH STORY

Helpern: Girl Was Strangled

—Story on Page 3

POLICE   DO

FINAL DAILY NEWS 8¢
NEW YORK'S PICTURE NEWSPAPER ®

Boy Friend Quotes Alice:

'FORGIVE ME; I KILLED HER!'

She Screams: 'How Could You?'

He Says She Opened Heart During Tryst

Joseph Rorech (left), a Huntington, L.I. builder and father of seven children, leaves Queens County Court after his bombshell testimony in the Alice Crimmins murder trial yesterday. He electrified the packed courtroom by testifying that accused daughter-slayer Alice Crimmins told him during a motel tryst that she had killed her daughter. Later, at a dinner date, he said Alice started crying and told him: "There's no reason for them to be killed. It was senseless. The reason had been eliminated."

Story on page 3

FINAL DAILY NEWS 10¢
NEW YORK'S PICTURE NEWSPAPER ®

WINDOW WOMAN ACCUSES ALICE

'You Liar! You Liar!' Screams Raging Mother of Slain Girl

The Crimmins Trial dominated headlines in May 1968.
(*N.Y. Daily News Photos*)

FINAL **DAILY NEWS** **10¢**

NEW YORK'S PICTURE NEWSPAPER ®

Vol. 49. No. 287   New York, N.Y. 10017, Friday, May 24, 1968   WEATHER: Occasional rain, cool.

ALICE TELLS OF LOVE AFFAIRS

Denies She Confessed Slaying

FINAL **DAILY NEWS** **8¢**

NEW YORK'S PICTURE NEWSPAPER ®

Vol. 49. No. 290   New York, N.Y. 10017, Tuesday, May 28, 1968   WEATHER: Occasional rain, windy, mild.

12 MEN RULE ALICE IS GUILTY

She Collapses, Sobs at Verdict

Convicted Of 1st Degree Manslaughter

Mrs. Alice Crimmins holds her hand to her head as she leaves court for lunch break after judge charged jury. With her is her husband, Edmund. Jury of 12 married men found her guilty. The shapely, red-haired defendant, 28, collapsed as the verdict was read. Final courtroom drama after 14 day of trial occurred shortly before 2 a.m.

Story on page 3

Crimmins Trial star witness Sophie Earomirski walks triumphantly through courthouse after giving testimony. (*N.Y. Daily News Photo*)

Below, workers excavating a sewer in Queens searching for the dismembered body of Barbara Lofrumento, who died during an illegal abortion operation. (*N.Y. Daily News Photo*)   Facing page, top, Dr. Carl Coppolino and his second wife stand with defense attorney F. Lee Bailey before Coppolino's trial for the murder of his first wife in Florida. (*N.Y. Daily News Photo*) Facing page, bottom, playwright Arthur Miller celebrating with Peter Reilly after the latter's successful appeal of his murder conviction. (*Wide World Photos*)

Chapter 15

Pitfalls for the Pathologist

Experience in forensic pathology and a full knowledge of all the surrounding circumstances are both vital in my profession, if miscarriages of justice—or even just red faces—are to be avoided.

A particular case in 1971 taught me rather late in my career not to give offhand expressions of agreement in a casual situation, without knowing all the medical and pathological facts. It was also a good example of the application of well-known principles in the analysis of a traumatic pathological situation.

I was invited down to Louisville, Kentucky that year, to give a lecture to a hospital staff and medical school audience. While I was there, and at the end of the day, some of the residents in pathology projected some small color transparencies of several medico-legal cases for me to see, including those of a dead woman in a bathroom, with plenty of blood about and some severe scalp injuries. At that time I was told only that the gory scene was from a homicide, which I accepted without having any opportunity of studying the other details of the autopsy. The case was demonstrated briefly, and I carried no recollection of it away with me when I returned to New York.

Well, as it developed, I should not have been so offhand and casual about agreeing with those doctors, because some months later that bloody bathroom scene came around like a boomerang and hit me on the head.

What happened was this—on December 4, 1970, some time before my lecture in Louisville, a middleaged architect in that town, William Banton Moore, had gone to Standiford Field Airport to pick up his wife Louisa from the New York plane. William Moore was descended from a distinguished family— some of his ancestors were among the early settlers in Kentucky and another relative was the distinguished district attorney of New York County.

Louisa had a drinking problem, to put it kindly. She was giving her husband a hard time, although there was no evidence at all to suggest that he took it other than quite stoically. Mrs. Moore would go off to New York alone, shopping, visiting art galleries, and indulging her alcoholic tendencies. This time, while she was away, they spoke on the phone on a few occasions and, as usual, the topic of conversation was divorce. Louisa Moore was always nagging William for a divorce, but as he was a prominent professional man in the town, and as they had a pair of twelve-year-old twin daughters, he always refused, citing their mutual responsibilities.

This particular night, William Moore met his wife with the car at the airport, drove her home, and dutifully carried her bags into the house. The children came to greet their mother, then vanished back to their television program.

Moore and his wife went upstairs, and for an hour they had another session on divorce. On the way back from the airport, he had taken her to a hotel for dinner, and she had had about three drinks there. The divorce argument reached its usual stalemate, and Moore offered to sleep in another room, apparently a very common state of affairs. He went downstairs and watched television for some time. The twins went to bed, and eventually Mr. Moore took his wife's luggage up to her bedroom. She wasn't there, but he noticed that the bathroom door was ajar.

He went back downstairs until about midnight; then he came up again. His wife still wasn't in her room, and the bags remained unpacked on the floor.

William Moore went to the bathroom to see if Louisa was there and found the room splashed with blood; his wife was lying alongside the tub, knees up, and either unconscious or dead.

Panic-stricken, he tried to revive her and spent half an hour giving her artificial respiration and the mouth-to-mouth "kiss of life." He said later that he was afraid to leave her to get help; the time he spent away might have been vital for resuscitating her. During his efforts, he turned her over onto her stomach and attempted to prop her against the bath, further spreading the blood that was coming from her scalp, soiling the room and himself.

Finally, he saw he was getting no response from his efforts and left her to telephone a physician, Dr. Burford Davis, who lived next door. It was soon obvious that Louisa Moore was dead, and the police were called to the scene. Since they were confronted with a bloody body, a husband with bloodstained hands, and a blood-smeared bathroom, they immediately suspected murder.

They kept asking him whether any other person could have entered the house and done this terrible thing, and Moore denied this possibility. He explained to them that his wife fell quite frequently, even after only a few drinks, but the police seemed unimpressed by his explanations. Soon, William Banton Moore was indicted for the murder of his wife.

By one of those coincidences that thread through life, his brother was a New York lawyer whose wife worked in our gift shop in New York University's University Hospital. One thing led to another, and by the time the trial came along the following June, I had been requested by the attorney in Louisville, Frank Haddad, to give evidence for the defense. Mr. Moore got in touch with me in the city. At this time I had no recollection at all of the colored photographs I had seen projected from small transparencies some months earlier at the hospital. The trial began, and Moore gave his straightforward account of all that had happened that night. A police officer testified that Moore had told him no one else could have done it, as no one could possibly have entered the quiet house without his knowledge.

The assistant district attorney, Carl Ousley, challenged Moore from across the courtroom, "Isn't it true, Mr. Moore, that you went into the bathroom; you struck her; she fell; then you picked her up and dashed her head against the bathtub, time and time again?"

From now on, the whole thing hinged on how the injuries were caused. The police alleged that they found pieces of scalp and tissue mixed with hairs on the bathtub and on a white three-legged milk stool, but a special agent from the FBI laboratory testified that there was nothing on the stool in the way of human tissue. All the blood stains on the bathroom surfaces and on Moore's clothes were Group 'O,' the same as the dead woman's.

The pathologist who did the autopsy also testified that there was no scalp tissue missing, so there could have been none in the bath. The case now depended on the prosecution's medical witnesses' explanation of the mechanism of the head injuries. Mrs. Moore had a very large circular flap of scalp torn loose from the skull, except along one arc of its circumference. Nowhere was the margin of this laceration bruised or contused, as would have been the case if it had been caused by impact by or against a blunt weapon. This wound had bled torrentially, as all scalp wounds do. She also had a linear fracture of the skull—a straight crack without any shattering or depression.

The autopsy had been done by Dr. Lawrence Boram, a resident pathologist at the general hospital belonging to the University of Louisville Medical School. His findings were correct, but his interpretations of those findings were not in line with my opinion. Boram, supported by Dr. Allen Lansing, a cardiovascular surgeon from Louisville, maintained that the damage to the scalp, which had torn a large area away from the skull, could only have been caused by repeated blows from a blunt instrument.

He rather spoiled the effect of this statement by testifying that there was only one laceration of the scalp, and then during cross-examination by defense counsel, he agreed that the laceration could have been caused by her falling once or several times and striking her head in the process. He also agreed that she could have moved about the bathroom after the injury, accounting for the spreading of the blood, and he further admitted that the bruises found on Mrs. Moore's arms, shoulders, legs, and face could have been caused by her falling about and striking against hard objects.

The net result was that he agreed with everything the defense was contending, though he still maintained his opinion of repeated blows by a blunt instrument, which was never described or identified.

After the prosecution had rested, I was the first witness, followed the next day by Dr. Cyril Wecht, coroner of Allegheny County, Pennsylvania, a very experienced forensic pathologist, whose opinion was similar to mine. I had not had the opportunity to study the body, since the death had taken place six months earlier, but I had seen Dr. Boram's autopsy report, the laboratory results, and various other documents, including the big color prints of the scene of death. I testified to these findings. At that time I still did not recall that these prints were of the same case as the one casually shown to me by the hospital residents months before, projected from small 2 x 2 transparencies. However, the hospital doctors had not forgotten, and I was later accused by the prosecution of changing my testimony for a monetary consideration, now that I was appearing for the defense. "But Doctor Helpern," said counsel. "When you saw these pictures before you were retained by Moore's attorney, you said 'homicide.' Now you're on the stand, you're telling us it was an accident!" I was never given the opportunity to explain on the stand. I had no one to blame but myself for the rushed look at the transparencies at the school lecture. I had not declared that the scene was a typical homicide but was told this without knowing all the facts to challenge that conclusion. I learned a lesson from that case.

During my examination, I gave my opinion about the head injuries, and it was based on the classical findings that occur in different kinds of brain injury.

When a stationary head gets a heavy blow from some object, like the traditional "blunt instrument" beloved of detective story writers, the impact causes bruising and splitting or laceration of the scalp. Sometimes this injury resembles a slash from a sharp instrument; even a blunt injury of the skin over unyielding bone beneath can cause a clean-cut gash, but close examination will show crushing of the edges, hairs driven into the wound, and strands of tissue bridging the depths of the cut. Most times, there is very obvious damage to the surrounding skin, depending on the profile of the weapon.

Even more important is the effect on the skull and its contents. With a direct impact on a fixed head, the skull fracture is often jagged, shattered, and frequently, depressed, bits of bone being separated from each other and sometimes driven deeply into the skull to damage the brain underneath. This certainly had not happened to Mrs. Moore.

Furthermore, a blow to a fixed head usually causes damage to the brain directly under the impact area—the so-called *coup* injury, a term of French origin.

But if we look into what happens not when a weapon hits a fixed head, but when a rapidly moving head strikes a fixed object or hard surface, we see a very different effect. The sudden, single impact may rip the scalp cleanly, and as in the case of Louisa Moore, actually "avulse" it—that is, shear it away from the underlying bone over a large area, due to a tangential strike. The moving skull may come into contact with a hard surface, like a tiled floor of the bathroom or the edge of a bathtub. Instead of a shattering, denting fracture, the force is spread over a wider area and causes a line crack, running away from the point of impact.

But the most characteristic feature of all is one that has caused a lot of argument, experimentation, and discussion among pathologists and neurosurgeons for many years. Instead of the brain damage being confined to the area immediately beneath the outer injury—the *coup* mentioned earlier—there is usually damage diametrically opposite on the other side of the brain. This may be present either in addition to or frequently instead of the *coup*, and it may be very severe and extensive. For instance, the typical case is of a drunk who teeters over backward after coming out of a saloon and falls full length onto the sidewalk. He cracks the back point of his head on the concrete and gets massive pulping of the frontal lobes of his brain, to such an extent that the thin bone forming the roof of his eye sockets gets fractured by transmission of the force of the impact into the undersurface of the frontal lobes of the brain.

This opposite-side damage is called the "counter coup", usually known as *contre-coup* by knowledgeable pathologists, and is a cardinal sign of damage to a moving head by impact against a hard, stationary surface.

Louisa Moore did have classical counter coup or *contre-coup* damage to her brain, and as far as I am concerned, that established that the prosecution theory was wrong about the mechanism of the brain injury.

There were no bruises around the edges of that cleanly-torn scalp wound, and when it came to the point, Dr. Boram honestly agreed that all the postulates of the defense could have occurred; though rather illogically, I think, he stuck to his first conclusions.

Moore was convicted and sentenced to twenty-one years in prison. Feeling in the town was strong against the young architect from the North, and his appeals were rejected.

His charming and intelligent sister, Elizabeth Green of Texas, adored her brother; she, his children, and her brother from New York were all convinced of his innocence and worked to set him free. His sister consulted two of my colleagues, Dr. William Q. Sturner, who was than a medical examiner in Dallas, now chief medical examiner of Rhode Island, and Dr. Frank P. Cleveland, coroner and forensic pathologist of Cincinnati, who both concurred with me that the prosecution's explanation of how the brain was injured was wrong. Mrs. Green never rested until she finally brought the case to the attention of the governor, and after William Moore had languished nineteen months in prison, on December 27, 1974, his sentence was commuted to time served, and he was freed. He is living happily at home with his children, who adore him, and he is slowly making a comeback in his profession. Moreover, he has set the wheels in motion to clear his name and set the record straight.

Another fertile area of trouble for forensic pathologists involves recognition of the difference between injuries that occur before death and after it. In many fatal traumatic incidents, the injuries take place either just before death or at the moment of death—but sometimes quite a variable time after life has become extinct.

It is difficult and frequently impossible to differentiate immediately ante-mortem injury from that occurring simultaneously with death or immediately after death. For instance, though bleeding is naturally associated with injuries before death, while the heart is still beating, undoubtedly post-mortem wounds may be followed by quite a lot of bleeding, especially from the scalp. If a person survives for a time after an injury, then there will be a recognizable "vital reaction" in the edges of the wounded tissue, amounting and similar to the early signs of inflammation. There are new techniques, not yet widely used, to detect very early changes of this nature by means of enzyme activity in the skin and tissues. Burns also provide difficulties in interpretation, if survival has been very short term.

These matters require all the expertise and experience of a pathologist or medical examiner with a lot of professional mileage behind him—and even then, at times he falls flat on his face.

There was a case some time ago in which a girl was made pregnant by her boyfriend, a fact that later helped to raise the suspicion index. The girl and boy drove off for a picnic one day and ended up in a natural pond in the country, where they decided to go swimming. After a time, he said he had to go off into the woods to relieve himself, leaving the girl swimming around in the pond. When he got back a few minutes later, she had vanished, presumably beneath the surface. He dove in and found her submerged at the bottom and dragged her out. He then tried to revive her without success, panicked, and then carried her back to the road to take her to the hospital, though by now she was almost certainly dead. He got her into his car, and a person who was driving by in a truck helped him place the girl on the rear passenger seat of the car.

The boy leaped into the driving seat and roared off, with his foot flat on the gas pedal, crazed to get to the hospital in record time. But he was so frantic not to lose a second, that he skidded on a corner and smashed his car into a tree, wrecking the vehicle. He was injured, and when assistance arrived at the scene of the crash, he and the girl were taken off to the hospital by ambulance, which was not the way he had intended to get there.

While the young man was being treated in the hospital for his injuries, the medical examiner did an autopsy on the girl, and quite rightly stated that something was odd about the case. Not knowing exactly what had happened, he interpreted the injuries to the girl as ante-mortem, and as a consequence, the police arrested the boyfriend, who was charged with homicide. There was no way the pathologist could use the usual criteria: he has to be told by a reliable observer that the injuries were or were not present before the collision took place. The fact that the couple had been swimming, and that the autopsy also disclosed that the girl was pregnant, and the other circumstances as to how her body was found submerged strengthened the feeling of suspicion against the boy. It was alleged that he had assaulted the girl, caused her to drown, and then deliberately wrecked his car with the girl in it on the way to the hospital, to confuse and obscure the nature of her injuries, which he was accused of causing while drowning her in the pond. Were it not for the witness who had passed by in his truck and helped the boy place the girl on the rear seat and who testified that the girl did not show any injuries when he first saw her, the defendant might have been convicted instead of acquitted. This kind of difficult situation can easily arise when the pathologist does an autopsy without the benefit of full information.

It happened again in our Office in New York, in connection with a baby. We had a routine "crib death" autopsy one day, but when the head was examined, we were surprised to find a grossly fractured skull and extensive meningeal bleeding between the membranes of the brain—two features that are so commonly seen in the "battered child syndrome." So immediately, our thinking was diverted from an innocent crib death to suspicion of parental violence and possibly homicide.

I went down and confronted the father, who was waiting in the office. He was staggered by even the hint of such an accusation. He told his story, and very soon it became evident that he was blameless. He told me that he had thought it was a little odd that, when the mortuary attendant called at his apartment after the medical investigator had been there to collect the baby's body and transport it to the medical examiner's building, he had wrapped the body in a blanket like a parcel and then tossed it over the banister of the tenement house stairway to his assistant on the lower landing, who caught it like a football.

Thinking that maybe this was the way that "morgue men" always acted, he drove off to the Medical Examiner's Office in his own car, and arrived there ahead of the mortuary vehicle.

He was in a room in our Office, which looked out into the yard where the bodies are delivered, and saw the same vehicle drive in and the attendant again throw the bundle containing the body of his baby from the back of the van to his assistant, who this time failed to catch it and let it drop onto the concrete pavement of the yard!

We then confronted the employee, who was very contrite and said that he "didn't know that you can do any damage to a dead body." He was strongly reprimanded, but if the father had not happened to see the events and we had not got the attendant to confirm them, he might well have been in very serious trouble.

We always have to be on the lookout for such spurious injuries. One that is so well known that every pathologist knows it—or should—is the so-called "undertaker's fracture," which occurs in the neck. When the heavy, unsupported head of a cadaver is allowed to drop back, as the body is moved from a bed or a house or even the mortuary refrigerator to the autopsy table, the strain can cause separation of two vertebrae in the neck. This has been mistaken for a genuine fracture of the spine. The location and absence of bleeding around the "fracture" should tell the doctor to disregard it, but now and then it crops up as a spurious allegation of injury.

All kinds of artifacts lurk in the body to trap the inexperienced and unwary pathologist, which is why it is so unsatisfactory for those without the necessary experience to get involved in legal medical work. In clinical autopsy practice on hospital deaths, there is not the same risk of serious consequences if any such misinterpretation is made, but if the same pathologist dabbles in forensic practice, then trouble is sure to arrive eventually.

It isn't a question of paper qualifications or certification—these are satisfactory, but it's the person who counts. Has he the experience, has he common sense, and does he know what he's trying or expected to do? If he hasn't these attributes, then all the certificates and titles and academic appointments will be wasted. Give me a conscientious physician with a good basic knowledge of autopsy pathology, who is interested and possesses common sense and integrity, and I will train him to be a good forensic pathologist in a few years. That person will be far more reliable and safer in a medico-legal situation than some longserving assistant or associate professor with a string of organizational diplomas as long as your arm, including membership on the local board of trade. It is a question of orientation, specialization, and experience, not of titles. The academic professor and staff hospital pathologist might be excellent in diagnosing the rare and unusual tumor of great importance for the patient but they may also be menaces when let loose on a homicide autopsy.

I have also found that an intelligent non-forensic pathologist, using the scientific method, can be instrumental in helping determine a homicidal poisoning that was overlooked by another pathologist.

This case occurred some years ago and was that of a young child of four years who suddenly developed convulsions and died. Two years before, its mother, who was pregnant at the time, had died—also after severe convulsive seizures. The family physician arranged for an autopsy to be done by the pathologist of a large hospital, and the findings were negative except for the intact pregnancy. The death was not reported to the medical examiner and was considered natural and related to the pregnancy.

When the child died, the family physician again wanted to have the pathologist do an autopsy at his hospital, where the body of the mother had been done, but my pediatrician friend Dr. Milton I. Levine arranged to have the autopsy done at Rockefeller Hospital by Dr. Joseph Smadel, who at that time was the pathologist at that institution. The body was brought there by the funeral director for the autopsy. As in most cases of death after sudden onset of prolonged convulsions, the anatomic findings were negative, and samples of the brain and other tissues were injected into hamsters and other appropriate small laboratory animals, to determine whether a viral infection had caused the death of the child. Now Dr. Smadel didn't just sit back and wait expectantly for the animals to die, but rather he had the imagination to anticipate that the animals might *not* die; therefore, he removed the child's stomach and its contents for toxicologic studies. This had not been done in the case of the mother when she died after her convulsions, which were written off as a manifestation of a toxemia of pregnancy and not looked into any further. It was too late, after two years, to test the mother's organs, something which should have been done at the time and would have saved the life of her four-year-old child.

When the hamsters and the other animals did not show any evidence of a viral or other type of infection, Dr. Joe Smadel called Dr. Levine to tell him what the results were. He also said that he had saved the child's stomach and its contents intact and indicated that it would be a good idea to have a chemical analysis for the sake of completeness. I then spoke to Dr. Alexander O. Gettler, the toxicologist at the Medical Examiner's Office, and he said he would do the analysis. The intact stomach was delivered to me by Dr. Smadel, and I turned it over to Dr. Gettler. The next day, I could tell from the expression on his face that he had found something.

With a look of consternation, he told me that he had found the stomach to be loaded with strychnine, which readily explained the fatal convulsions. This was a homicidal poisoning and in all probability the mother's death was, too, but it hadn't been considered such at the time. The other pathologist and the mother's physician were thunderstruck. The ability to suspect or carry out that extra step, so that a chemical analysis, if necessary, could be done to provide the solution to an unsuspected poisoning death, is the quality of a thinking man. Hospital pathologists and forensic pathologists do not have a monopoly on brains. Dr. Smadel had never been in a courtroom in his life.

Every man should stick to what he does best. As a chief medical examiner, I wouldn't presume to perform a delicate brain operation or replace heart valves. Why should a man who has spent all of his professional time directing a hospital clinical laboratory suddenly decide he is competent to perform an autopsy and testify at the trial on forensic pathological matters? Misinterpretation by the pathologist can cause endless trouble, not only for the relatives at a time when their bereavement is already a burden, but most important, for the fair administration of justice.

I remember being involved in a case concerning the death of another infant, this time a genuine case of the battered child syndrome. The baby had been admitted to the hospital, *in extremis* or dead, after what in retrospect were seen to be severe abdominal injuries due to parental assaults. The child was placed in the intensive care unit, with teams of doctors and nurses working on it as hard as they could. There was no evidence to prove that the child was alive during that period, although the attempts at resuscitation were continued, with intravenous drips set up in the fruitless attempt to accomplish this. Eventually, it was pronounced dead. Now for some reason, an intern assigned to this unit thought that an autopsy would not be done. He had a bit of a brainstorm and remembered something from his medical school lectures: that in the absence of an autopsy, punctures of the four quadrants of the abdomen with a syringe and needle with aspiration might reveal the presence of blood in the belly. Using a good-sized needle he followed this procedure—which seemed a peculiar thing to do. He inserted the needle through the belly wall and recovered only a few drops of blood, but the large bore needle produced four easily visible punctures through the skin.

The body of the infant was then taken to the hospital mortuary. The intern who did the four-quadrant tap of the abdomen had not recorded it on the chart. The coroner decided to have an autopsy and engaged the hospital pathologist to do it.

There was a deep laceration of the liver, with evidence of

infection and infarction, referring to the presence of dead areas of liver in the margins of the severe laceration. The gross and microscopic appearance of the liver indicated that the injury must have been inflicted many hours before the child had died. There were other abdominal injuries, including bruising and bleeding from the intestines and their attachments. The autopsy disclosed frank evidence of severe, blunt force injury to the abdomen, and any forensic pathologist should have recognized that they must have been inflicted hours before the child died— the second most common way in which battered children are killed.

But in spite of these typical findings, the pathologist stated that death was caused by the four needle punctures performed by the intern with his syringe, at a time when the child had already been pronounced dead! He reported this to the police and the poor intern was then charged with manslaughter. I was consulted about this case at this point by the district attorney and, after seeing photographs of the autopsy, explained the findings to him and advised him that the liver and bowel injuries were considerably older and must have occurred before the four-quadrant tap was done, which obviously occurred after death. I suggested an investigation of the persons who brought the child to the hospital. It was a typical traumatic death and obviously the result of a severe battering that the child had received. There were also scars on the skin and penis consistent with the final stage and healing of burns. These have been known to have been produced with a lit cigarette, as punishment for the infant having wet itself.

But the next incredible thing was that there was no investigation of the child's injuries that caused its death. Once the intern was released from custody, the matter seemed to have been dropped. What was even more incredible, the parents— who should have been investigated for homicide—came back and instituted a suit against the hospital and the intern for malpractice for causing the death of their child! You know, if you read that in a novel or magazine you just wouldn't believe it.

Chapter 16

A Strange Death in Texas

Texas has the reputation for doing things in a big way, and this extravagance even extends to homicide—it was Dallas that provided the spectacular tragedy of the Kennedy assassination. As far as my personal involvement is concerned, there was another case in Houston that was equally extraordinary. As in the Kennedy case, the major suspect was himself murdered before the processes of the law had been completed—by a killer from Dallas, who in turn was gunned down before he could be tried!

In true Texas style, the autopsy which I performed at the invitation of the chief medical examiner and district attorney of Harris County was witnessed by no fewer than eleven doctors— as I say, everything seems to be done in a big way in Texas.

This case was like a scenario from a Hollywood film or T. V. show—the people concerned were the "jet set" of the Southwest, with one of the leading characters a rugged oil millionaire and another a leading plastic surgeon. It seems rather strange how many medical men I've seen tried for homicides of various sorts over the years; far more than, say, accountants, lawyers, or bankers. Names come to mind easily, like Coppolino, Sander,

Montemerano, Singer, Glasberg, most recently Friedgood—and Dr. John Hill.

John Hill was a well-known plastic surgeon in Houston. He had a first-class professional reputation—and an income to match, which was reputed to be in the region of $250,000 a year. In 1958, soon after he was graduated from medical school, this tall, good-looking young surgeon made an advantageous marriage to an attractive blonde from the best social set in the state. This was Joan Robinson, adopted daughter of an astute, independent, self-made oil tycoon named Ash Robinson, who had a wide circle of important friends in the professions and business. Ash Robinson and his wife deeply loved and adored their only child, who had become an internationally-known horsewoman—in fact, she was to the equestrian world what her husband was becoming in the field of plastic surgery in America.

There are conflicting opinions as to what extent this marriage was responsible for John Hill's rapid rise to fame and fortune in the cosmetic surgery sphere. Probably his own professional skill was the major factor, but no doubt the entrée his wife gave him into the sophisticated world of potential clients was by no means a hindrance, especially as Hill came from much more humble origins along the Rio Grande, whereas Joan Robinson Hill was a River Oaks girl, with all the advantages of wealth, schooling, and social status.

Be that as it may, all seemed to go well for the better part of ten years. They lived in suitable style in a large colonial mansion in Houston's exclusive River Oaks—a house on which Hill, with the help of his father-in-law, spent a hundred thousand dollars merely for a music room, which gives some idea of their life style.

But around 1968, when Joan was thirty-six, the marriage seemed to go wrong. John Hill appeared to be indulging a long-lasting "seven-year itch" and was undoubtedly having affairs with other women. It was his first marriage, though for Joan it was already her third when she married him at the age of twenty-six.

They separated for a time in 1968, but then came together again, perhaps for the sake of their nine-year-old son. (It seems in retrospect that Ash Robinson had never been overjoyed at the marriage, but it is later on that he comes into his own in the story.)

Joan Hill became more and more preoccupied with her

equestrian activities. She was often away at horse shows with her champion mount, Beloved Belinda, and she had her own horse farm in Houston—maybe a cause or perhaps a compensation for the roving eye of her handsome husband.

In 1969, Joan Hill was in apparent good health until March 17. On March 14, a Friday, she went to a benefit dinner where her husband was playing the tuba in a doctor's musical group, the Heartbeats, whose members included Denton Cooley, the heart transplant surgeon. On the next day, she had two house guests over for the weekend, and again she seemed all right.

On Sunday morning, March 16, she complained of some sickness and threw up her breakfast; diarrhea and a chill sent her back to bed. She stayed there while the guests went out to dinner that night. The next morning, Monday, the guests left, and Joan appeared dehydrated, asking for ice water only. Her father came over and left under the impression that she had influenza.

Her maid, Effie Smith, was worried about her mistress all that day and into Tuesday. John Hill went about his work as usual, and there was later conflicting evidence as to what steps—if any—he took to treat his wife. On Tuesday, the maid found her weakened and almost stuporous. She sent for Joan's parents and summoned Dr. Hill back from his office at the hospital in the mid-morning. Hill drove his wife to Sharpstown General Hospital, a small hospital in which Hill had some financial interest. There he placed her under the care of a physician, who had not been called to see her at home and was now seeing her professionally for the first time. She was found to be in an advanced state of shock, with a barely recordable blood pressure, and was considered by the physician there to be already dying. In spite of all supportive therapy, she died early Wednesday morning, March 19.

Now, as I've so often said, the medico-legal mistakes that frequently screw up a case begin right at the start. Here was a previously healthy, vigorous young woman, brought to a hospital in a moribund state and expiring in a matter of hours after admission.

By any medical examiner's office regulations, such a death should have been reported to it immediately—for it obviously called for an investigation by the medical examiner, who in this case happened to be my old pupil and friend, Dr. Joseph Jachimczyk. But no, it was not reported! The first he heard of it was two days later, on Friday, and the route that the news took was via the district attorney, who had been disturbed by some rumors that were flying around town. Joan's father, Ash Robinson, was furious in his despair over her death and the way her illness had been treated.

Jachimczyk then discovered that the body had been embalmed and was already in a coffin in a funeral home waiting for burial that very day. There had already been a hurried autopsy, carried out at John Hill's request by Doctor Morse, the Sharpstown Hospital pathologist, who performed it on the embalmed body in the funeral home—hardly the best conditions for investigating such an obscure death. The body should not have been released to the funeral director by the hospital administrators and should not have been embalmed before the cause of death was determined and certified. There is a purpose to such procedures! Unfortunately, such mistakes are made in many jurisdictions.

Joe Jachimczyk was furious at this short-circuiting of his jurisdication and later held a full inquiry among the doctors and administrators at the hospital—but now he had to move fast to beat the hearse to the cemetery. He rushed over to the funeral home and managed to get a look at the coffined body of Joan Robinson Hill. All he could do was a partial external examination to check for obvious surface injuries, but he could see none. Dr. Morse had promised to show him the slides of the tissues he took for microscopic study at his hasty autopsy, and the medical examiner had to settle for that and allow the burial to proceed. I know he later regretted letting this happen, but we can all be wise after the event. One must consider that a complete autopsy was done before the death was reported to the medical examiner. To have held up the funeral might have been considered unreasonable and arbitrary. Had there been no autopsy, Jachimczyk would have had no hesitancy about performing one. Nevertheless, the fact that the body had been embalmed would have interfered with its complete success.

So far, the diagnosis had jumped like a grasshopper, from the effect of snails eaten the week before to "turista" caught on a trip to Mexico three weeks before, then to "acute pancreatitis," which was Morse's diagnosis. Now here, the hospital pathologist fell into a common trap that catches almost every unwary autopsy surgeon of limited experience. The pancreas, a glandular digestive organ lying behind the stomach, produces the most powerful digestive juices of all—and after death, when the vital protective mechanisms fail, it promptly starts to digest itself. This auto-digestion often produces a hemorrhagic appearance in the gland, and the incautious pathologist, if he's short of some more obvious cause of death, may be misled into conveniently thinking that he is dealing with a case of acute pancreatitis. Morse made this mistake, though he was ready enough to retract this cause of death when Jachimczyk challenged it. The medical examiner retrieved slides of stomach, kidney, liver, heart, brain-covering, and blood from Doctor Morse and examined them carefully himself. He came to the conclusion that Joan Hill died from a severe liver infection, hepatitis. But he couldn't at that stage go any further to identify what had caused it. The body had been embalmed and buried, so there was no hope of isolating any bacteria or viruses, which the very process of embalming is designed to kill, in order to preserve the body. A dozen causes of hepatitis could have been the culprit, whether viral, bacterial, or toxic from some outside poison.

Dr. Jachimczyk felt that the most likely cause was a virus, and though he wasn't too happy or certain about it, he signed the case out as "virus hepatitis."

Well, if Joe Jachimczyk wasn't too happy about it, then Joan's father, millionaire Ash Robinson, was a great deal less satisfied. It was he who had raised the issue with the district attorney of Harris County immediately after the death, and when the funeral and the medical examiner's investigation were over, he still refused to accept the stated natural cause of death. He haunted the district attorney and spent large sums of money on private investigators to collect evidence about the last days of his daughter's life. He was outspoken in his opinions and began openly to accuse his son-in-law of deliberately allowing Joan to die, not giving her treatment and leaving her to lie about the house for three days without arranging for hospitalization.

When Dr. John Hill, three months after the funeral, married a woman with whom it was known he had been having an affair for the past year, Ash Robinson became more vociferous, suggesting that there might have been sins of commission in Hill's behavior toward his wife, not merely sins of omission.

Hill had married an attractive divorcée, Ann Kurth, for whom he had maintained a separate apartment in town. Joan

had known about her, because a friend, Mrs. Maxwell, later
testified that just before her death Joan had been upset that her
husband had bought a new car for his mistress. As it turned out,
this second marriage of John Hill's was to last only a few
months, and in April of the next year Ann Kurth gained an
uncontested divorce. Hill soon married for the third time.

By now, Joan's father was raising hell all over the place, and it
got to the point where Dr. Hill set his lawyers on the old man,
with a five-million dollar lawsuit for slander and libel. Hill
claimed that Robinson's malicious and spiteful actions had
severely damaged his surgical practice and drastically reduced
his income. Hill's complaint stated that "Robinson initiated a
conspiracy and spent thousands of dollars on secret investigators, electronic equipment, attorneys and scientific experts, all to
the end of damaging and injuring him." He alleged that Ash had
stated that he would destroy Hill's medical practice by any
means possible and destroy him economically. He also said that
Robinson was attempting to obtain custody of his grandson
Robert, as well as Hill's home and other possessions.

This was a civil suit, but criminal matters were developing.
Between the death of Joan in March 1969 and August of the same
year, no fewer than three grand juries were convened to consider
the case. Two of them faded out, but the third had the benefit of
additional medical evidence, and this is where I came on the
scene in this curious affair.

In August 1969, due to Ash Robinson's persistence and the
statements of witnesses that his investigators had assiduously
collected, the district attorney of Harris County, Carol Vance,
requested the medical examiner, Dr. Jachimczyk, to carry out an
exhumation to try to clarify the medical position.

My first knowledge of the death of Joan Robinson Hill came
from her father, who telephoned me from Houston to ask
whether I would be available to perform a second autopsy on the
body of his daughter, who had died several months before. He
said I had been recommended to him by a physician friend as
someone who was qualified as a forensic pathologist to do this. I
asked him why the autopsy was needed, and he voiced his
suspicion that Joan had died as the result of foul play. I
explained that I could not intrude in such a case as a private
medical examiner, and that such an autopsy would have to be
done officially by the county medical examiner or one of his

deputies. I did say that I would be willing to serve as his observer, but could only do so on invitation and with permission from the district attorney and the medical examiner to observe or assist as an official deputy to the medical examiner, who at the time was out of the country on holiday. Although I expected to receive a fee for my services, the amount was not discussed with Mr. Robinson. He agreed that he would pay for the expense of my trip to Houston. After the district attorney and the grand jury and Dr. Jachimczyk agreed that the body of Joan Hill should be exhumed for another autopsy (the expense of which would be borne by Ash Robinson), arrangements were made for me to perform the autopsy as the official deputy of Dr. Jachimczyk and to send my report to him when it was completed. Also to be present at the autopsy were representatives of Mr. Robinson and of Dr. John Hill.

Now, such big issues were at stake at Joan Robinson Hill's autopsy that Jachimczyk wisely decided to spread the responsibility as widely as possible. Two teams of doctors were recruited, one group representing the interests of the dead woman's husband, and the other her father.

I was invited down from New York to take overall direction of the actual examination of the exhumed body. Joseph Jachimczyk gave me the temporary status of deputy medical examiner in his jurisdiction and appointed me chief pathologist for this particular occasion. The autopsy, which took place on Saturday, August 16, 1969, lasted a full seven hours, and in addition to myself and the two pathologists Jachimczyk and Morse, there were Dr. Edmund Gouldin, a hematologist; Dr. Paul Radelat, a pathologist; Dr. Grady Hallman, a cardiovascular surgeon; Dr. Howard Seigler, a local physician; Dr. Bertinot, the physician from the hospital where Joan Hill died, who had been given the hopeless task of treating her; and Dr. William Fields.

In addition, Hill's lawyers, Richard "Racehorse" Haynes and Michael Ramsey, had sent four doctors to represent him; namely, Dr. Robert Bucklin, the Galveston County medical examiner; Dr. George Thoma; Dr. Berne Newton; and Dr. Robert Nelson.

So, as you can imagine, it was quite an event, with all these people milling around in the autopsy room.

Well, the body had been buried a few months, but because of the embalming, it wasn't in too bad a state, though naturally the previous autopsy didn't help our task. But after the time that had elapsed and the embalming, it was quite out of the question at that late stage to get any clue from microbiological or the more sensitive toxicological tests, so we had to rely on visual appearances, the microscopic sections that Dr. Morse had made at the first autopsy, and those which I prepared.

One controversial matter arose at this stage. Dr. Morse, the Sharpstown Hospital pathologist, arrived at the autopsy with a brain in a container, fixed in formaldehyde, which he said he had retained from the first autopsy.

Now, there was quite a debate as to whether this really was the brain of Joan Robinson Hill and not some other brain that had got confused with it during storage in Morse's laboratory. This dispute reached the newspapers and there were big headlines in the Houston *Post*: "DOUBT CAST ON MRS. HILL AUTOPSY— WRONG BRAIN HINTED."

Morse indignantly denied any possibility of a mix-up, which was first suspected because the brain he brought showed a definite inflammation of the covering membranes—a "meningitis"—whereas the upper end of the spinal cord, which was originally continuous with the stem of the brain before it was cut during the autopsy, was quite normal and free from any meningitis. Now, opinions were divided among the medical team as to whether this was possible. I thought it peculiar and rather unlikely that the inflammation should be present in one place and absent in the adjacent part, but I was willing to give Morse the benefit of the doubt. Two of the other doctors there had stronger misgivings.

The main doubts were cast by a statement that Jachimczyk issued, in which he said that he had received a letter from a Houston brain specialist—not one of the autopsy team—who said that the brain could not be the one from Mrs. Hill's body because of the discrepancy in the meningitis.

Dr. Morse was naturally in a flaming temper at this insinuation by someone whom the medical examiner would not name. "I wish this individual would stand up and identify himself, so I can take him to court where he belongs," he said to reporters. He vehemently denied any possibility of an error. "All the information I had, both clinical and anatomical," he went on, "was given to the coroner's office and the D. A.'s office and was a hundred percent correct. There was no tissue switched, no

attempt at any kind of subterfuge.'' He also attacked the
Houston *Post* for publishing news stories saying that he
attributed the cause of death to hepatitis and meningitis. He said
that he had never said that ''in those terms''—and we know that
he had originally called the death acute pancreatitis.

Well, after many hours of work, I finished the autopsy and
returned to New York. My findings were dictated for everyone to
hear and agree or disagree with. All of us were going to make up
our own minds on what we had seen at the autopsy, and make
our own interpretations.

It was many months before I submitted my full report, which
ran to twenty-four typewritten pages. In fact, when I came down
to the resumed grand jury hearing the following April, I still
hadn't finished the final two and a half pages as there hadn't
been time to have my dictation transcribed before leaving for the
airport, so I gave oral evidence as to my conclusions. I said that,
in my opinion, ''death resulted from an acute inflammatory and
probably infectious disease, the origin of which could not be
determined. In view of the severe vomiting and diarrheal
manifestations it is most likely that the portal of entry was by
way of the alimentary tract.''

I concluded my report: ''If any death should have been
reported in time for an official investigation, this one obviously
should have been. Failure to have done this leaves the origin of
the fatal illness undetermined. Failure to provide adequate
medical attention at home and the resultant delay in hospitalization for diagnosis and effective therapy aggravated a situation
which proved fatal. The hospital, the attending physicians, and
the pathologist were all remiss in not having reported the death
originally to the medical examiner's office for investigation.''

How often have we seen this sort of thing? Not infrequently:
the entire matter shrouded in mystery forever because of some
careless administrative slip-up right at the start.

Jachimczyk himself concluded in his own summation, ''The
exact cause and manner of death cannot be established from the
autopsy alone. However, in view of the unusual circumstances
surrounding this death and the questions raised following the
death and a review of the hospital chart [which first became
available at the time of the exhumation], a thorough grand jury
investigation is herewith recommended.''

My report took into account all the surrounding circumstances, a frame of reference that I have repeatedly said is the legitimate province of the autopsy pathologist, who cannot produce a meaningful report and interpretation if he is blinkered to looking merely at what lies on the autopsy slab. My long report took account of the preliminary clinical features of Joan Hill's illness, as described by the various witnesses, including her maid and the two houseguests. I took into account the medication—or lack of it—that she had had before going to the hospital, as a legitimate part of trying to understand how the fatal processes came about. And I concluded, as I saw it in quite valid terms, that she had died of a now-undeterminable infection, but I was actually appalled at the conditions surrounding her death. Her state of shock and moribund condition on arrival at the hospital were evident from my examination of the hospital chart. My assessment of her pathetically ill state while still at home was derived from reading the statements of her maid and the two houseguests.

The other doctors, apart from Hill's representatives, agreed with my conclusions, with the notable exception of Paul Radelat, who dissented strongly. He contended that we were there only to give an opinion on the pathological anatomy of the body and criticized my exploration of the clinical circumstances that led to my disquiet about John Hill's neglect of his wife's moribund condition. Well, Radelat is entitled to his opinion as to what a medico-legal investigation is supposed to be, but Jachimczyk agreed with my findings and conclusions. Two doctors, William Gouldin and William Fields, entered documents expressing their doubts that the brain brought to the autopsy by Dr. Morse was in fact that of Mrs. Hill. I've already said that the John Hill defense team had categorically stated that she died of meningitis, so from their point of view, everything hung on the correct identity of that brain, which I've explained I was prepared to accept.

The grand jury hearing was quite a performance, in many ways. There was an allegation that one of the female witnesses had reported an offer of a bribe of $10,000 to go before the jury with certain information. This allegation was made by one of John Hill's attorneys. Assistant D. A. McMaster confirmed that a witness in the first grand jury hearing had in fact reported this to him, but he refused to identify her. There was talk of an investigation, but the whole thing faded out. I was hounded quite a bit by the press in this case—it was not long after the Coppolino affair, and the media smelled another sensational homicide case. And they were right, though not in the way anyone expected at that stage. I had to dodge them as much as I could, as I didn't want anything I said—or they imagined I said—spread over the papers before the case came to trial.

They called me "the grey-haired eminence of American pathologists, who testified in an aura of mystery" and such like. The grand jury cooperated to shield me as much as possible. They left their usual room on the sixth floor of the county courthouse, supposedly for "a tour of inspection." But in reality, they went up to the eighth floor and listened to my testimony there. When it was finished, they supplied a bogus Dr. Helpern to confuse the press, and a photograph of him appeared in that next morning's paper. The D. A. walked out with a man looking rather like me, carrying a briefcase and shielding his face with a hat. In fact, it was a Mr. Bogart, one of the grand jurors, trying to decoy the photographers. A few minutes later, I came out, with the rest of the jurors clustered around me, trying to keep me insulated.

Well, the Robinson-Hill case wasn't over yet, not by a long way. The woman had died in March 1969, the third grand jury hearing was in April 1970, and the bill of indictment was most unusual. It was based on nineteenth-century Texas law, charging John Hill with the death of his wife by "murder by omission." They alleged that he had killed her "by malice aforethought by failing to provide and by witholding proper medical treatment and timely hospitalization." By the law existing in Texas in 1970, he could face the death penalty if convicted.

Hill, who by now had been divorced by Ann Kurth, denied the charge but was brought to trial in February 1971. He was represented by his famous lawyer, Richard "Racehorse" Haynes, the state prosecutors being McMaster and Erwin Ernst.

A lot of the early testimony was about Hill's family troubles: friends of Joan recounted her despair at his philandering. Guests at the Hill home that weekend told a curious story of how John Hill brought home eclairs, cream puffs, and tarts; he personally selected which pastry was to be given to which person, including his wife. He did this for three nights.

The prosecutors then called his recently estranged wife, Ann

Kurth, who told how she found some pastries in the refrigerator of their illicit apartment, a week before Joan Hill's death. She was about to eat one, when John Hill stopped her. In the bathroom of this apartment, she found three Petri dishes, used in medical laboratories for growing bacteria. She saw that they were under a lamp for warmth, but Hill crowded her out of the room and closed the door.

It was Ann Kurth who, in her apparent enthusiasm to testify against her ex-husband, unwittingly saved him from conviction. While still giving testimony, she alleged that he tried to kill her a month after they were married, by deliberately crashing his car against a bridge abutment, with her sitting in the passenger seat on that side. That having failed, she said he twice tried to inject something into her with a syringe. The defense screamed objections, and the judge declared a mistrial.

Now John Hill would be in jeopardy again when the retrial came up—but it never did, not for him. Two years passed, and legal wrangles delayed it too long, during which time the death penalty was abolished by federal Supreme Court ruling.

The trial was eventually scheduled for November 1972, but John Hill didn't show up—by then, he was dead. In September, a gunman burst into his house in Houston and shot him dead. He had married for the third time by now, but his new wife managed to escape the assassin.

This new twist in the story had further ramifications, which are no part of my story, as I had nothing to do with them; but for the sake of completeness, I must tell you the outcome.

The killer had thrown away his gun after the murder, and the Texas Rangers traced it. They arrested the man, a Dallas crook named Vandiver, a contract killer who had been hired by a former brothel madam in Galveston to shoot John Hill. Another woman, a heroin addict and call girl, was later convicted of procuring the gun for Vandiver. Before Vandiver could incriminate any more people, he jumped bail and was pursued by a police sergeant into a café in Longview. Each held a pistol in his right hand, and when the police officer jumped the man, they became deadlocked, each gripping the other's gun hand. The sergeant, with great presence of mind, fired his revolver into the ceiling, and because Vandiver was actually gripping the gun barrel, the suddden heat of the discharge made him let go, and the policeman shot him dead. But now he was silent forever, unable to implicate any more people.

When the two women were tried, they named Ash Robinson as the man who put out the contract for John Hill's death. A daughter of the madam testified that her mother and Ash were old friends. Both women were convicted of complicity in the murder, but Ash, now approaching eighty and in poor health, was never indicted. However, John Hill's son, his new wife, and his mother filed a suit amounting to over seven and a half million dollars against him, alleging that he hired the killers of his son-in-law. Ash took a lie detector test later that absolved him from the guilt of complicity in the death of John Hill.

And we still don't know what really killed Joan Robinson Hill.

I'd like to clear up a misunderstanding about my consultation fee in this case. There was discussion with Mr. Robinson about the Milton Helpern Library of Legal Medicine, the only chartered library of its kind in the entire country, which was established in 1962 and named in my honor on my sixtieth birthday. Mr. Robinson showed great interest, and without being asked, offered to make a generous contribution for the support of the library. I indicated that I would be happier if he did that instead of paying me a fee for the autopsy. Because of a combination of circumstances at the time and the fact that a libel suit for several million dollars had been instituted against Ash Robinson, the contribution for the support of our library was postponed. Neither I nor the library ever received any payment or contribution from Ash Robinson for the services which I rendered in connection with the autopsy. The only money which I received from Mr. Robinson was a check for $500 that he sent me to pay for my expenses to Houston to perform the autopsy and in connection with the second trip when I testified before the grand jury months later. Again, in all fairness to Mr. Robinson, I never did send him a bill, and I don't doubt that he would have paid one.

In an interesting book by Thomas Thompson of Houston, entitled *Blood and Money*, about the deaths of Joan Robinson Hill and Dr. John Hill, it is stated that I had received a fee from Mr. Robinson in an amount "in six figures." This seems to be an appropriate opportunity to correct the statement in Thompson's book, and to quash the many rumors which have been current in this regard (and I hope that what I have just written will keep the Internal Revenue Service away from my door), but I have not given up the expectation that Ash Robinson will remember his generous offer of help in the way of a contribution for the much-needed support for the library.

Chapter 17

An Abortion
Horror Story

In these days, when abortion is available virtually on demand in New York State, it's hard to visualize a case like that of Barbara Lofrumento.

It happened in Queens back in 1962. It was dealt with primarily by one of my assistant medical examiners, Dr. John Furey, but the whole affair came under my jurisdiction as an exercise in identification. Eventually, I was called to testify at the trial, which followed a very newsworthy international manhunt.

The whole thing concerned the Lofrumentos, a well-to-do closely-knit family, with Dominick Lofrumento, a Yonkers pharmacist, very much the dominant father figure.

Dominick had a daughter, Barbara, who was a pleasant, easygoing girl of nineteen. She was very much overweight, at a hundred and fifty pounds to her five feet one in height. Maybe it was this plumpness that concealed from her family the fact that she was five months into a pregnancy before it was discovered at the end of May 1962, after an examination by Dr. Bertram Moore. He found then that she was a healthy girl and that there was no sign of any tampering with the pregnancy at the time he saw her.

The father, understandably upset, decided to have the unhappy situation terminated, both discreetly and immediately. A friend gave him the name of a doctor who would be likely to give the help needed in such an emergency, and on the very next day, Dominick Lofrumento telephoned for an appointment with Dr. Harvey Lothringer.

Lothringer was a physician who lived in an $85,000 ranch-style house in the expensive Jamaica Estates, in Queens. He listened sympathetically to the agitated pharmacist and asked him to come across to his office, taking the precaution of telling Lofrumento to park his car five blocks away from his house at 185-01 Union Turnpike and to walk the rest of the distance. At the interview, Dr. Lothringer agreed to perform an abortion on Barbara for $500. On the next day, Saturday, June 2, he examined the girl.

After some changes of arrangements to diminish the chance of any suspicion of what was going on, Barbara eventually went to the house on Union Turnpike—which was also Lothringer's office—to have the "operation."

Originally, the abortionist had said that he would bring his equipment by station wagon out to the Lofrumento home in Westchester County, but this plan fell through. Lothringer reassured them that this would be merely a routine case, with no risk at all. "I wouldn't take a case like this if I was going to have any trouble," he told the father. When the change of plan to come to Queens was put to the Lofrumentos, the doctor explained that he had a furnished bedroom at his house, which was available to his patients for recovery and rest if it were needed. It contained a well-stocked refrigerator, he said, in which there were fluids that a patient might require after such an experience.

Lothringer explained that his method was to give an injection of pituitary extract to induce artificial labor, so that there would be very little bleeding. Mr. Lofrumento explained on his part, that his daughter had a penicillin allergy, so the doctor promised to use a different antibiotic to prevent post-operative infection.

So far, all was going well. Then Lothringer telephoned to change the arrangements and said he would phone around midnight with details. At eleven on the night of June 2, he phoned again and told the father to meet him with Barbara near Grand Central Station at 1:30 in the morning. At 1:50 a.m., the doctor, with a female companion, drove his car up to Park Avenue and Forty-first Street. Mrs. Lofrumento and the daughter changed cars, and Lothringer drove off toward Queens, leaving Dominick Lofrumento to drive home alone.

It was about three in the morning of June 3 by the time that Dr. Lothringer arrived at his house on Union Turnpike. He put Barbara into a small room, from which she emerged holding her underclothes. "I feel sick," she said, and Lothringer told her that the pituitary extract was beginning to work. A little later, he said, "Well, now we'll get started," and took her into another room, leaving her mother waiting in the living room.

Mrs. Lofrumento remained there, waiting and worrying, until after seven that morning. No doubt they were endless, fearful hours, as she wondered what was happening to her daughter at the hands of this stranger. She had already handed over the $500 in bills, and when she next saw Lothringer at about five o'clock, he told her that Barbara was all right, but he was giving her some oxygen. Hardly reassuring words!

A couple of hours later, he again told her that the daughter was all right, and that she was resting. "I've telephoned your husband to meet you back at Grand Central," he explained. "I want you to come back and pick up Barbara at noon, on the grounds of Terrace Heights Hospital."

Dominick Lofrumento had received a call from Lothringer, who told him that Barbara was "a little miserable," but that everything was fine. He gave his instructions to pick her up at noon.

However, when the father met Mrs. Lofrumento at Grand Central at eight o'clock that morning, they decided to drive straight back to Queens. Arriving there at nine o'clock, they found the house quiet, and they could get no response from the doorbell.

Mr. Lofrumento went to a nearby call-box and telephoned the house, but again there was no answer. Becoming worried now, they went to Terrace Heights Hospital, then back to Union Turnpike—but not a twitch of response could they get!

All that day, they rang Lothringer's number every ten or fifteen minutes, but all they received was a resounding silence.

At ten that night they gave up until the following morning, Monday June 4. By nine o'clock, Dominick Lofrumento was on the doorstep of the house in Jamaica Estates. He found a number of patients waiting outside, also trying to see Dr. Lothringer, but the house was locked up and no one could get access to it. The father hung about for a couple of hours, then went home. Naturally, by now he was desperate to know what had happened to his daughter, but he was afraid to go to the police because of the illegal nature of the business that had been going on.

Now it turned out later that Dr. Lothringer had not left the neighborhood, but was still lurking around at that time. On Monday, June 4, he telephoned a Queens police officer, Patrolman George Harchack, whom he had known for many years.

"Do me a favor, George," he said. "Get hold of the sewer maintenance people, Roto-Rooter, and have them take care of my house sewers. I've got a service contract with them. I can't do it myself; I'm away from home on business."

Obligingly, Harchack contacted the sewer men and the next day—by now it was Tuesday—he let them into the house. Robert Busch, one of Roto-Rooters technicians, found that a toilet was backed up, with water spilling on to the floor. There was more water in the cellar.

He took the cap off the main house trap, but no water came out. He then removed the inside cap and found the cause of the trouble. It was completely blocked by a mass of debris.

Harchack had wandered upstairs while he was waiting, but now Busch yelled for him to come down.

"Come and look at this!" shouted the worried sewer man. He dug out a lump of sinister-looking sludge from the trap. "Looks like flesh and bones!"

Harchack wrapped the material in aluminum foil and put it into the freezer, then notified his colleagues on the police. At one o'clock Detective Collins arrived and took the foil-wrapped parcel to Queens Central Hospital, where it was seen by a Dr. Mendelson. As a result of this doctor's opinion, Collins went back to the house and called the Medical Examiner's Office. Dr. John Furey, one of the assistant M. E.'s in Queens, went to the house, where the other sewer lines were now being opened.

More flesh and bones, pieces of a cloth coat, and parts of female undergarments, including a brassiere and girdle, now came to light.

The search of the drainage system went on into the next day, and eventually our Office had a horrendous collection of small fragments of human body laid out for examination, all of which had apparently been passed through the disposal, or flushed directly down the toilet.

I had the remains and the disposal unit brought over to the museum, where they are now on exhibit—the only disposal case we have ever had.

Recognizable parts were few, and the largest pieces were only a couple of inches long. However, Dr. Furcy was able to identify parts of upper and lower jaws and a number of teeth, some still embedded in the jawbone. All this material was taken to the Queens general morgue. Fragments of the cloth were identified by the horrified relatives as being part of the clothing that Barbara Lofrumento was wearing when she was last seen with Dr. Lothringer.

A dental expert identified the teeth in the jaw, as well as some loose teeth from the sewer lines, as belonging to Barbara, having checked them against her old dental records.

Even more significant, as well as more pathetic, was the discovery of parts of a human foetus among the debris in the traps and sewer lines. There was the right foot and ankle and part of a thigh of an unborn child, about the expected age of maturity of around five months.

Our Office was now able to certify that the fragments of flesh and bone in the sewer lines belonged to a pregnant woman; that the foetus was the result of this pregnancy; and that the duration of the pregnancy was about five months. Naturally, in the circumstances it was quite impossible to hazard even a guess at the actual cause of death.

Now the question changed from "Who was dead?" to "Where is Doctor Lothringer?"

And not a trace of him was to be found—nor was there for several months. The Federal Bureau of Investigation worked like beavers to retrace the steps of Harvey Lothringer and to establish his whereabouts. They were also very keen to know where the female companion in the car on Park Avenue had gone, This was his receptionist, an attractive, darkhaired woman called Terry Carillo, a Cuban former airline stewardess.

Nothing more was heard until September 11, 1962, when the newspapers burst forth with the news that Lothringer had been arrested three thousand miles away, in Perpignan, France!

The assistant district attorney of Queens flew out to arrange extradition, and three D. A.'s officers were standing by to fly to Europe, together with a female police officer to chaperone Terry Carillo, who, though not charged, was wanted as a material witness.

Lothringer protested his innocence when arraigned in France, but a laconic French prosecutor warned him about further outbursts in the court. "I'm not guilty of what I'm accused," protested Lothringer, but the French told him impassively that they weren't concerned with that, but only with the fact that he was the man sought by the F.B.I.

Lothringer and his girlfriend had been hiding out in Andorra, that tiny state tucked away in the Pyrenees, on the Franco-Spanish border. They had rented a house and were calling themselves "Mr. and Mrs. Victor Ray." A French official said that they had picked the wrong place to try to hide, because everyone in Andorra knew everyone else, and they were as prominent there as sore thumbs.

The Spanish and French police had cooperated with the federal agents in tracking down the pair—it never became clear how they were actually arrested in a French border town, away from the false security of Andorra.

After extradition, the trial took place, and I went to give the fairly straightforward evidence about the identity of the grisly remains in the house sewers. At the trial, Lothringer completed the story by his own admissions. (He eventually pleaded guilty to second-degree manslaughter.) He said that after giving the injection to Barbara, he began the operation itself. She was disrobed and on the table when he began preliminary probing with an instrument.

There was an immediate torrent of blood—probably he dislodged an embolus into her bloodstream, for she died immediately. He used strenuous resuscitation, giving numerous injections and oxygen, but all to no avail. Lothringer alleged that there had been some previous tampering with the pregnancy, which had led to the dangerous condition, though there was no confirmation of this. I think that the most likely reason for Barbara's sudden death was an air embolism, but how do you prove that after a body has been through a disposal?

On the Monday night, the doctor and Terry Carillo left Queens for Cleveland by train, then bussed to Detroit. Using a circuitous route, they went to Windsor, Ontario, and then flew to Montreal. From there they flew to Paris, then to the south of France, on to Spain, and then doubled back to Andorra, where it took the F.B.I. three months to find them.

From the Sunday morning to the Monday night, they had been lying low in Queens—and it was all through the Sunday evening that Lothringer went about his macabre task of shredding up the body of the poor, fat, unfortunate Barbara Lofrumento into pieces tiny enough to stuff down the drains of the elegant house.

In many ways, the Lofrumento case was very similar to that other abortion death back around Christmas 1955, when the dismembered body of Jackie Smith was disposed of without trace in dozens of small packages wrapped in Christmas paper and dropped into the litter baskets and hauled away by the New York City sanitation department.

Chapter 18

The Survivors

The treatment of a dead body should not be personalized. It should be conducted with dignity and respect, remembering that any person, in any walk of life, through circumstance may require post-mortem examination. The autopsy room is the great democratizer. Each case is important, not because of who the individual was in life, but because of the circumstances of the death.

Facetiousness is completely out of order and an indication of the height of irregularity. Nor should the individual who is autopsied become a topic of discussion at a cocktail or dinner party. Religious beliefs of relatives and friends should be regarded as far as possible, even in the absence of the relatives. When the family and friends request the opportunity of remaining with the body, this can easily be arranged for. Why not comfort the bereaved relatives by providing a chair near the mortuary compartment containing the body of the deceased, as in the case of some groups of Orthodox Jews?

When autopsy is objected to by the next of kin, in a death in which the procedure is deemed necessary for legal reasons, invite the religious group to have a medical representative witness the autopsy to assure the family that the procedure is being done with dignity and with regard to the restoration of blood and tissues. I have had some very interesting experiences in this type of situation.

One that I recall vividly concerns the death of a very orthodox member of the Hassidic and Mizrachi sect of Jews, who live in the borough of Brooklyn, where they moved from the crowded Lower East Side section of Manhattan after the Delancey Street Bridge was built across the East River. The victim was a rabbi, and as in ancient biblical days, he worked at a trade for a living. This rabbi was robbed and assaulted on the street, knocked down, and sustained a fracture of the skull. He was taken to the hospital in a coma and operated on for the skull fracture and severe intracranial injuries. Despite the best neurosurgical care, he died, and the death was properly referred to the Medical Examiner's Office. The police had already been notified, and the body was sent to the mortuary for examination and autopsy.

The next morning a large number of men friends and relatives were at the Medical Examiner's Office, and they decided that there could not be any autopsy, which they would consider an offensive and sacrilegious desecration. About ten people, members of the family and their spokesman, a leader of the group, were in the lobby of the building. It resembled a page out of the ghetto, beautifully drawn by Szyk, or a setting for *Fiddler on the Roof*. The feeling of grief was intense, angry, and vocal and they were worried that there would be an autopsy. The spokesman was very articulate. I invited the entire group into my large office and discussed the matter with the spokesman, patiently explaining that an autopsy had to be performed even though the diagnosis was evident. It had to confirm the injuries and exclude some other cause of death. I asked the spokesman whether or not he was anxious to have the perpetrators taken into custody and brought to trial. He indicated that he was, in which case failure to perform the autopsy could lead to a miscarriage of justice. I did not want to embarrass him. He was eloquent and quite sincere, and the family hung on his every word.

Before this discussion took place, my old friend William F. Martin, a distinguished lawyer who was general counsel for the Medical Society of the State of New York, was in my office to ask me about a case he was interested in. Bill Martin was fascinated by the intensity of feeling of the Jewish spokesman and the members of the family. I then told the representative of the family that he could arrange to have the group's physician observe the autopsy, to assure the family that the autopsy was performed with dignity, and that all the organs and tissues and blood would be returned to the body after it was completed. This offer was accepted, and the physician, who was very busy at the time with an office full of waiting patients, was told to come right over to witness what had to be done. He came right over. Meanwhile, the spokesman went out of my office, to meet someone in the lobby of the building.

While he was gone, Mr. Martin, a devout Catholic, remarked on his sincerity and eloquence and said that if he needed a lawyer, he could call on him to represent his interests. Martin then left, and when the spokesman returned I told him who Mr. Martin was, that he was the lawyer for 25,000 doctors in New York State, and that if he needed a lawyer he could call on him to plead his case. The spokesman was obviously pleased and asked me, "Did he say that?"

The important thing in dealing with bereaved relatives and friends is to be compassionate with them and not officious, explaining, when there are objections, why the autopsy has to be done. This requires patience, but the family is entitled to know what is going to be done and why it has to be done. I have always been successful in avoiding deceit and being considerate. If physicians haven't the patience to do this then they shouldn't work in a medical examiner's office.

One's friends and associates may ask facetiously, "How are your patients?", insinuating that you have it easy because they are all dead. The "patients" are dead, but the relatives are very much alive and want answers to their questions. They can be very helpful, for sometimes without them, an autopsy with many conspicuous findings remains obscure and meaningless.

A thirty-seven-year-old man was admitted to the hospital on a Monday, having been found unconscious at home. His condition worsened, and despite careful study by the physician, including X-rays of the head, the diagnosis remained obscure, and he died eight days after admission. The death was reported to the Medical Examiner's Office, where a complete autopsy was performed. The brain revealed a fresh acute purulent meningitis and a large hemorrhage in the temporal lobe of the brain on the left side. The history from the hospital where the patient died contained nothing revealing. Thus, the autopsy contained ample findings—namely, an acute meningitis and a large brain hemorrhage. Were they related or was one a complication of the other? Cerebral hemorrhages are rarely complicated by meningitis. The remainder of the autopsy was essentially negative.

After two hours of deliberation and muddling, I was notified by the Office that a cousin of the deceased had come to identify the body and that she was in a hurry because she had to return to work. I went to the Office to fill out the death certificate. The clerk-receptionist asked what I had found. She was told meningitis and a cerebral hemorrhage, whereupon she blurted out, "That's funny, because the cousin told me that the deceased had been stabbed in the eye with a screw driver." I asked the clerk why she hadn't mentioned it before, while the autopsy was being done. Her answer was that I was doing the autopsy, and she assumed, as many persons do, that I would find this out for myself!

Well, the truth is that one finds things out, but the meaning of the findings may not be evident until a young cousin comes by to give you the important clue, without which the case has no meaning whatsoever. I then spoke to the cousin and asked her how she knew this. She said the deceased had told her on the day it happened, which was two days before he was taken to the hospital, unconscious. She happened to see him walking along the street, and he was weaving along his way—which was not unusual the day after payday. She assumed he had been drinking, but she also noticed a gauze patch covering his left eye. She had the curiosity to ask him what happened, and he told her he had gone over to visit his girlfriend after deciding to break off with her. He went to take back the gifts he had given her on more pleasant occasions. An argument started, and he got mad and began to break things up. When his anger and destruction continued and he smashed the television set he had given her, she got real mad and picked up a two-inch long screw driver and poked him in the eye with it. The blade went through the upper lid. Somewhat subdued by this assault, but without any disability as a result, he left the flat and went to the large Municipal Hospital emergency room for treatment. This is where the surgical patch was placed over his eye, after the wound was cleaned. No one suspected that the weapon had penetrated beyond the skin. He was told to return to the eye clinic two days later, but in the interim, while he was home alone, he became unconscious for the very good reason that the weapon had penetrated the eyesocket above the eyeball; the track continued through the superior orbital fissure into the brain. There was no immediate disability—that didn't happen until two days later, when secondary hemorrhage developed in the temporal lobe of the brain. The dirty weapon also infected the covering of the brain; hence, the purulent meningitis. Both conditions resulted from the same poke in the eye. I dare say that similar occurrences take place without suspicion of their severity, but without complications as in this case. We re-examined the eyelid through which the two-inch screw driver had passed. All I could find was a tiny scar, almost concealed by the skin fold, no more conspicious than the many other undistinguished scars on the face of an active thirty-seven-year-old man, who sometimes horses around with friends.

This case teaches an important lesson: the forensic pathologist can not keep himself aloof. He must learn to talk to people who can give him important information, and encourage his staff to do the same thing. If Miss Cavanough, our receptionist, didn't chat with people, or our mortuary assistant, Betty Forman, didn't exhibit some kindly curiosity, we would be deprived of information, and many a case would be lost. Betty looked like a Gibson girl at the turn of the century, and indeed she used to pose for Gibson. In this work it is important to train the staff to be outgoing. One never knows what will be gleaned by this.

Members of the clergy of all faiths are always helpful and usually reasonable. They should always be treated with great consideration, and over the years I have come to know many of them. Our relationships ordinarily have been most cordial and mutually respectful. One of the most antagonistic groups, though, as far as acquiescence to autopsy is concerned, was the really Orthodox Jewish community.

Now, I am deeply conscious and respectful of the right of every national or religious minority to preserve their customs and beliefs, and wherever possible would discuss the matter with them and try to get them to see and understand the wisdom of a proper post-mortem investigation. It has worked both ways, and occasionally, they would get me to see their point of view. Generally, it's better, and often easier, to come to an understanding after a full explanation, rather than use the big stick of authority and brush aside sincere protests.

Having said that, I would never be dissuaded from an investigation if I felt it really needed to be pursued. I was appointed by the mayor and was under a legal and moral obligation to the community to carry out my duties as I thought best—this has been tested in the courts more than once, when relatives brought civil actions against me and the Medical Examiner's Office for carrying out official autopsies against their wishes.

Neither the English coroner system nor the systems elsewhere in Europe have this potentially disturbing come-back. The coroners in England have absolute authority to order an autopsy, and they are completely protected by law from any form of litigation from relatives.

The medical examiner system in the United States does not have this absolute immunity, and on occasion, other jurisdictions have found it to be a restricting factor in investigating a case in the depth that was really required.

This may act as a brake on the autopsy rate, although I don't think that it is a good thing for any medical examiner to feel inhibited by fear of a law suit. You can't do your best work when you are looking over your shoulder all the time, as the medical and surgical professionals have found—to their cost—during the current epidemic of malpractice suits that is sweeping the country.

I was marginally involved in a case of this sort, where a hospital was sued, even though our Office was the agency that ordered the autopsy.

A woman was admitted to a hospital in this city with abdominal pain of considerable severity. She underwent nine days of extensive diagnostic tests and procedures, which revealed that she had air in the abdominal cavity, collected under the diaphragm. The physicians felt sure that she had perforated an organ, but before any more could be done, she died.

The medical staff of the hospital requested an autopsy, to discover what actually had happened, but the family refused consent; so the doctors filled out a death certificate to the best of their ability, guessing that the woman died of peritonitis due to a ruptured organ.

The Department of Health, which receives and scrutinizes all certificates, refused to accept this one, on the grounds that it was too vague: the cause of death was still obscure.

The case was referred to the Medical Examiner's Office and an autopsy was performed—a quite reasonable procedure, as otherwise we had no magic means of getting any more information than was already available, and the possibility of some internal injury had to be considered.

Then the husband sued the hospital, alleging that the autopsy had been performed without his consent, on the pretext that it was done by the medical examiner.

The jury awarded him no less than $12,500, which was reduced to $3,500 by the appellate court.

As a matter of principle, the hospital took the case to the Court of Appeals, the highest court in the state of New York, which unanimously reversed the decision of the lower court and dismissed the case. They determined as a matter of law that the plaintiff did not have a valid complaint.

The remarks of the court, given through Judge Bergen, are worth recording, because they gave us valuable precedents for future disputes of this kind, and helped to reassure us that every decision to carry out an autopsy need not be accompanied by that uneasy feeling that somewhere around the corner, a relative was sharpening his knife ready to stab us in the back for doing our duty to the city.

The judge said, "The medical examiner of New York City is authorized to perform an autopsy on the body of a person dying in any unusual manner. The question must be determined by the situation confronting the medical examiner before he makes his decision to perform the autopsy. In this case, the records showed the wide range of investigation made in the course of treatment, and the inability of the physicians to diagnose the illness or the cause of death was an unusual termination of life.

"The medical examiner was acting within the frame of his authority, when having a report of a death not acceptable to the Health Department and finding on investigation no satisfactory explanation in the hospital records, i.e., a definite diagnosis, he determined that an autopsy was necessary.

"Such a determination in such circumstances is protective to public health and an additional safeguard in hospital care. If a hospital uncertainly or indifferently explains how a patient in its care died, it is manifestly the duty of the medical examiner in the public interest to find out if he can."

This was plain speaking on the part of the highest court in the state, and in this instance, it carved out an exception to the general rule that an autopsy cannot be performed without valid consent. After this, a medical examiner would be able to carry out an autopsy without consent, if the attending physicians were unable to determine the cause of death and exclude traumatic injury as its basis.

Getting back to groups in the community who are opposed to autopsies, I've already mentioned the Orthodox Jews. It was all the more surprising then, that one morning in 1974, I was consulted on the phone by a group of very solemn speaking rabbis who had called to ask me to actually carry out an autopsy on one of their congregants! It certainly was a unique experience for me, as so many times, my staff and I had spent hours persuading this same group and explaining to them why an autopsy was necessary.

But the story here was pretty unusual and involved a very prominent Orthodox Jewish family who lived in New Jersey, just across the Hudson River. The deceased person was twenty-nine-year-old Berel Weinstein, a brilliant young millionaire, who had made quite a name for himself as an inventor and manufacturer, mainly in the medical field. He was a real wonder boy—a real *mensch* as the newspapers called him—the pride of his Orthodox Jewish family. He was a scientific whiz kid whose genius for gadgetry made him rich in a relatively short time after graduating from Brooklyn College. He invented a disposable clinical thermometer, a disposable intravenous feeding device, a portable electro-cardiograph, an electronic device for blood-pressure recording, and a machine for continuous monitoring of the temperature of patients in intensive care units. To market these, he founded Biomedical Sciences Inc., a small company with research laboratories and a production unit in Fairfield, New Jersey.

All went well with him for a time. He had a beautiful wife,

Julie, and owned a luxurious penthouse in a thirty-story apartment house at Fort Lee, on the Palisades overlooking the Hudson.

But in the last year of life, ill fortune began to dog him. He developed a number of illnesses affecting his heart and his nervous system; he became involved in illegalities over company shares so that his business career was in ruins; then, his father died suddenly on the same day that his mother, Rachel, underwent surgery for lung cancer.

The sequence of events surrounding his death seemed to be these: One night early in 1974, Julie phoned the police at Fort Lee and requested assistance, because her husband had been suddenly taken ill. Two police officers and a police surgeon were sent to the penthouse, and the surgeon pronounced him dead and notified the medical examiner. He summoned the family physician, Dr. Schorr, who issued a certificate of death from natural causes, and later informed the Bergen County medical examiner, Dr. Lawrence Denson, that Berel had suffered from a long-standing heart complaint.

So far there was nothing too unusual in what happened, but at four in the morning of the next day, the Bergen County prosecutor, Joseph Woodcock, was awakened from sleep by a phone call from Weinstein's uncle, Rabbi Reimann, one of the very strict Orthodox sect to which the Weinstein family belonged. The rabbi was very disturbed about certain aspects of the death. He was speaking on behalf of the relatives, as well as himself, when he reported that they were suspicious about the whole affair. He said that the body had been removed to the medical examiner's office, but the wife then obtained a release of the body from the medical examiner's office, saying that she did not want an autopsy on Orthodox Jewish religious grounds. She then arranged to have the body taken to a funeral chapel in New York City.

Woodcock, still half asleep, must have wondered why on earth the rabbi was ringing him at four in the morning to tell him this, but he soon realized the significance of it when Reimann went on to say that Julie Weinstein had instructed the funeral directors in New York *to embalm and then cremate the body*! Now if autopsy is anathema to Orthodox Jews, then embalming and, above all, *cremation* are the ultimate desecration and abomination. It violated the very foundation of their beliefs—and Julie must well have known it.

Woodcock promised to look into the situation right away—he checked with the police at Fort Lee and with Dr. Denson, the medical examiner. Then he called the New York authorities and asked them to hold up the cremation already planned for that day, and to return the body to New Jersey for autopsy. Rabbi Reimann had told him that the family wanted a full investigation, and the first I knew about it was the calls from the five or six Orthodox Rabbis asking me if I would perform the autopsy. I told them that I had no jurisdiction in New Jersey, but it soon turned out that I was invited officially by the Bergen County, New Jersey authorities to act as an observer for the family and the rabbis at the autopsy.

It certainly was paradoxical to be asked by these rabbis to do this, after all their usual resistance to autopsies throughout the years, but they were very unhappy with the actions of Weinstein's wife, and undoubtedly there had been some pretty tough discussion within the family circle.

Well, Berel's mother, Rachel, and his brother Eli went to the funeral parlor in Manhattan, and after a twenty-minute service, the casket was closed. Eli asked for it to be opened again so that he and his mother could view the body for the last time, after which it was taken out of the chapel. Outside, various factions of the family had lined up, about fifty of them. Instead of going through with the cremation, the funeral attendants put the casket aboard the hearse for the return trip to New Jersey and the official investigation. Then, trouble broke out among the mourners—so much so that some tried to prevent the vehicle from leaving. The police had to be called, and a dozen patrolmen broke up the crowd and cleared a path for the hearse. It was a near riot, according to the newspapers that day, with the Orthodox camp berating Julie—an extraordinary spectacle for a section of the community normally so restrained.

When the body arrived at the Bergen County morgue, Woodcock asked the mother to identify the body, and then the autopsy was begun by Lawrence Denson, with myself as the observer. I offered the toxicologic facilities of our Office in Manhattan, and it was this analysis by Dr. Milton Bastos that actually came up with the answers, as the autopsy itself was inconclusive without it. The press were banging on my door wanting information, but I explained to them that I couldn't release anything until the drug tests were completed.

Joseph Woodcock was very understanding and helpful in encouraging the cooperation between New Jersey and New York. He told the press that he was very happy to have me working with them to assure the family that everything possible was being done to clarify the matter. The embalming didn't help things, in the sense that it obscures the presence of alcohol, but since we were looking for drugs and other poisons, the procedure didn't interfere too much. We always try to do our autopsies before the embalmers have had the opportunity to get at the bodies, and with some poisons, like cyanide, the analysis is interfered with and becomes impossible—but in the Weinstein case, we had no difficulties.

Our toxicology laboratory in New York found high levels of Darvon, a prescription, pain-killing drug. There was also evidence of Valium, a tranquillizer, although this was not present in lethal quantity, as was the Darvon. Nevertheless, the Valium might have increased the effect of the Darvon.

Well, we had a conference at the Bergen County medical examiner's office. I must admit that I didn't see eye to eye with Lawrence Denson on the question of accident, suicide, or homicide, but there was no disagreement on the cause of death, which was attributed to the large amount of Darvon found. Denson said he couldn't rule out the possibility that Weinstein had kept on taking the Darvon to get relief from whatever he was taking it for and, not remembering how much he had already swallowed, had continued to take additional repeated amounts of the medication. I cannot go along with that old story of automation which has been thrown up for years as a completely theoretical excuse to avoid a suicide verdict. I said that if Weinstein had been a four-year-old imbecile, then maybe I would buy that story—but he was a near-genius. While I couldn't exclude anything, I just didn't believe that he could have taken such a large dose by accident. Someone asked me if the death could be a homicide—all I could answer was that we get very few homicidal poisonings with this type of drug, but that the question was undeterminable.

Prosecutor Woodcock said he would carry on with his investigation—Weinstein did have some arteriosclerotic heart disease, even at the age of twenty nine—and he had some kidney disease, but Darvon and Valium were not drugs used for either of these illnesses. He said it was impossible to know how much of the drugs had been taken.

In any event, the investigation came to a dead end and no charges were ever filed. But what stands out in my memory of that case was the group of Orthodox rabbis calling on me and asking me to do the ultimate in forbidden things—and for a very good reason.

Chapter 19

Forensic Offshoots

Over the years, the Office of the Chief Medical Examiner in New York City developed a number of offshoots, which had no real official origins so far as the city administration was concerned.

Even though these were relatively "fringe" activities, I feel that they have contributed greatly to the status of legal medicine in the country. The first was the legal medicine library that was set up by a group of my friends and colleagues. Like Dr. Bill Eckert, whose center in Wichita I'll be mentioning again, they did me the honor of naming it after me, and the official opening ceremony of the Milton Helpern Library of Legal Medicine took place on my sixtieth birthday, April 17, 1962.

Until that day, there was no specific collection of books and other material on legal medicine in the United States, no reservoir of knowledge and references such as existed in some of the European institutes. Naturally, there were departmental and personal collections scattered around the country, but I had felt for a long time that there was a real need for a centralized, accessible library to bring together an extensive, properly catalogued collection of all available material on legal medicine and the rather rambling sister disciplines that make up the subject of medical jurisprudence. The nucleus of such a collection was already there, in the shape of my own extensive personal library, which included some rare volumes.

An impressive group of people arranged the opening ceremony on that birthday in 1962, at which Robert Wagner, mayor of the city of New York, was the guest of honor. The library was housed on the top floor of the new building on First Avenue, and it provided a full-time service for doctors, lawyers, and any other authorized people who needed to use it.

Howard Craig, director of the New York Academy of Medicine and one of the library's original trustees, ably summed up its aims at the opening ceremony:

> Osler once said practicing medicine without books was like navigating a sea without charts. With the plethora of material published these days, only a common library, properly manned and efficiently administered, can provide that without which no good doctor can practice good medicine. It assures a tool for daily practice, resource material for research, and abundant material for teaching. This library shows clear promise of filling the urgent need in this city for a specialized collection devoted to legal medicine.

Well, the Milton Helpern Library seems to have achieved these aims in the years since its foundation, and it has been used extensively by all kinds of people involved in medicine, law, and law enforcement.

The library is kept going financially by grants from various organizations and by the efforts of the "friends of the library," who hold annual social events of considerable elegance and success, which raise both funds and interest to keep this worthwhile service in operation. In recent years, these events have included the showing of various films that have both a popular and a medico-legal content. Examples include the Yugoslav film "The Tragedy of a Switchboard Operator," and some of Chris Steinbrunner's "Festival of Mad Doctors." In 1976, the Consulate of the People's Republic of China loaned the library a wonderful film of an archeological exhumation of an ancient royal tomb. On another occasion, the Circle Theatre of New York gave a performance of Dylan Thomas's "The Doctor and the Devils," appropriately about the notorious Edinburgh bodysnatchers who used to kill victims in order to sell their bodies to the anatomy department of the medical college.

Another development that I feel was a considerable asset to the status and practice of legal medicine in New York was the founding of the Institute of Forensic Medicine. This was another example of the harmony and cooperation which came about between the academic world and the city authorities of New York, for it is a joint organization between New York University and the city of New York.

In the United States, we never had any specific identity for any institution that was involved in legal medicine, as has been so common in Europe since the early part of the last century. In New York, we had the Office of Chief Medical Examiner, which was basically a working service devoted to a large volume of routine investigation and disposal of deaths in the community. On the other hand, the academic presence was represented by the New York University Schools of Medicine, which were basically concerned with the teaching of students.

What was required was something which partook of both these activities and yet added to them so that there would be more opportunity for research and training in our speciality rather than the two somewhat watertight compartments of student teaching and routine service commitment.

In September of 1968, we took the opportunity of a double anniversary to set up an organization that would link the two interests. It was the fiftieth anniversary of the founding of the Office of Chief Medical Examiner and it was the thirty-fifth anniversary of the establishment of the Department of Forensic Medicine at N.Y.U., an appropriate date on which to fuse the interests of the city and the university in a common institute.

In fact, this idea was by no means new in 1968—it was some twenty-eight years old by then! Back in 1940, the Public Health Committee of the New York Academy of Medicine had proposed just this. As a result, all the medical schools in New York endorsed the establishment of an institute within the geographic boundaries of the N.Y.U. Medical Center, on the condition that every school should have free access to the teaching facilities. A piece of land was set aside for the purpose at the corner of Thirtieth Street and First Avenue, and though World War II intervened, it was this piece of ground that was eventually donated to the city of New York for the erection of our new Office in 1960.

So in September 1968, the institute was formally declared open by Mayor John Lindsay for the city and by President James Hester for the university. Once again, another of my long-awaited ambitions had been fulfilled.

Now I'd like to mention one of the nicest things to happen to me in the few years since I retired from my official appointment, the naming after me of the Milton Helpern International Center for the Forensic Sciences.

The man behind this project is someone I must tell you about—Dr. William G. Eckert, a man with terrific drive, and a wonderful person with a most unusual personality. Originally from Union City, New Jersey, Bill Eckert majored in history; was a semi-professional football player; graduated in medicine; was in both the army and the navy, and ended up a pathologist.

When he was in medical school at New York University, he came to my pathology laboratory in the Hospital for Special Surgery as a laboratory technician. I believe that at that time he roomed with Joe Umberger, my toxicologist at the Office. The influence that Bill received turned him towards pathology with a strong medico-legal bias. He later worked as a medical examiner in New Orleans and then in Dade County, Florida, with Dr. Joe Davies, but for some years now, he has been out in Wichita, Kansas, as a clinical and forensic pathologist and deputy coroner.

Now Bill Eckert is one of those restless, sleepless, fellows who must always be involved in some project, some new development. He found his niche in life in communications, which he has applied to legal medicine and forensic science. From a place like Wichita, which is about as far as you can get from anywhere else, he has built up an extraordinary organization, which now covers the world like some forensic Interpol or medico-legal United Nations.

This is INFORM, short for Internationl Reference Organization in Forensic Medicine, a unique outfit that is a cross between the C.I.A. and Rotary International!

At an international forensic convention in Copenhagen, Denmark, in 1966, Bill Eckert got together a group of people from a number of countries, irrespective of politics, language, or race, and sold them on the idea of a collaborative organization designed to break down distance and frontiers as far as the interchange of medico-legal information, personal contacts, and cooperation was concerned.

He went home from that meeting and singlehandedly (apart from the conscripted labor of his wife and kids) began circulating to almost a hundred countries a deluge of newsletters, reference material, and information about what was happening on the medico-legal scene all over the world. His co-worker on the project was another extraordinary man, Dr. Tom Noguchi, the chief medical examiner and coroner of Los Angeles.

Well, in the decade since 1966, INFORM has flourished and has put out a lot of valuable information. One of Eckert's preoccupations is the assembly, retrieval, and dissemination of reference information, and through INFORM, he has published dozens of compilations of worldwide references on various forensic topics ranging from aircraft accidents to alcoholism, from child deaths to drowning. These are partly made up from print-outs from computer sources and are in use all over the world, in forensic institutes, university libraries, and government establishments.

Bill Eckert, again through INFORM, has arranged numerous visits and lecture tours for foreign experts coming to the United States and has generally done more singlehandedly in a few years to establish contacts between colleagues in a hundred countries than has ever been done before.

Well, all this culminated in 1975, in the establishment of a permanent International Institute of Forensic Medicine and Sciences in Wichita. The state university there has given him a building and facilities, with promises of more, and there is hope of further support from state and possibly federal funds to build up this center into something big. The idea is to house the world's largest collection of reference material on legal medicine and forensic science, so it can be instantly available by computer links to enquirers from anywhere in the world by letter, Telex, or telephone. In addition, it is hoped to establish archives of famous criminal and civil cases, provide facilities for visiting foreign students and professors, and provide research facilities as well as teaching functions for all grades of law-enforcement officers as well as for medico-legal practitioners.

When the time came, in 1975, to celebrate the opening of this unique center, Bill Eckert and his colleagues at Wichita University did me the high honor of naming the whole complex after me, in recognition of what I guess they felt was my long service record in American legal medicine. I went out there to a dedication ceremony in October 1975 and had a real Midwestern celebration, which included the presentation to me of an Indian blanket by the local Indian Chief. A photograph of this ceremony has been whisked around the world in one of the INFORM newsletters!

Chapter 20

Who Killed Barbara Gibbons? The Peter Reilly Case

Once again—and this time very recently—the New England states provided another odd case, where circumstantial evidence, such as it was, caused a conviction that was quite unjustified.

The first I knew of it was a letter from a playwright living in Roxbury, Connecticut. But no ordinary playwright, for this was Arthur Miller, probably the most well-known stage writer of the present day.

In a sober, modest note, he kindly expressed his admiration for my own work over the years and asked if I would be interested in looking at the medical evidence in a murder case in which he felt there had been a miscarriage of justice.

The homicide concerned was that of a middleaged woman in Canaan, Connecticut, as a consequence of which her eighteen-year-old son, Peter Reilly, had been convicted of her murder. The crime was a brutal, sadistic, perverted affair, and most of the township refused to believe Reilly was guilty.

Arthur Miller began to take a personal interest in the case some eight months after the murder. He called together some of his prominent neighbors, including William Styron, the novelist, and Mike Nichols, the director, to form an action group to raise money for Reilly's defence. This interest was originally aroused by an article in a magazine suggesting that Peter Reilly had been coerced into a confession by the state police.

After the trial ended in a conviction, Arthur Miller asked a prominent attorney, Gilroy Daly, to press for a new trial, and in the fall of 1975, he stimulated the *New York Times* to conduct an independent investigation into the Reilly affair.

For Mr. Miller, it was more than a specific miscarriage of justice—it was almost a philosophical situation demonstrating his concern for the way in which the machinery of society can overwhelm the individual.

Well, I readily agreed to do what I could. This was in December 1974, though the business had started in September 1973 and is still going on now, as I'm writing.

The facts were these, though "facts" can be very fluid concepts and vary both with time and the angle at which different people view them.

Peter Reilly was a lanky youth, eighteen years old at the time of the death of his mother, Barbara Gibbons. She was brutally killed on her fifty-first birthday, in the small clapboard house where she and Peter lived, in this little township of Canaan.

On the night of September 28, 1973, Peter was at a teen center meeting in the town. He left there at 9:40 p.m., with a friend, whom he dropped off at the friend's home at 9:45 p.m. Peter drove in his car to his own home, a ride that takes at least six minutes. He locked his car, entered the house, and then found his mother lying, badly mutilated, on the floor of her bedroom. She was still breathing, and he immediately summoned help.

He went about this by first phoning for an ambulance. Then he dialed Information to ask for the telephone number of a doctor. He rang the number and spoke to Jessica Bornemann, the daughter-in-law of Dr. Carl Bornemann, for about two and a half minutes.

She advised him to ring the Sharon Hospital, so Peter again had to dial Information, to get the hospital number. He then rang the hospital and spoke to a duty nurse who asked him three or four questions.

The hospital then called a second ambulance and also rang the state police, who recorded having received the call at 9:58 p.m.

Trooper McCafferty, who was in a prowl car, was notified by

radio, and arrived at the scene at 10:02 p.m. He found that the woman appeared dead at that time, and he could feel no pulse at her wrist.

The object of these detailed records of time will become apparent later on. They were a central issue in the whole case for a retrial, and were the major facts on which I gave my testimony in January 1976.

To go back to the events of that September night, the police, and subsequently the medical examiner, Dr. Ernest Izumi, found that Barbara Gibbons had shocking injuries which had resulted in very extensive bleeding from several parts of the body. She was clad only in a shirt and undershirt, and she had been brutally battered and stabbed. The cause of her death was established as gross loss of blood due to wounds in her neck and body, and also to a blockage of the air passages by blood that had been breathed into her chest.

Dr. Izumi found at the autopsy that she had been stabbed through her right hand, a typical defense wound due to her attempts to ward off a weapon. Her elbow was injured, her nose was broken, she had a brain injury and three broken ribs. More serious were two slashes of her throat with a sharp weapon, severing her jugular veins. She also had multiple stab wounds on her back, a gash in her abdomen, two broken thigh bones, and deep penetration of her vagina with an unknown object. The weapon or weapons which caused these horrific injuries was never found, another factor that later had relevance.

As soon as the police arrived on the scene, Peter Reilly automatically came under suspicion, and from then on he was effectively in police custody. There seemed no logical reason why they should immediately suspect him, but that was the case.

Not long afterward, he was stripped and searched by a detective, Lieutenant Shay. This revealed that there was not a single spot or stain of blood on his person or clothing, in spite of the bloody scene where the body was discovered.

Reilly was taken away by the police to Hartford at about 1:45 a.m. and subjected to prolonged interrogation, lasting more than six hours. He was still being questioned at 8:00 a.m. in the morning and had been given a polygraph lie detector test.

It was during this stressful period that he made certain confessions, which he soon retracted, but he was placed under arrest for murder. The police reckoned they had the matter all sewn up.

Dr. Izumi, the medical examiner, told the detectives that Reilly could have performed all these maniacal acts on his mother without getting contaminated with her blood. They also established that the boy sometimes quarreled with her—though it would be an odd pair living together that didn't have an occasional row.

The prosecution also offered testimony at the trial that the call to Sharon Hospital was received at 9:40 p.m. and that the meeting at the teen center ended at 9:15 p.m.

With this circumstantial evidence, Reilly went to trial in May 1974, and Judge Speziale gave him six to sixteen years imprisonment, after the jury had found him guilty of first degree manslaughter.

No one in Canaan, or indeed in Litchfield County, seemed to believe that Peter was guilty, and the defense committee became active in agitating for a retrial. Not long after his conviction, Reilly was released from jail on $50,000 bail, mainly raised by the Madow family, who had taken Peter in after his mother's death. They mortgaged their own home to raise the bail, but legal fees were an added problem toward getting a new trial. Neighbors organized a Peter Reilly bond fund, and held bake sales and spaghetti dinners to collect money.

Mr. Miller added his considerable weight to this campaign, and made many inquiries among witnesses himself. At first, he says, he wasn't sure whether Reilly was guilty or not, but as the investigations went on, he became convinced of his innocence.

A former New York policeman turned private investigator was hired, and this man, James Conway, worked indefatigably to gather new evidence, sometimes with a marked lack of cooperation from the state police—to put it kindly.

At the first trial, the defense alleged that a family living nearby was involved in the death. There were bad relations between Barbara Gibbons and some of the sons, especially one in particular, but he had been given an alibi by a girl with whom he was living in a trailer nearby. She said he had not left her all night.

Then at the hearing for a new trial, the girl changed her story and admitted that the boy had not slept with her in the trailer that night. He had come back at 8:30 in the morning, upset, shaking, and nervous.

The family denied any involvement, but the judge pointed out in his memorandum the possibility of robbery and the animosity that existed between two of the brothers and the deceased.

James Conway and T.S. Gilroy Daly, the attorney for Reilly, eventually produced enough background evidence to begin the fight for a new trial. They needed someone to look at the medical evidence and asked me to do this for them.

My main impression, which was so strong that it seemed incontrovertible from common sense as well as from medico-legal experience, was that there was just not enough available time for the accused to have perpetrated this act. The new investigations had made a much tighter, more accurate schedule for Reilly's movements on the night of the killing.

First of all, Barbara Fenn, the night supervisor at Sharon Hospital, had testified at the first trial that she had received the call from Reilly at 9:40 p.m. But Peter had already telephoned his friends the Madows before that, to call for an ambulance. Marion Madow remembered that she had been watching a film on T.V. called "Kelly's Heroes," and recollected that the call from Peter came through during a particular scene. The defense then got evidence from an offical at C.B.S. Television that stated beyond any doubt that that particular scene had been transmitted at ten seconds past 9:50 p.m. Faced with this, the night supervisor conceded that the call may have come through later. So it had to be *after* the call to the Madows, and it had to be *after* the call to Dr. Bornemann's house. The switchboard operator at the hospital said she logged the call at approximately 10:00 p.m.—and we know that the state police were notified at 9:58 p.m. and arrived at 10:02 p.m.

Now, several people at the teen center, including two priests, were quite sure that Peter had not left until between 9:40 p.m. and 9:45 p.m. He had then taken his friend home, and the friend's aunt was sure that her nephew had entered the house at 9:45 p.m. She had heard a car outside just prior to that. So as it was a six-minute drive to Reilly's home, he had barely enough time to fit in all the phone calls before the state police arrived. So when did he get time to kill his mother—inflicting all those injuries, taking her clothes off, and disposing of the knife?

It was quite impossible! I said at the hearing for the retrial, when I went up to Litchfield in January that it just couldn't be done.

The next medical matter was the complete lack of bloodstains on Peter's clothing or body. The medical examiner had denied that there need have been any such staining, but I flatly refused to believe that. This woman had been slashed twice in the throat, had large veins cut, stabbed in the back, slashed in the abdomen and punched in the face sufficiently hard to smash her nose. Yet there was not a mark on Reilly—not even a bruise or graze on his fist, though the facial injury was said by Dr. Izumi to have been caused by a fist or soft weapon.

It was just not reasonably possible for him to have done this thing and remain utterly uncontaminated. There was not time enough for him to have committed the multiple injuries, let alone go and get cleaned up. Even if he had washed his hands, any bloodstains on his clothing would have been easily detectable by laboratory techniques. The police and their laboratory tested all the sink traps and drains for blood by a very sensitive method—and found nothing.

The only weapon that they suggested was a sheath knife, hanging in a scabbard on the kitchen door. One expert said that tests showed that there was bloodstaining on the blade, but so little that they could not even get a blood group to prove it was Barbara Gibbons's blood. It was hardly likely to have been the instrument that caused such devasting injuries a short while before.

I said at the hearing that, "Reilly would not have had time to commit the crime and appear the way he did when the police arrived. Medical experts frequently disagree, but it depends on the experience of the individual."

The prosecutor, John Bianchi, gave me a pretty stiff cross-examination, but I felt so resolute about the impossibility of this lad doing this crime, that I was able to stick to my interpretation of the situation. Bianchi asked me if I would come to a different conclusion if Reilly had arrived home ten minutes earlier. As he didn't, I can't see what that had to do with it, but it made no difference to the issue. What could he have done in ten minutes to change all his clothes, dispose of the old ones, clean himself off, and yet not get a drop of blood into the sinks or drains? But ten minutes he didn't have, according to the new timetable established by the defense investigators—hardly ten seconds, by the sound of it!

Bianchi tried to get my evidence stricken from the record, because this was something that should have been raised in the first trial; the Connecticut rules state that only matters which could not have been discussed at the first trial can be offered as grounds for a new trial. But the judge—the same one who presided at the trial when Reilly was convicted—ruled that my evidence could stand.

The autopsy had shown that Reilly's mother had had her thigh bone broken in a sideways direction, yet the spurious confession that Reilly made after the all-night grilling had described him jumping up and down on her body— incompatible with the direction of the fractures.

The defense also introduced psychiatric evidence to show that Reilly's nature was such that he would be easily confused by an authoritarian questioner, and could be led into accepting as fact some supposition that was put before him with sufficient force. He had withdrawn the confession the next day, once the impact of the police interrogation had subsided.

After a six-week hearing in early 1976, Judge Speziale decided that a new trial was necessary, and in an unprecedented statement, said that Reilly's conviction "represented a grave injustice." He said that the state statutes would be thwarted if the conviction were allowed to stand. After citing "the unusual, bizarre, and complicated nature of this case," Judge Speziale predicted that "Mr. Reilly would never be convicted of the murder again."

Strong words from the very judge who handed down the first sentence, which could be taken as a hint to warn off the district attorney from putting Reilly in jeopardy again for the killing of his mother. "It is readily apparent" he said, "that a grave injustice has been done, and that upon a new trial, it is more than likely that a different result would be reached."

Yet within days of the verdict of the hearing, the state police arrested the defense investigator, James Conway, on a technical offense of bringing a loaded gun into the courtroom during the hearings, which could get him five years in prison. He gave the gun up to the sheriff on entering the court, got a receipt, then, when he reclaimed the gun later, was told the receipt was invalid! On the day following Judge Speziale's verdict, the prosecutor, Bianchi, announced his intention of bringing Reilly to trial again. Attorney Daly said that this was obvious harrassment of one of the key witnesses in the case.

Eventually, yet another curious turn in events occurred. John Bianchi died of a heart attack in the early part of 1976, and his job was filled by a new state's attorney, Dennis Santore. In spite of the strong words of Judge Speziale mentioned above, a new trial for Peter Reilly was set in motion, but at the pretrial hearing in November 1976, before Judge Simon S. Cohen, the new state's attorney announced his discovery of evidence that had been lying in the papers of his predecessor. On the strength of what he found, the judge declared, "I believe, in the best interests of justice, that the case should be dismissed."

What had been found in Bianchi's files? It was evidence that placed Peter Reilly miles from his mother's house at the time of the killing, just as the defense had maintained throughout.

Arthur Miller, the man who had remained convinced of Reilly's innocence all along, was in the courtroom in Litchfield to hear the proceedings, and seemed outraged that such dubious actions had unnecessarily prolonged the final clearing of Peter.

The new evidence, never handed over from the State's Attorney's Office to Gilroy Daly for the defense, was a vindication of the time scale of the period around the murder—and consequently bore out exactly what I had said in my testimony, that it was impossible for Reilly to have done all those things in the time available. Bianchi's files contained two previously unknown sworn statements by a Mr. and Mrs. Finney, who definitely saw Peter Reilly in downtown Canaan at 9:40 p.m. that night. Frank Finney, an auxiliary state trooper and a fireman, said that he and his wife had left a drive-in movie theater in Canaan, and had met Peter in his distinctive blue Corvette sports car at a downtown intersection at 9:40. Mrs. Finney had re-enacted the encounter for the state police a few days later, and they found that the encounter had occurred at 9:39 p.m.

The Finneys said that they had never been asked to testify about this matter, which made the evidence of the telephone supervisor at the Sharon Hospital quite incompatible with the rest of the testimony, as regards timing.

The new state's attorney showed these statements to Judge Speziale, who is now presiding judge of the Superior Court, who gave the opinion that they were exculpatory.

At the pre-trial hearing on November 24, Judge Cohen read out the new evidence into the record, and in conclusion said "In order to write f-i-n-i-s to this case and in the interests of justice, the case is dismissed."

So is it all over at last? It was thought to be when Judge Speziale delivered his blistering opinion almost a year before, but it wasn't. After Judge Cohen had dismissed the case, the state's attorney asked permission to reinstitute prosecution of Mr. Reilly at some future date—many thought it just a formality, but it means that the lad is still in legal jeopardy.

Arthur Miller was not too convinced—he was quoted in the *New York Times* as saying, "Here we are several million words later and back where we started from. So who killed Barbara Gibbons?"

Well, that's another matter. I found the medical issues clear-cut, and had no hesitation in believing that Peter Reilly was innocent, because he just couldn't have done what he was alleged to have done in the time available—and kept as spotless as he was—in the face of the mayhem that went on in that little house in Canaan, Connecticut.

Chapter 21

Defining Death–
The Transplant Question

Elsewhere in these pages I've mentioned the Latin motto I had the architect place in large metal lettering on the marble wall of the reception lobby of the New York City Chief Medical Examiner's Office, part of which, translated, says, *"This is the place where death delights to help the living."*

This has been my credo throughout many years as a medical examiner. Many interpretations can be read into these words, but basically I suppose they refer to the public health aspects of the investigation of deaths such as those caused by carbon monoxide emissions from gas appliances, and the malaria transmitted artificially by the intravenous heroin addicts. But in recent years, an even more direct connotation has arisen in connection with great advances in surgery and the complex techniques utilized in transplanting human donor organs from suitable bodies. The medical examiner frequently plays an important role in facilitating the procedure, always with the cooperation and sometimes even the insistence of the deceased's family, who are solaced by the thought that he or she helped another person in need. In homicide cases, permission for the donation must also be obtained from the district attorney.

Understandably, there has been a "feedback" mechanism from organ transplant into the realms of legal medicine and medical ethics; one might even say that philosophical and even religious questions have arisen from these commendable new activities of surgeons in many parts of the world.

Until a decade or two ago, the determination and definition of death were fairly straightforward matters; certainly, in the majority of cases, any doubt of its occurrence rarely continued longer than a few minutes. If a motionless person stopped breathing, and his heart also stopped, that was it! Within moments, he was recognized as dead by all the usual criteria available at that time; the signs of death progressed and were recognized as part of an irreversible phenomenon.

True, there were occasional, exaggerated, horrific tales of persons supposedly pronounced dead waking up in the mortuary or even in their coffins, a real worry which had some people, who could afford a physician's service, arrange for the doctor to insert a long needle into the heart after death to make sure that death was real and final and not simulated. Many a young physician starting out to practice in Vienna earned some of his first fees in this way. This was before embalming became stylish. Embalming was reserved for persons whose bodies were to be laid out in state.

My friend and colleague, the late Dr. Georg Strassmann, who had been professor of legal medicine in Breslau and who came to New York after he had been displaced from his position by the Nazi regime, told me that in some of the old morgues in Central European cities, the bodies of persons who had died suddenly were placed on a table in an open room, and a string was tied to one finger and extended over a pulley into an adjacent room, where it was attached to a small bell within earshot of the attendant, in the event that the deceased came to!

In these apocryphal situations, it was not that the process of death had reversed itself, but that there are times when the signs of life are so difficult to detect that death is simulated and pronounced prematurely. Today, with the availability of more sophisticated equipment, like the electrocardiograph and encephalograph, such an occurence is almost unknown, although now and then, acute barbiturate poisoning can mimic death very closely. It was this drug that was involved in a curious case, in which an old, retired nurse was certified dead no less than three times.

But to return to true "deaths": the old situation, where cessation of breathing and heart beat were the sole criteria of mortality, has now gone overboard. When someone asks, "Is he dead?", we now have to reply, "What sort of 'dead' do you mean?," because in the context of the use of organs for transplantation, there are several stages of death.

Death occurs when there is irreversible cessation of the vital processes which maintain the physical integrity of the body, but if we take this to its logical conclusion, the only true sign of death is the onset of decomposition.

This fundamental change in definitions began with the development of equipment which could sustain first the breathing processes and then the circulatory functions of the body. The old "iron lung" for victims of polio might be thought of as one of the forerunners of this revolution, but now there are machines which will keep patients who years ago would have died in a state which must be called "alive," for an almost indefinite period. The most well-known example in New York, of course, is the much publicized case of Karen Ann Quinlan. At the time of this writing, the situation still hangs in the balance, but I have been retained by the family, either to conduct or represent them at an autopsy and to advise them on the medico-legal implications when the time comes.

Since April 1975, following the ingestion of liquor and tranquilizers, the unfortunate Karen has been unconscious, with evidence of extensive brain damage, the precise nature and origin of which are not altogether clear. She had been connected to life maintenance equipment for over a year and was in a progressively deteriorating, vegetative state, with no hope of ever recovering consciousness. There had been a prolonged legal battle of worldwide interest to give to her parents in Trenton, New Jersey, the right to have the respirator disconnected so that their daughter might "die with dignity." Eventually, a court ruled that this might be done at the request of the parents. It *was* done in May 1976, and the patient began to breathe spontaneously without the respirator and suffered no abrupt worsening other than the further gradual, general deterioration in her condition. She is unresponsive, but electroencephalograms continue to reveal abnormal but definite brain wave activity, along with spontaneous respiration and heart action.

At the suggestion of Dr. Julius Korein and its attorney, Paul Armstrong, the family requested that I should make a full examination when death eventually takes place, to "insure the highest degree of medical and scientific objectivity," to use the attorney's own words. I intend to recruit the best expert assistance available, as the examination of the cause of the prolonged coma may require the most sophisticated techniques.

Getting back to generalities on the question of what is death, we have reached the state exemplified by poor Karen Quinlan, where death cannot necessarily be defined by failure of the function of heart and lungs, as these functions were at first assisted and then replaced by sophisticated machinery and then restored by spontaneous action after removal of the patient from the life maintenance equipment.

When death of the individual occurs, the tissues and organs do not all die at the same time. Different tissues survive for different periods, which is the basis for their transplantation into a live recipient. When the heart and lungs stop, oxygen is no longer transported to the cells, and waste products are no longer cleared from the tissues. This stagnant situation very rapidly causes the death of certain organs, and the brain is the most sensitive and vulnerable of all. If the heart stops for more than a couple of minutes, the brain cells are severely damaged, and this damage is irreversible after a few more moments. If, at this stage, the heart is stimulated by electrical impulses or cardiac massage, it may begin to beat again. Similarly, if a modern "iron lung" or an even more sophisticated machine is connected up, the heart and lung function may be simulated and artificially maintained in a practically normal manner. But the brain may already have been damaged beyond recovery, as demonstrated by clinical tests and the electroencephalograph. If so, that person is already "dead" in some respects. If he is unconscious, cannot communicate with his fellow men, is unaware of their very existence or of the existence of the world, and—most vital criterion of all—this unawareness is permanent and irreversible, then surely this state can be designated as "social death," as in the case of Karen Quinlan. The persistence of spontaneous breathing and heart action and the evidence of some electroencephalograph activity indicate the narrow margin between evidence of life and the time when death may be pronounced by the physician. In addition to lack of oxygen from a temporarily failed heart or lungs, many drugs such as barbiturates and general anesthesia also may cause such brain death, and the end result is the same.

Many efforts have been made to establish fixed criteria for this irreversibility, but none are absolutely foolproof. Even the electroencephalograph has on rare occasions shown a flat tracing in cases of barbiturate poisoning where the patient has recovered.

It is in this state of limbo, where the heart and lungs are being supported but where no sentient life is present, that the twilight zone exists that causes so much dispute and discussion on medical, ethical, philosophical, and religious grounds. The person lying in bed like a vegetable, wasting away to a human skeleton, connected with wires and tubes to complicated machines, but silent and utterly oblivious of relatives or the outside world—is he or she "alive" or not?

I shall not attempt to answer that, but I have sympathy with those who, like the Quinlan parents, prefer seeing the machines removed and allowing nature to take its course.

But what has this to do with organ transplants? Obviously, the type of patient who has undergone slow, progressive, gradual deterioration of the entire body would never, when death finally occurred, be selected as a source of donor organs. It is the one with an acute injury or brain illness, in whom death is rapid, who provides the opportunity for donation of an organ like the kidney to the recipient requiring this frequently successful lifesaving donation. Although heart transplants and other major transplant organs (like lung and liver), have been important and exciting news ever since Dr. Christiaan Barnard did the first one in Cape Town, South Africa, it is the kidney transplant that has been the most frequently successful lifesaving donation. Both in survival time and sheer numbers, it is with this organ that the whole transplant program is mainly concerned. For a transplant of a kidney to be a success, the organ must be taken out of the donor body either while the circulation is maintained, or removed within thirty minutes of the cessation of the heartbeat. It is far more likely to be successful if the support machine is kept running while the kidneys are being taken out. On the continent of Europe and, increasingly, in Great Britain, this technique to prolong viability of the donor organ is used to ensure the success of the operation.

Now we run into the problem. Who decides when to switch off the machine and to remove the donor organs? This is too big a subject to tackle here, but it is accepted now that the two teams of doctors, the donor and the recipient teams, must not be in any sort of collusion. The decision that brain damage is irreversible must be made by a totally different set of physicians from those who wish to use the kidneys for transplant.

The medical examiner's office does not begin to participate in this matter until after the decision has been made that death can be pronounced and that brain death has been demonstrated with or without other organs being irreversibly damaged. Most of the potential donors are cases which have to be referred to the medical examiner. The majority of these are acute, unnatural deaths or natural ones that cannot be certified by a regular physician because he was not in attendance on the deceased for a sufficiently long time. The gamut of reportable deaths includes certain traffic accidents, drug overdoses, cerebral or subarachnoid hemorrhages, and, of course, some suicides and homicides. These are the types of cases in which brain deaths occur, and yet the viability of organs utilized for transplant can be maintained with mechanical support for variable amounts of time until the procedure can be performed.

A problem that arises in these cases—especially the homicides—is that the medical examiner has an official responsibility to investigate them and perform an autopsy for the purpose of determining or confirming an apparently obvious cause of death and interpreting any injuries and other findings. Obviously, if this were to be done first, the time factor and unsterile autopsy would make the donor organs useless for transplant. On the other hand, the removal of the donor organs before the body is delivered to the medical examiner might be said to distort the subsequent autopsy appearances. However, the difficulties are more apparent than real, for in the great majority of these cases, the fatal damage is confined mainly to the head and brain, with no involvement of the abdomen and kidney region.

When I was chief medical examiner, I resolved these difficulties by agreeing to the prior removal of organs for transplant, but I always sent a medical examiner to observe and record the procedure, so that he could testify, if necessary, to the original intact state of the body in the donor region. Thus, there was a continuous chain of official scrutiny from the donor organ removal to the subsequent autopsy, and never once did any difficulties arise from this practice.

I have always felt, and still do feel, that it is incumbent on us in the Office to do all we can to cooperate in and not obstruct this vital and humanitarian procedure, which can bring such relief to sufferers from kidney disease, many of whom are young and active members of the community and often at a time of life when they have heavy family responsibilities. To do anything to obstruct this transplant program would, in my view, be a most undesirable attitude, and I have been saddened in the few years since I retired to see that things are no longer running as smoothly in the handling of these cases.

Recently, some medical examiners in New York City have insisted on doing the autopsy on homicides before allowing the surgeon to remove the kidneys for transplant. This was done although permission was given by the relatives, who naturally have to agree with or request the procedure, especially if the deceased had left instructions during his lifetime that he wished to donate his organs. All the technicalities for transplant procedures are in accordance with the Anatomical Gift Acts, which have been adopted by all fifty of our states. There is naturally never any attempt to effect removal of donor organs without permission of the parties concerned. Indeed, I have found that relatives are usually more than willing to allow organs from their deceased kin to be used for the benefit of others and for at least a small part of their loved ones to live on in someone else. When the more recent, obstructive attitudes developed, I am certain that there was considerable disquiet and even anger among relatives when they found that their wishes to allow the donation were being thwarted.

The supply of donor organs lags far behind the need for transplants. There are vastly more potential recipients than there are donors, and this makes it all the more unfortunate that bureaucratic attitudes have reduced even further the trickle of suitable donor material for those desperately in need of kidney replacement. So acute has the problem become, that some New York hospitals have in desperation broken the medical examiner's rules in an effort to get the law modified.

The Health and Hospitals Corporation and the Medical

Examiner's Office in New York went to court in 1975, over a dispute concerning kidney removals performed in defiance of orders issued by the acting chief medical examiner. This was a test case, and the two kidneys removed from a homicide victim were successfully transplanted into two recipients. Both the family of the deceased and the district attorney had approved the procedure. The donor in this case was a twenty-two-year-old homicide victim who had been shot in the head, and by no stretch of imagination could the condition of the kidneys have had any bearing on the cause of death. In my day at the Office, I would have sent an assistant medical examiner to watch and record the removal of the organs, considering this to be an "interlude in the autopsy," as I termed it. But Jacoby Hospital, where this happened, had been forbidden to carry out the procedure. Only one day before, another victim of a gunshot wound in the head had been passed up as a donor because of this embargo.

I was interviewed on the whole affair and said that I thought it was unfortunate and unnecessary that such scarce, vital donor material should be lost because of official technicalities that were easily made compatible with the donor program. The case went to court, and the Health and Hospital Corporation asked that death be legally defined as cessation of brain function. The American Medical Association has recognized that brain death is a valid additional criterion to determine that death has occurred but is opposed to a legal definition. They consider it unnecessary, holding that the pronouncement of death is a medical responsibility and should remain so. Cessation of brain function has never been statutorily accepted in New York State, though six other states have so defined death.

Justice Mary Johnson Lowe of the Supreme Court presided over the case, and Dr. Samuel Kountz of Downstate Medical College in Brooklyn explained to her that the previous chief medical examiner—me—had permitted removal of donor organs before autopsy. He also said that he recalled a case in Brooklyn where the assistant chief medical examiner had refused permission, and the mother of the patient had gone to see Dr. Helpern to get the order countermanded. Dr. Kountz also said that the ban on using homicide victims was the last obstacle to the widespread acceptance of kidney transplants. "There are up to 1,800 homicides in New York City each year," he said. "The majority are healthy young people, the best kind of donors. If we could use only a third of these, it would eliminate the need for dialysis treatment and for taking kidneys from living volunteer donors. On four previous occasions this year, transplants could have been made, because the relatives had willingly given permission, but the acting chief medical examiner objected. It was after the most recent of these that the surgeons agreed to make a test case of the next one."

The court proceedings continued for a time during 1975. The head of the Research and Development Division of the New York State Health Department at Albany testified that to require the demonstration of brain death as a criterion of death in every case would be unnecessarily cumbersome; but still no definite resolution of this important problem has been made.

Chapter 22

When Autopsies Fail

Most people, including many medical men, have an almost religious faith in the infallibility of the autopsy. They believe that a body is like a watch or clock and that if you take it apart carefully enough, you can always discover why it stopped working. I am afraid this is not always so, but this is not a valid basis for not performing an autopsy in every case in which one is indicated. The fact remains that in a certain proportion of these cases, nothing sufficient to explain the death can be seen after even the most searching examination with the naked eye, the microscope, or the most sophisticated laboratory procedures.

Negative findings in an autopsy are important, not only in immediately excluding a large variety of conditions that may have been suspected originally and could have involved or incriminated an innocent suspect trapped by circumstances, but also in suggesting the possibility of unusual conditions in which death may occur.

For instance, some chronic alcoholics may embark upon a prolonged binge during which large amounts of alcohol such as whiskey or gin are consumed and then, for various reasons, abruptly stop drinking. They might survive long enough afterward for metabolic processes to eliminate all the alcohol in their systems within a twenty-four hour period. The disappearance of alcohol during the hangover period does not, however, mean that the individual has returned to normal. Such persons may die after convulsive seizures or suddenly after a period of rapid, irregular heart action and chest pain, without the existence of coronary artery disease. Again, the known coronary case with significant disease in the heart may die suddenly after excessive drinking. Such delayed sudden deaths after bouts of drinking, simulating those caused by primary coronary heart disease, are often not appreciated by the pathologist. He may not attribute a death to alcoholism unless alcohol can be recovered in the body and alcoholic changes are visible in the liver By no means do all alcoholics develop fatty livers and liver cirrhosis, although many do; when such liver changes are found, they are and should be recognized as indicators and manifestations of longstanding over-indulgence in alcohol.

Chronic alcoholics also develop changes in the brain and its coverings. Shrinkage of the outer layer—the cerebral cortex— and replacement of the atrophied brain by a visible accumulation of fluid is a condition known as "wet brain" and is well known to the pathologist, who exposes and removes the brain himself at autopsy and doesn't depend on the "diener" (autopsy assistant) to do this in his absence. "Wet brain" can only be appreciated when you are there in the autopsy room to see it. Few pathologists know what or where it is, but it is a real entity and an important finding in the chronic alcoholic.

There are other rarer and more subtle changes in the body of some chronic alcoholics, especially a degenerative and inflammatory process in the voluntary muscles called rhabdomyolysis, but in the conventional autopsy these muscles are not examined, and the condition is not recognized. Along with these visible muscle changes, there are fascinating microscopic findings in the muscle fibers, which become fragmented and distorted into a pattern that resembles that of a crude fingerprint.

Another example of the negative autopsy is encountered in the well-known phenomenon of "crib death," or sudden infant death syndrome, which is responsible for the sudden tragic loss to young parents of thousands of apparently healthy infants in the first year of life. Among the many infant deaths of this kind investigated by the Medical Examiner's Office in the City of New

York was that of Andrew Menchell, the son of Vicki and Lou Menchell, two delightful, dedicated, talented people, who are nightclub performers. Instead of perpetuating the grief which had initially overwhelmed them, they came to us and offered to support research on baby deaths by the Medical Examiner's Office and the Department of Forensic Medicine of New York University School of Medicine. As far as I know, the only privately funded research organization for this purpose in the United States is the Andrew Menchell Foundation for Infant Survival, named after their deceased infant son.

Intensive research into the cause of these infant deaths has been carried out in America and in Europe, and many leads have been assiduously followed. Claims have been made but have not been substantiated. Theories are numerous, but the cause or causes have not been determined to the satisfaction of the research teams. These unexpected deaths are as reportable as any others to the medical examiner and coroner for investigation. This should be mandatory and not optional, and a complete, meaningful autopsy should be carried out. The circumstances of many of these deaths repeat themselves, but the autopsy may exclude the case as a crib death. It may reveal an abundance of unsuspected natural disease, such as an infection or a congenital malformation or a tumor; or it may disclose traumatic injury as the cause of death of a type requiring careful investigation to determine whether the traumatic findings are indicative of an overt act of violence, placing the death in the category of the battered child syndrome, child abuse, or neglect.

In post-mortem examinations on all types of subjects, too often the autopsy is performed by a pathologist who is not too experienced or interested. This is difficult to recognize, unless one has had the opportunity of witnessing the autopsy. The conventional report may follow the usual descriptive pattern, with much unimportant verbiage about the autopsy incisions but practically nothing about the details of the wounds, which are often inaccurately described and labelled.

A common failing is a gross description and misinterpretation of the nature of an occlusive or blocking process in a coronary artery (to say nothing of actually overlooking the occlusion), unless there is a microscopic followthrough on the blocked segment. Another source of error is failure to recognize the nature of intracranial hemorrhage (bleeding within the skull), a critical differentiation of the natural case from the traumatic. Too often, the pathologist mislabels what he sees and does not understand or is influenced too much by what he is told about the case. Descriptive terms are omitted that would indicate the age of hemorrhages, which is important in corroborating or excluding the likelihood of involvement of a suspect. Miscarriages of justice can easily occur due to the pathologist's misinterpretation of what he sees.

Another source of difficulty is failure to distinguish ante-mortem from post-mortem injuries and to conclude erroneously that hemorrhage into the tissues in an area of trauma is always evidence that the injury is ante-mortem. I have seen so many examples of proven post-mortem injury with an erroneous conclusion that it was ante-mortem that I am appalled by the frequency of this common error. The truth is that the differentiation of the ante-mortem from the post-mortem wound may be impossible, except as the problem may be resolved by circumstances and a reliable history. This is not news, but the old mythology of legal medicine and forensic pathology dies hard and is dangerous to the administration of justice.

The only solution is day-by-day experience, acquired by application to routine cases. They must be carefully investigated as to circumstances and then examined post-mortem and autopsied—each case presenting an individual problem—not to be short cut as to completeness by a preconveived, premature conclusion about the answer. Promotion to a supervisory official title does not automatically and immediately endow anyone with knowledge and is not a substitute for application and experience. There is too much cockiness and indifference—admixed with arrogance and ignorance—encountered among some—not all—inexperienced men too rapidly and recently appointed as supervisory professionals. This attitude is contrary to the public interest.

But advocates in our adversary system of jurisprudence seem only to be upset when on the wrong side of criminal and civil litigation. The legal profession is interested in winning its case before a judge, or judge and jury; but merit and justice are not always on the winning side. Medical experts, including the pathologist, are supposed to explain and clarify medical findings and issues but not to color their opinions to win the case for the lawyers who call on them in the interest of their clients.

There should be no expectation that the expert will play an adversary role, in the sense of giving favorable answers to the lawyer who calls on him to testify and hostile replies to his opponent. The witness should be alert and responsive to all questions from both sides, for the benefit of the court and jury. If an expert witness cannot clarify the issues and medical questions, he should not testify. If he does, he should not assume the role of a reinforcement called up in desperation to save the day for the losing side.

Common occurrences in litigated cases are what I can designate as "fragmentation" and an oversimplification of the facts. These are indulged in by lawyers who want to confuse the issue and by judges who want to simplify it. The apparent onset of a disabling illness may in this manner be related causally to a death, and the intrusion of an intervening cause may be disregarded.

The following case illustrates how an initial injury of fractured ribs was misinterpreted by the process of oversimplification, with failure to recognize intervening complications of chronic alcoholism and delirium tremens. I shall always remember this case, in which I was consulted almost forty years ago, when I was only a young medical examiner in New York. Dr. Peter Denker was an assistant medical director of the Equitable Life Assurance Society. The medical director was Dr. Edwin Beckwith, who occasionally, on Denker's recommendation, would call on me for my opinion in some medico-legal problem in a death case having to do with the issue of the double indemnity feature of an insurance policy. Now, there are some persons who believe that the title of "chief" or "deputy chief" automatically provides one by osmosis with qualifications and wisdom to understand such issues, but I wish to point out that when I was only a lowly assistant, I had already acquired a reputation for understanding the medical issues of causal relationship that frequently arise in connection with the death of insured individuals, especially when the complication of traumatic injury had to be evaluated. There are physicians and surgeons, medical examiners and pathologists—including the newer breed of "forensic" (legal) pathologists—who never acquire the ability to carry out such evaluations. I did this work well—to the satisfaction of those who consulted me—from the very beginning, applying rules of logic which I had learned in my college days, under the tutelage of a great and stimulating teacher of that subject, Professor Morris Raphael Cohen, in the College of the City of New York.

In any case, Dr. Beckwith called and asked me to go to Detroit in connection with a double indemnity claim on one of their life insurance policies. In such cases, as everyone knows, the insurance contract—the face amount of which had been paid—provides double payment if death results solely from or as a direct complication of a traumatic injury, and the company was being sued by the beneficiary for the double indemnity benefit.

The insured was the proprietor of a bowling alley and drinking establishment in that city. He was an obese, heavy-set man, who was chronically inebriated. One day, a young man with the appropriate name of Tank visited this place of recreation and sat down at one of the tables with some friends, all in high spirits because Tank was celebrating his birthday. When the waiter came over, Tank explained to him that the proprietor had promised him and his friends a friendly round of drinks on this joyous occasion. The waiter went to verify this and the owner, though not too pleased, rather sullenly agreed to the request. But when Tank requested another round, not realizing that as far as the owner was concerned, Tank's birthday was over, the angered, besotted boss came over to the table, grabbed hold of the birthday boy, called him a son-of-a-bitch, and ungraciously indicated that he was going to throw him out.

Tank responded by pushing him away. The tipsy, unsteady proprietor was propelled and staggered back against the wall, and then fell into a sitting position on the floor. He became stuporous and was taken to the hospital. Tank was careful to explain the circumstances, emphasizing that he was not the aggressor, but was only reacting to the aggressive moves of the owner. In the hospital, it was found that he had two fractured ribs, and shortly thereafter his stupor turned into a clear-cut case of delirium tremens, which in turn was complicated by a bronchopneumonia. Death occurred within a few days.

After an autopsy performed in the hospital under a coroner's system that existed in Detroit at that time, the death was incorrectly attributed to cirrhosis of the liver. But the liver had not yet become cirrhotic: as is commonly found in many chronic alcoholics, it was large and fatty. The death was certified as having been caused by bronchopneumonia secondary to cirrhosis of the liver, contributed to by rib fractures. As is often the case in deaths from chronic alcoholism and one or more of its complications, the word alcoholism—a dirty word to many physicians—was not even mentioned, despite the clear-cut history and clinical record of delirium tremens.

The beneficiaries of the insurance policy made a request for the double indemnity payment on the basis of the rib fractures, but the amount of money was substantial, and the company refused payment because of the intervening delirium tremens, which was a complication of the long standing chronic alcoholism, of which there was also ample evidence in the large, fatty liver. In the state of Michigan, the double indemnity provision in a policy is voided if it can be shown that the deceased provoked an attack that resulted in a fatal injury.

I went to Detroit and reviewed the history and clinical and autopsy reports and other documents. I spoke to various physicians who knew the deceased and were familiar with his last illness, but they didn't seem to understand what I was trying to point out, in as tactful a way as I could as a visitor from New York. They equated a death from chronic alcoholism with either one from delirium tremens or cirrhosis, but chronic alcoholism as the primary cause of these two conditions was not included in the death certification. They just assumed that a fatty liver was a cirrhotic liver. Yet obviously, the liver was only fatty and not cirrhotic; a chronic alcoholic dies of alcoholism, not of a fatty liver, which is only an indicator of that condition. I had to be very careful not to talk down to them—I had come in from New York, and there is always an understandable tendency for the locals to say, "Who the hell is this guy trying to tell us our business?"

The case was heard in the federal court in Detroit, as the insurance company was based out of the state. The first witness was Tank, who was playing it very careful indeed. He knew he was still being considered as possibly liable to a criminal charge for assault. He said that the owner had come over to the table and grabbed him forcibly in anger and that he just pushed him back and away to get clear. His story was good ammunition for a defense of provocation, and the counsel acting for the defendant's insurers moved for a dismissal under the state law, which negated double indemnity under this provision. The judge granted the motion, and it was all over without my being called to the stand.

I returned home to New York and told my friends in the Equitable, "Well, you have won your case, but not for anything I have done; it was purely a legal point and would not have applied in New York State, which does not have this provision about provocation."

If the case had gone through the court to the bitter end, it is hard to prophesy what the outcome would have been. If the deceased had not been an alcoholic, a reasonable expectation would have been that he would not have died, as the injuries were trivial and at most no more than a precipitating cause of his death from chronic alcoholism.

But to explain the entire medical situation to a lawyer, or even to an experienced judge, is very difficult. The legal profession tends to see only black and white, whereas in medicine there is a whole range of grey between those two extremes. Lawyers have a habit of breaking up a situation into small fragments and concentrating on each fragment to get a definite answer. Thus, they tend to lose the overall coherence of the picture that a medical man views.

I think there is a basic difference in the way that a lawyer's mind works compared with a doctor's. It is no doubt a product of training, as well as of daily practice, but time and again the lawyer goes single-mindedly for a "yes or no" answer to every question, a concept that is quite alien to anyone working in the medical or biological fields, where natural variation and a whole host of other variables make it impossible to give an unqualified answer to so many questions. Then, when you try from the witness stand, to explain the difficulties, the attorney tries to cut you off short and pin you down to a nice, convenient, snappy affirmative or negative. Well, over the years, I have learned to deal with this situation, and a lawyer is not going to tie me down or pressure me into saying something that I don't feel fits the circumstances. In the nicest way possible, I offer to help him rephrase his question so that it is compatible with the sensible medical answer, and if he still doesn't like it, then I appeal to the judge for a fair chance to expand on my answer. The autopsy certainly doesn't finish with the writing of the report or the giving of a straight narrative testimony in court. You have to learn in the hard school of experience the best way to conduct yourself during cross-examination so that you remain fair minded and not unduly partisan while not letting the opposing counsel trample you into the ground. This is another reason that the dilettante medical witness is a hazard; because whatever his clinical pathological knowledge, unless he is experienced in the peculiar medico-legal aspects of the work and in conducting himself on the witness stand, an astute lawyer can turn his testimony into a travesty of what he intended to convey, no matter how technically perfect his autopsy technique might have been.

Sometimes you hear such pathologists complaining of the roasting they were subjected to under cross-examination by a skilled opposing counsel and how their evidence didn't seem to come across as they had hoped it would. Well, all I can say to the medical expert is: if you can't stand the heat, you don't come into the kitchen!

Afterword

Despite all the advances in the American medico-legal system, we must not merely congratulate ourselves for what we have done but must think of what we should do in the future. There should be more uniformity in the different jurisdictions in their medico-legal investigative systems. Large training centers should be set up so that everyone may receive the proper education. There should be some way for the busy and less active centers to communicate so that one can learn from the other. Most important, we need more qualified, well-trained doctors with the right attitude in this field. This is a growing area, but it should grow even more. Not everyone likes this kind of work, and it is very strenuous physically, but more doctors—including female doctors—should be encouraged to join us.

A good medico-legal department in each jurisdiction of the country can prevent deaths. For example, the medical examiner often serves the community in the capacity of a public health officer. He may be the first to detect and warn of deaths signaling the onset of epidemics from disease, from food, or from other types of poisoning that are of direct concern to the public health authorities and the community. Properly trained, well-qualified medical examiners and coroners, with the right attitude of acceptance and curiosity, are also important for the family and friends of the deceased; for the detection of criminal violence (including the protection of the innocent and the apprehension of the guilty); and for the health, safety, and well-being of all of society.

Index

Bertinot, Dr., 203
Bevilacqua, Rocco, 128
Beyers, A.J., 155
Bianchi, John, 241-43
Biddy, Carolee, 79-83
  background of, 79-80
  and death of Mona Lee, 81-
    82
  trial of, 82-83
Biddy, Mona Lee, 79-83
  autopsy of, 81-82
  death of, 79-81
Biddy, Mr., 79, 80
Biddy, Mrs., 79
Biron, Dr., 161
Body storage facilities,
  modern, 47, 48
Bogart, Mr., 207
Booysen, Owen, 152-53
Boram, Lawrence, 187-89
Bornemann, Carl, 237, 240
Bornemann, Jessica, 237
Borrero, Mrs., 145, 147
Borroto, Abbie, 158-67, 169
  autopsy of, 162-63
  death of, 158-60
Borroto, Mr., 158-60
Boyer, Ross, in Coppolino
  case, 17, 18, 20, 26-28 40
Brouardel, P.C.H., 65
Byrnes, Detective, 126
Bucklin, Robert, 203
Busch, Robert, 214

Camps, Francis, 150-52
Capital punishment, 106
Carbon monoxide deaths, 106,
  176-81
Career Girl murders, 142-47
Carillo, Terry, 215-17
Carpozi, George, 138
Cavanough, Miss, 221, 222
Chasnoff, Julius, 2
Children's deaths, 49, 50, 175-

76, 192, 255-56
Childs, Richard S., 11
Civil Service rules, medical
  examiners under, 13
Cleveland, Frank P., 190
Cohen, Isidore, 153, 156
Cohen, Morris Raphael, 259
Cohen, Ronald, 153-56
  and death of Susan, 153-54
  trial of, 154-56
Cohen, Simon S., 243, 244
Cohen, Susan, 153-56
  death of, 153-54
Colabella, Vincent, 133, 138,
  139
Collins, Detective, 214
Conway, James, 239, 240, 242
Cooley, Dr. Denton, 199
Coppolino, Dr. Carl, 16-44,
  197, 207
  background of, 18-20, 25
  and death of Carmela, 23-25,
    27-28
  and death of Farber, 21, 26-
    28
  investigation of, 16-18
  trials of, 35-44
Coppolino, Carmela, 18-33,
  35-37, 40-44
  autopsy of, 28-33, 36
  background of, 20-22
  death of, 23-25, 27-28
  and trials of Carl, 35-37, 40-
    44
Coppolino, Mary (Mary
  Gibson), 22
Coroner system
  evolution and uses of, 5-13,
    105, 223
  pathologists unused by, 78-
    79
  See also Medical examiner
    system
Corsi, Chief, 24